D0939685

Brian Cody

Form
Follows
Energy

Using natural forces to
maximize performance

Birkhäuser
Basel

TO HATICE

WITHDRAWN
UTSA LIBRARIES

THE IMAGINATION IMITATES.
IT IS THE CRITICAL SPIRIT THAT CREATES.
OSCAR WILDE

Library
University of Texas
at San Antonio

CONTENTS

PREFACE

This book speaks to both architectural and engineering audiences and offers a concise interdisciplinary overview on the subject of energy and the built environment. It explains and examines the complex relationships between energy and architecture and shows how energy design strategies can be used to maximize the energy performance of our built environment, while at the same time leading to new aesthetic qualities and new forms in architecture and urban design. It is intended to be equally useful to both students and professional architects and engineers in research and practice.

The book's philosophy is based on the guiding principles underlying nearly 30 years of work in practice, research and teaching. I believe in a holistic approach and as a result I do not believe that architects need to be – or should be – kept away from differential equations or engineers from spatial and aesthetic design considerations. To illustrate the theory and principles outlined in the text, examples from both research work and experience on real projects are used.

The goal of the text is to explain the principles in simple yet precise language with diagrams showing the essential elements to promote understanding. The approach of using hand-drawn sketches to illustrate the ideas is the result of experience in teaching and lectures for both professional and non-professional audiences. For some reason, complex themes are more readily understood when illustrated in a simple hand sketch. Some of the diagrams were specially drawn for the book, others are based on diagrams and sketches used for teaching and lectures. The majority are taken from sketches done on real projects. All of the diagrams were redrawn for the book in order to pull together over twenty-five years of work into a cohesive graphical style without any changes to the original content. Some of the sketches represent conceptual ideas and approaches used to inform the architectural concept during the design process, but do not necessarily reflect the final architectural design.

The phrase "Form follows energy" originated in my mind in the early 1990s when I was working on the "Low Energy Building" project in Berlin, and in 1998 I wrote a contribution for a journal about that building using this title, describing how energy strategies and concepts influenced the form finding process in its design. Now, when I talk about "Form follows energy", I am thinking about the relationship between energy and the built environment in much broader terms, as outlined above and expanded upon in the ensuing chapters.

All the research projects mentioned in the book were carried out at the Institute of Buildings and Energy at Graz University of Technology in Austria. The energy concepts for the projects described were developed during my time as an engineer with Arup in the period up until 2009, and thereafter with my own engineering design firm, Energy Design Cody.

It is possible to start anywhere in the book and read an isolated chapter. However, the book is intended to be read from the beginning through to the end and I would recommend this approach.

INTRODUCTION

Architecture not only uses energy. Architecture is energy. Lines on paper or a computer screen representing an architectural concept imply decades, and sometimes centuries, of associated energy and material flows. This book is about the relationship between energy and the form of our built environment. It examines the optimization of energy flows in building and urban design and the implications for form and configuration.

Energy is quite possibly the defining issue of our time, and a large portion of the world's energy consumption is attributable to buildings. The potential for solving the energy problem with solutions in architecture and urban design is therefore very significant. Building design professionals today are confronted with substantial challenges, but are at the same time offered enormous opportunities to increase the societal relevance of their professions to an unprecedented level.

Against the prevailing background of global warming, rapidly depleting energy resources, exponential population growth and the mounting geopolitical instabilities that arise from the insecurity relating to future energy supply sources, it is clear that energy performance is one of the most important design criteria for building design. Achieving sustainability and energy efficiency in building design must not be seen as a problem which constrains creative freedom, but as a challenge which can lead to new architectural qualities.

Over time, building professionals have become preoccupied with the protective functions of buildings. The phrases and terms used in the building industry show the thinking behind the design and construction of our structures; thermal protection, solar protection, wind protection, vapor barriers etc. It is now time to adopt a paradigm shift in thinking. Instead of devising ever more effective means of protection against the prevailing natural forces, why not use them? Instead of concentrating on minimizing the negative impact on the environment of the buildings we design, we should look to maximize their positive impact – buildings which give and don't just take!

In the energy design of a building, strategies and concepts are developed, which use the building's form, configuration and construction along with it's envelope, climate control and energy supply systems to minimize building energy demand, while at the same time optimizing the internal environmental conditions in the spaces.

After building an understanding of the physical laws of nature underlying energy use in buildings and urban design in the initial chapters, ways and means of allowing the consideration, analysis and manipulation of natural forces in the field of design in the built environment are explored. Strategies for maximizing energy performance in the design and construction of buildings and cities are then expanded upon.

It is interesting to note that, although energy is one of the most important topical issues of our time and many varied professions are involved in some way with finding solutions to the energy problem, many people if pressed would be stuck to define what it is. What is energy? In fact, this question is not that easy to answer and we will return to a more detailed discussion of it in the first chapter. Although we talk of energy being consumed, most people are actually aware of the conservation of energy principle, that "energy cannot be created or destroyed" but merely transformed from one form into another. This is in fact a simple statement of the first law of thermodynamics. The second law – which is unfortunately less well understood – is equally important, as we shall see. A basic understanding of the physical principles behind the use of energy and how energy is converted from one form into another is essential for all those involved in the design of buildings, and in the first part of this book the reader is introduced to these principles in a non-technical way. The goal is critical thinking, and this is only possible with a basic grasp of the physical principles.

A walk through a city is probably the best way to obtain a feeling for energy use in the built environment. Hong Kong is a city which is particularly suitable for this purpose. Go into any cafe or shop and look up at the ceiling and you will see an array of exposed pipes, cables and ducts through which flow hot and cold water, fresh and stale air, electricity, data, waste water. Energy flow in the built environment is visible, almost tangible. Walk out onto the sidewalk and you will see on many façades exposed vertical pipes, ducts, cables. At eye level on the streets, you will find technical plant rooms, substations and air intakes. Cars, trains, trucks, buses, trams, boats, people moving at different levels make the energy associated with transportation visible. In Berlin, Vienna or London you will also see energy systems in operation. However, in Europe, mechanical systems in buildings tend to be hidden from view as they are deemed ugly. The particular aesthetic associated with exposed systems in cities such as Hong Kong has to my mind its own special quality. In some ways, there is a suggestion of raw physical power emanating from the systems on view.

Looking out the window of an airplane at the structures of cities, towns, villages, suburbs, streets, roads, motorways, railway lines, forests, fields, agriculture, electrical transmission lines, power stations and wind turbines also provides a good start for considering the relationships between energy and the built environment.

However, perhaps the most impressive way of obtaining a feeling for energy use today is to imagine the world for one moment without fossil-fuel-based energy. Wherever you are, observe what is taking place and try to imagine the origin of the energy flows involved. Imagine the energy supply is cut off. Cars, trains, trams would stop moving. In buildings, many rooms would turn completely dark, even during daylight hours. Essential air flows would stop; heating, cooling systems would cease to operate; not to mention nearly all the equipment we use for business and entertainment.

The basic premise of this book is that the relationships between energy and form in architecture, urban design and city building are omnipresent and that in solving the challenges posed by the energy problem, we will develop new forms which not only achieve higher energy efficiency but also improve our built environment and provide a higher quality of living. Energy strategies in the form-finding process of building design can lead to new architectural forms, so that the urgently needed increased energy efficiency of our built environment can lead to new aesthetical qualities in architecture. The influence of energy strategies is thereby not confined to a consideration of the interaction of sun and wind forces with a proposed building shape. It can go far beyond this to lead to completely new forms in urban design and even to a radical reconfiguration of our entire physical infrastructure.

Energy efficient architecture should be understood as a triad comprising minimized energy consumption, optimal internal conditions and excellent spatial qualities, both in urban design and architectural terms. The aesthetics, the architectural quality, the beauty of our buildings is a vital component of any architecture which claims to be ecological or sustainable. A loss in the aesthetic quality of our built environment has no place in the truly sustainable development of our society.

This book does not refer to national norms. My experience working in many different countries around the world has shown me that the differences between doing an innovative concept in Singapore and in Berlin are often exaggerated by people who cling desperately to norms and standard practice for fear of doing something wrong, or as a way of demarcating their territorial expertise. There are the laws of states and countries, the laws of lands and international communities and then there are the laws of physics. The laws of physics are universal.

Fig. 1.1
Global primary energy
consumption

Our point of departure is a brief look at the global **energy problem**. Given the extensive coverage on climate change in the media, one could easily equate the energy problem with the global warming problem. In fact, the challenges associated with energy supply and use go far beyond this single aspect.

Quantities can be helpful in describing and understanding a problem. The magnitude of worldwide primary energy consumption in 2015 was approximately 570×10^{18} J or 570 EJ[1]. The sheer size of this number, however, makes it difficult to gain an understanding of this problem in human terms. To help you grasp the physical magnitude of energy consumption in today's world, close your eyes and imagine that every single person on earth (and there are now over seven billion of us) is holding in each hand four 100 W light bulbs (of the old incandescent type), which operate continuously for the period of a whole year. The amount of energy consumed would be very close to the actual energy consumed by our real world. This picture in your mind's eye is shown graphically in Figure 1.1. To deliver the 800 W electrical output of the light bulbs, roughly three times as much fossil fuel energy is consumed at a thermal power plant somewhere. The horizontal axis represents the world population and the vertical axis the energy consumption rate per person, roughly 2445 Watts per person (W/P) in 2015. The shaded area gives a geometrical representation of worldwide primary energy consumption[2]. The idea of a fictive continuous energy consumption rate to aid understanding of the magnitude of energy flows in society and the unit of "Watts per Person" have been used in Switzerland since 1998 to help convey a vision to the population with regard to a sustainable future. At that time roughly 2000 W/P was the global average energy consumption rate.

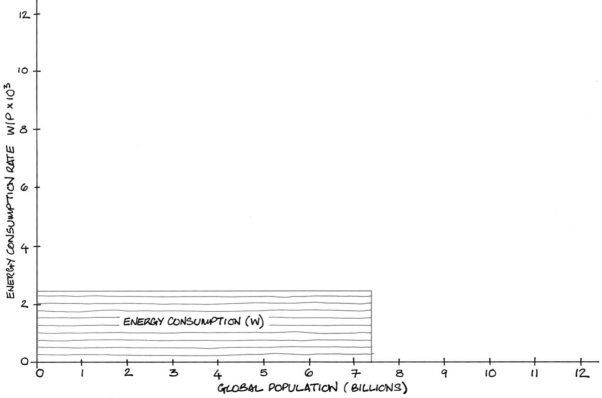

Fig. 1.1

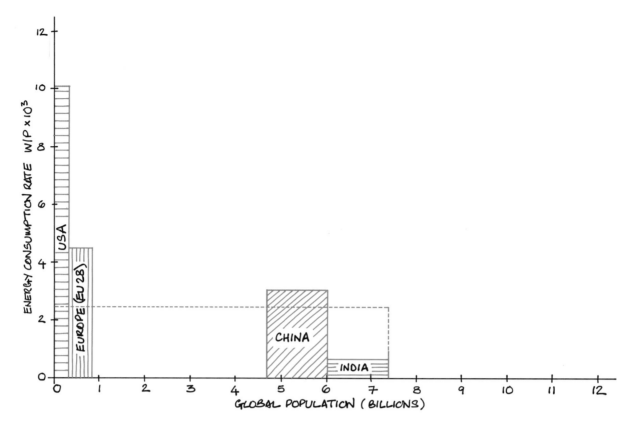

Fig. 1.2

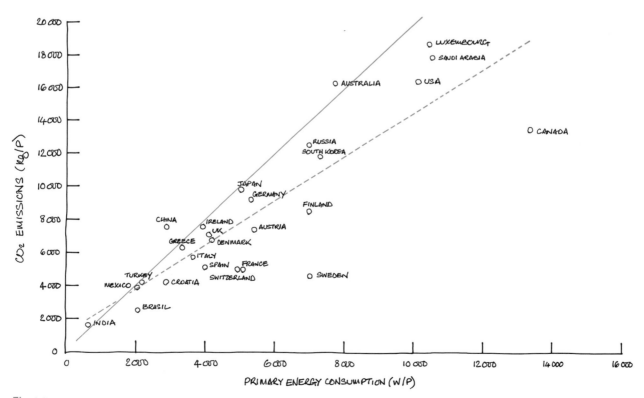

Fig. 1.3

Energy consumption is of course not evenly distributed across the globe. Figure 1.2 shows how energy is used at different rates in various regions of the world. An average US citizen consumes energy at a rate roughly four times greater than the global average; Europeans at a rate roughly twice as great and India at a rate which is lower than the world-wide average. When I first began to use this method of representation a decade ago, China too was significantly lower than the global average. The horizontal width of the respective rectangles represents the population size and it is therefore easy to see that moderate increases in energy demand in large countries such as China and India lead to a large rise in absolute energy demand, which cannot easily be compensated for by reducing specific energy demand in other regions.

Figure 1.3 shows the correlation between energy consumption and CO₂ emissions for various countries. Countries which lie above the dotted line emit larger amounts of CO₂ for each unit of primary energy used compared to the average value for these selected countries, while countries below emit smaller amounts. The full line represents the global average value. The position on this chart thus gives an indication of how carbon intensive the energy production processes in a given country are.

There is also a clear correlation between energy consumption and economic productivity as shown in Figure 1.4, where GDP (Gross Domestic Product, the monetary value of all goods and services provided by a country in a year) is plotted against primary energy demand. Here, countries which lie above the dotted line have a higher energy intensity; i.e., they use more energy to produce one dollar of gross domestic product, while countries below the line are more efficient. The import and export of

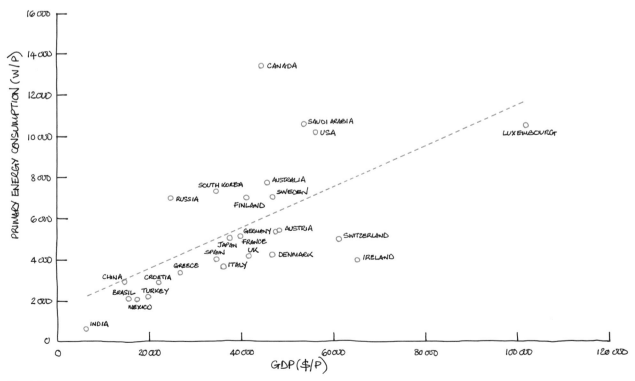

Fig. 1.4

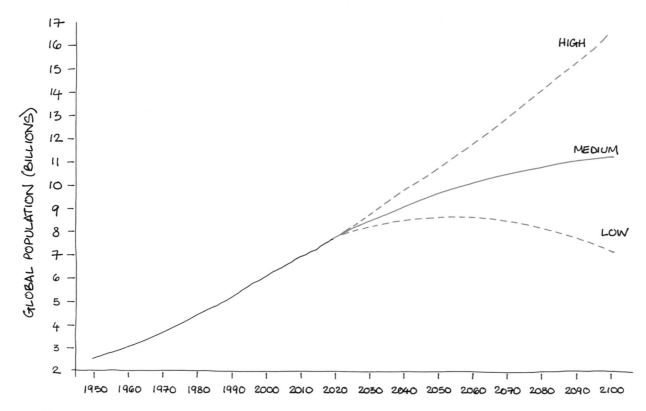

Fig. 1.5

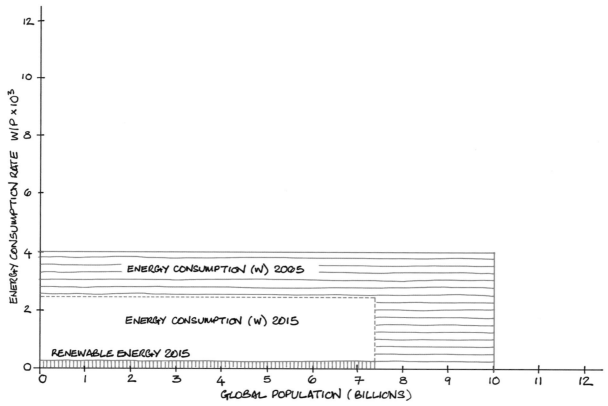

Fig. 1.6

Fig. 1.5
Projected population
growth (Source: UN,
esa.un.org/unpd/wpp)

Fig. 1.6
Projected worldwide
energy consumption 2065

manufactured goods of course distorts the picture. The global average energy intensity is 0.16 W/$ and is therefore slightly higher than the 0.14 W/$ calculated as an average value for these selected countries. Economic growth can to a certain extent be decoupled from energy consumption by increasing energy efficiency. However, while the slope of the curve can be modified, the basic relationship remains. Increasing economic productivity leads to an increase in energy consumption. High economic growth rates in large countries such as China will result in a significant increase in absolute worldwide energy consumption.

How can world energy demand be expected to develop in the future? To allow an insight into even the not-so-distant future requires knowledge of factors such as expected population and economic growth rates. Figure 1.5 shows various scenarios for projected population growth. Assuming a global population of 10 billion people in 2065 and an average energy consumption rate of 4000 W/P (calculated as the average of today's global rate of roughly 2500 W/P and a figure of 5500 W/P for a relatively energy efficient developed country), total energy consumption is estimated to be 1250 EJ (Fig. 1.6). More detailed estimates have been made by organizations as diverse as Greenpeace and Shell, where the projection for 2050 ranges between 800 and 900 EJ. Of course, some will argue that such a rate of economic growth is unlikely and that in 2065, half the world's population will still be living in poverty and more than one in ten people will not have enough to eat. To base our future strategies on such predictions is however deeply cynical and when we devise concepts for the future, we must assume as the basic premise that we will correct the global inequalities and squalor which is an unfortunate part of our world today.

How realistic is the figure of 4000 W/P used above? We can estimate it in a different way by starting with today's global average GDP of roughly $15 550 and an energy intensity of 0.16 W/$ and assuming a modest global economic growth rate of 2 % after inflation and an annual decrease in energy intensity of 1 %. This calculation also gives a figure of approx. 4000 W/P in 2065. Note that an annual decrease of 1 % in energy intensity over 50 years is equivalent to a total decrease in energy intensity of approximately 40 % and thus we are assuming that global energy efficiency, measured in $ per W, would increase by approximately 65 %.

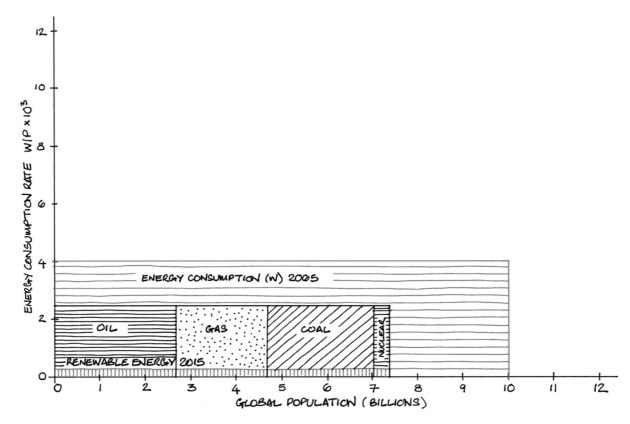

Fig. 1.7

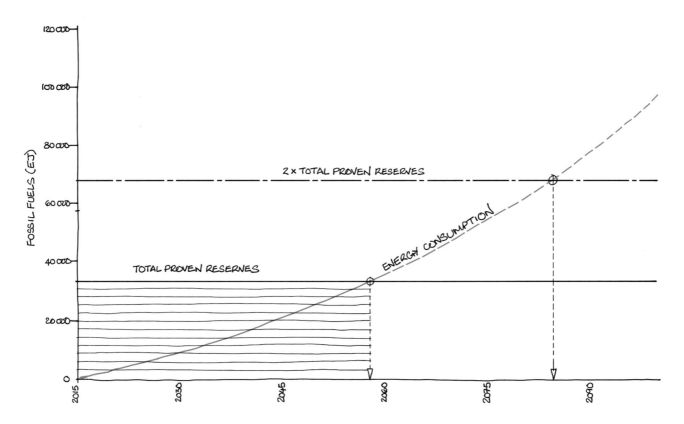

Fig. 1.8

Fig. 1.7
Energy mix 2015

Fig. 1.8
Fossil fuels expiration date

The amount of primary energy demand met by renewable energy sources today is also shown in Figure 1.6. The relative sizes of the rectangles for energy use in 2065 and energy production by renewable sources today should give you an idea of the magnitude of the energy problem and, as is hinted at in the opening paragraph of this chapter, global warming is only one of the many aspects of this problem alongside the pollution of air, land and water (oil spills, atmospheric pollution, smog, ozone, acid rain, thermal pollution of rivers etc.). It is also necessary to take into consideration the issue of rapidly depleting fossil energy resources and the geopolitical issues and tensions arising out of the struggle to control these.

Now consider the following. The vast majority of this annual energy demand is met today by basically setting fire to remaining reserves of fossil fuels found underground (Fig. 1.7). When you consider the daily struggle to meet our present energy demand represented by the small white rectangle in Figure 1.6, little imagination is needed to perceive that coping with the projected energy demand represented by the large shaded rectangle in 50 years' time may be a challenge.

Fig. 1.8 shows a plot of the predicted fossil fuel consumption rate against known reserves, assuming an annual increase in the magnitude of renewable energy production of 1% and the same assumptions as above, giving a fossil fuel expiration date before the end of this century[3]. Therefore, even if we were not concerned with global warming, someone born today will likely see the end of the fossil fuel era; at least in its present form. In the time it probably took you to read this far, roughly 2000 people joined us on the planet and an energy demand equal to roughly 2 million barrels of oil was consumed.

What is energy? Energy is, on a basic level, easy to understand: on a deeper level, notoriously complex. The brilliant American theoretical physicist Richard Feynman, known for his work in quantum mechanics and particle physics, famously said: "In physics today, we have no knowledge of what energy is," a year before he received the Nobel Prize for Physics in 1965.

In our everyday use of the word, energy suggests movement, power or potency. Energy makes things happen. Things move or change condition. Energy can be thought of as the potential to cause change. In classical physics, energy is the ability to do work and work is done when a

ENERGY

$$e = mc^2 \ (J)$$

m IS MASS IN kg
c IS SPEED OF LIGHT (3×10^8 m/s)

WORK

$$W = Fd \ (J)$$

F IS APPLIED FORCE IN N
d IS DISTANCE IN m

POWER

= WORK DONE
   PER UNIT TIME

$1 W = 1 J/s$

KINECTIC ENERGY

$$E_k = 0.5mv^2 \ (J)$$

m IS MASS IN kg
v IS VELOCITY IN m/s

POTENTIAL ENERGY

$$E_p = mgh \ (J)$$

m IS MASS IN kg $g = 9.81$ m/s^2
h IS HEIGHT ABOVE REFERENCE DATUM (m)

CHEMICAL ENERGY

$$E_c = mH_c \ (J)$$

m IS MASS IN kg
H_c IS HEAT OF COMBUSTION IN J/kg

THERMAL ENERGY

$$Q_s = mc\Delta T \ (J) \ [SENSIBLE]$$

m IS MASS IN kg
c IS SPECIFIC HEAT CAPACITY IN J/kgK
ΔT IS TEMPERATURE CHANGE IN K

$$Q_L = mh_T \ (J) \ [LATENT]$$

m IS MASS IN kg
h_T IS ENTHALPY OF TRANSITION IN J/kg

Fig. 1.9

Fig. 1.9
Energy formulae

Fig. 1.10
Converting kJ to kWh

force acting on an object causes it to move a distance in the direction of the force. Energy is measured in Joules. When a force of 1 N acts on an object and causes it to move 1 meter, 1 Joule of work is said to be done (see Fig. 1.9). The ability to provide this work can also be stored in a system. To get an idea of what 1 Joule of energy feels like, raise a cell phone from a table to your ear and you will increase the potential energy of the phone by approximately 1 Joule of energy. If you repeat this exercise once every second, you will be working at a rate of 1 Joule of energy per second (J/s) which is equal to 1 Watt. The rate of work or energy use is also called power. Energy use in buildings is often measured and stated in terms of kWh. 1 kWh is equivalent to 3600 kJ. This can easily be remembered by the representation shown in Fig. 1.10.

You may be wondering how the above definition can be applied to heat energy. After all, if we heat an amount of water from an initial temperature of 20 °C to, say, 40 °C, the water does not move; so where are the force, object and distance referred to in the above definition to be found? In this situation, although there may be no movement on a macroscopic scale, there are interactions between the atoms and molecules which involve forces and movement on a microscopic scale.

Albert Einstein showed that mass and energy are equivalent, and his famous equation is the mathematical expression of just that (Fig. 1.9). The essence of this discovery is that mass can be converted into energy. This phenomenon can be observed in a nuclear reaction.

Energy exists in many different forms. The form of energy which is probably easiest to understand intuitively is **kinetic energy**, the energy associated with movement. If you throw the cellphone mentioned above across the room at a velocity of 10 m/s (or 36 km/h), its kinetic energy will be 7.5 Joules (see formula in Fig. 1.9). Kinetic energy is mass in motion. Consider a 200 m tall high-rise office building. If a wind turbine with a

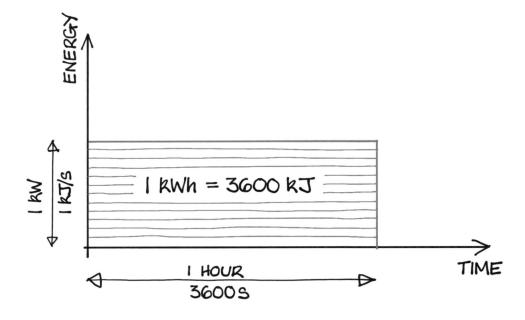

Fig. 1.10

SI PREFIXES

E	10^{18}	GLOBAL ENERGY CONSUMPTION 2015 = 570 EJ
P	10^{15}	
T	10^{12}	
G	10^{9}	FUKUSHIMA NUCLEAR POWER PLANT CAPACITY 4.7 GW_{el}
M	10^{6}	
k	10^{3}	BMW BUILDING MUNICH, PV SYSTEM CAPACITY = 824 kW_p
h	10^{2}	
da	10^{1}	
	10^{0}	= 1
d	10^{-1}	
c	10^{-2}	
m	10^{-3}	LASER POINTER LIGHT = 5 mW
μ	10^{-6}	
n	10^{-9}	WAVELENGTH OF VISIBLE LIGHT: 380 nm – 780 nm
p	10^{-12}	
f	10^{-15}	
a	10^{-18}	1 ELECTRON VOLT = 0.16×10^{-18} J

Fig. 1.11

Fig. 1.11
SI prefixes

diameter of 10 m – and therefore an area swept by the blades of 78.5 m² – is integrated into the roof design so that it faces into the prevailing wind with a wind speed of 3 m/s, the mass flow rate of wind approaching the turbine's swept area is approximately 283 kg/s (the volumetric flow rate of a fluid is the product of velocity and cross sectional area, and mass flow rate is obtained by multiplying by density, which is approximately 1.2 kg/m³ for air). In this case, we are interested in the power available; i.e., the energy flow per unit time. In the same way as above, the kinetic energy of the wind is calculated to be 1274 Joules per second or 1.3 kW. The wind turbine can, however, only convert a portion of this available energy into electrical energy which can be used in the building. Assuming an efficiency of 40 %, the electrical power delivered would be approximately 0.5 kW. If the floor area of the skyscraper is 100 000 m² (50 floors at 2000 m²) and we assume an electrical energy use intensity of 65 W/m², the proportion of the skyscraper's total energy demand which can be met by the wind turbine is about 0.01 %. Assuming that wind blows at a constant velocity of 3 m/s for the entire 8760 hours in a year, the annual energy yield of the wind turbine would be less than 4500 kWh and therefore barely able to meet the electricity consumption of a single-family household.

When you lift the cellphone (with an assumed mass of 150 g) you increase the **potential energy** of the cellphone with respect to the height of the table. The increase in potential energy is given by the mass of the phone multiplied by gravitational acceleration and the height difference; in this case assumed to be 0.7 m between the table and your ear (Fig. 1.9). Let us assume that the 200 m high building mentioned above has a swimming pool on the roof with dimensions of 25 m by 10 m and a depth of 2 m. The mass of water in the pool is the volume multiplied by a density of 1000 kg/m³ for water, which gives us 500 000 kg. Similar to the phone example just considered, this mass of water possesses potential energy relative to the ground. Using the same formula and the conversion factor explained above, the potential energy is approx. 273 kWh. If we allow this water to flow through a turbine on the way to the ground, we can convert the potential energy to kinetic energy and produce useful work. Assuming an efficiency of 80 %, the system could provide power for one 100 W computer in the office building below for roughly 2200 hours a year.

Chemical energy is the energy contained in the chemical bonds between the atoms and molecules in a substance. Energy is released in exothermic reactions, and must be supplied in endothermic reactions in order for the reaction to occur. A common endothermic reaction is photosynthesis; a common exothermic reaction is the combustion of a hydrocarbon fuel (Fig. 1.12). You will notice the mirror symmetry in these two equations. The burning of wood can be seen as the reverse process of its creation. Wood has an energy content of approximately 15 MJ/kg and a density of approx. 700 kg/m³. If we were to fill up the swimming pool on the rooftop of the tower considered above with wood, we could store approximately 1458 MWh of chemical energy. Assuming an efficiency of 90 %, we could combust the wood in a boiler and provide 1300 MWh of thermal energy for use in the building. This equates to approximately 13 kWh per m² office area which could meet roughly 50 % of the annual heating energy demand of a low energy office building in central Europe.

The energy released by the above chemical reaction is in the form of heat, a very common form of energy that flows as a result of temperature difference. The energy in a hot object is **thermal energy** which is a result of the kinetic energy of the atoms and molecules in the object. All other energy forms are eventually transformed into thermal energy. If we fill the swimming pool mentioned above with water from the city supply network at a temperature of 10 °C and heat it up to 30 °C, the energy required to do this is given by the formula for thermal energy in Fig. 1.9. The specific heat capacity of water is approximately 4200 J/kg°C, i.e. 4200 J of thermal energy are required to raise the temperature of 1 kg of water by 1 °C, and so we will require 42 GJ to heat the water by the required amount. To heat

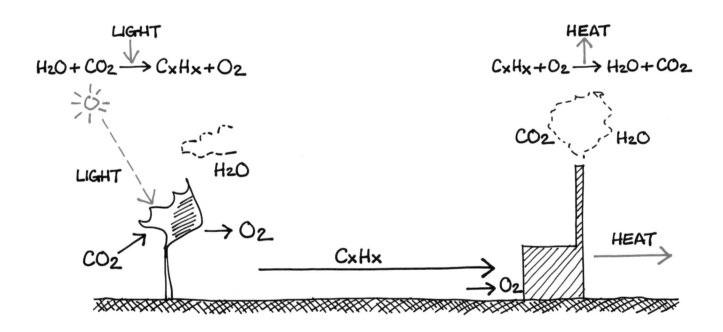

Fig. 1.12

Fig. 1.12
Chemical energy

the water to 100 °C we would need to supply a further 147 GJ. If we were to continue to supply heat to the water after that, it would remain at 100 °C and start to boil. A further 1130 GJ of heat can be added in a process during which the water temperature remains constant but the water changes phase or state from a liquid to a vapor (steam). This energy is called **latent heat energy** and is the thermal energy released or added in a process during which a substance changes state. We will discuss these energy forms – as well as other forms such as electrical energy and nuclear energy – in more detail in the next chapter.

Up to now we have talked about the energy problem. It is important, however, to realize that energy cannot be consumed and therefore there is, in a physical sense, no energy problem. Energy is in fact conserved and can be neither created nor destroyed (according to the theory of special relativity, it is actually mass-energy which is conserved; however in all practical cases, excepting the use of nuclear energy, the change in mass is negligible and therefore mass and energy are taken to be independently conserved). Energy can however be transformed from one form to another and every physical process on earth in which energy is transformed leads to an increase in **entropy**, which is a measure of disorder in our universe. This amounts to a continual reduction in the quality of energy resources and flows available to us. This is what we call the "energy problem", although "entropy problem" would be a much more exact description of the situation. This seemingly semantic issue has far-reaching practical consequences, and the lack of understanding of these basic scientific principles leads to misunderstandings and misguided developments in our society.

As we shall see in the next chapter, heat cannot be completely transformed into work and for this reason, real physical processes are not reversible. One important consequence of this is that the various forms of energy available to us in a given situation – e.g., chemical, thermal, electrical etc. – have different qualities. As an example, in a building design context the quality of energy available in one unit of electricity is much greater than that that available in one unit of the thermal energy associated with hot water in a heating system. Therefore, when comparing energy flows in various options, the quality and not just the quantity of energy needs to be considered. In a building, a unit of electrical energy can be used to power the motors needed to transport people in elevators, move water in pipes or air in ducts, or provide energy for artificial lighting; whereas hot water at 45 °C can be used to provide space heating or to take a shower but for little else. A unit of electricity can be converted entirely to thermal energy, whereas a negligible fraction of a unit of thermal energy at that temperature could be theoretically converted to electricity. It is therefore important to differentiate between thermal and electrical energy use in the analysis of energy use in buildings. Consider the following: the heat produced by 200 students in a lecture theatre for a period of 2 hours is approximately 145 MJ. The heat required for a warm shower is approx. 7 MJ. Yet even if we could completely capture the thermal energy in the lecture theatre, we cannot use this energy to provide enough warm water for even one shower. We will see why in the next chapter.

It is important to differentiate between primary, secondary, final and useful energy use. **Primary energy** use is the direct use of an energy

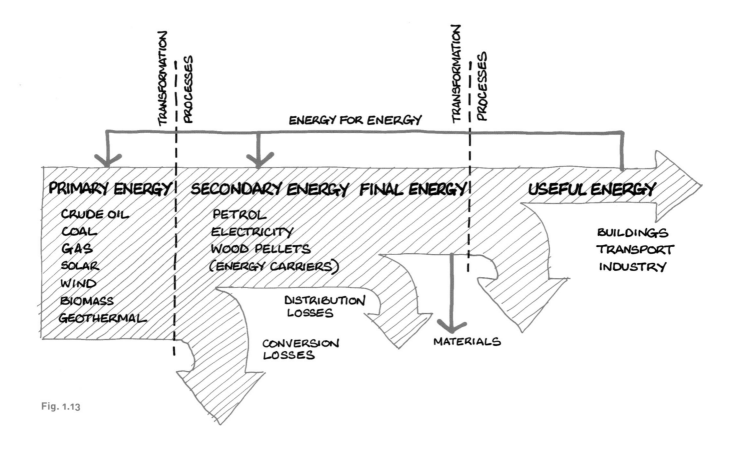

TRANSFORMATION PROCESSES

ENERGY FOR ENERGY

TRANSFORMATION PROCESSES

PRIMARY ENERGY

CRUDE OIL
COAL
GAS
SOLAR
WIND
BIOMASS
GEOTHERMAL

SECONDARY ENERGY FINAL ENERGY

PETROL
ELECTRICITY
WOOD PELLETS
(ENERGY CARRIERS)

DISTRIBUTION
LOSSES

CONVERSION
LOSSES

MATERIALS

USEFUL ENERGY

BUILDINGS
TRANSPORT
INDUSTRY

Fig. 1.13

Fig. 1.13
Primary, secondary,
final and useful energy

source which occurs in nature and which can be supplied to energy users without any conversion or transformation process. Primary energy can be renewable (solar energy, wind, geothermal, biomass) or non-renewable (crude oil, natural gas, coal). Energy obtained after a transformation process, such as electricity or refined petroleum products, is called **secondary energy**. The actual energy delivered to an energy user or consumer, e.g., the electricity at the main building switchboard or the natural gas connection to a heating boiler, is called **final energy**. The resulting warmth, cooling, light, motion etc. available to the end user (which is the aim of the whole process), is called **useful energy** (Fig. 1.13).

Of the fossil fuels, gas is the cleanest in terms of CO_2 emissions, whereas coal is the least clean and has by far the greatest reserves. Fossil fuels only began to be used on a large scale about 200 years ago and their use to meet energy demand on the present scale cannot be expected to last even another 100 years. Therefore, in the history of mankind, the age of fossil fuel use will have been a short period. There are no CO_2 emissions associated with the electricity produced by nuclear power plants. There are however many other problematic issues, including risks due to accidents, use of nuclear waste for terrorism purposes and unresolved waste disposal. In addition to the geopolitical issues associated with the security of energy supply, nuclear power plants as targets for terror attacks are also a concern. Energy sources are regarded as renewable if they are not expected to be depleted on a human timescale.

How much energy could we supply ourselves with using only our own muscles? If we look up one of the many reference sources for diet, health etc., a figure of about 500 Calories "burned" per hour for intense physical activity is often quoted. Assuming the human body is approx. 20 % efficient in converting the chemical energy of food into useful mechanical work, we arrive at approximately 100 W (1 Calorie is equal to 4 184 kJ). Therefore, we could assume that a person used to physical work could supply approximately 100 W of mechanical power over a sustained time period. In a world powered by human muscles, an average European's primary energy consumption of approx. 4400 W would require roughly 44 muscle-bound "Energy Delivery Specialists" working around the clock.

A human being can supply roughly 100 W with muscle power. A 1 m² photovoltaic panel can supply roughly the same at times of peak sunshine. On the other hand, if you pull up at your local refueling station and fill up a 70-liter tank with fuel within a time interval of 2 minutes, you are transferring 2100 l/h of fuel with a density of roughly 710 kg/m³ and an energy content of approximately 13 kWh/kg (or 45 MJ/kg) from the pump to your car. Energy is being transferred at a rate of approximately 19 MW or 19 000 000 W! As we will see in future chapters, these differences in energy density between our present fossil-fueled society and a world running on renewable energy sources in the future is one of the major challenges we face as we develop the energy systems of the future.

Fig. 2.1
Temperature and pressure
of a gas in a container

Fig. 2.2
Thermodynamic system

Movement is the natural condition of all things. If no external force acts on a moving object, it will continue its movement eternally. As you read this book, photons are supplying the necessary light at a speed of 3×10^8 m/s (the fastest speed possible in our universe) to enable you to see the text. The molecules of the air surrounding you are darting around in random motion. The higher the temperature of the space, the faster the motion of the air particles (Fig. 2.1).

All matter is composed of a large number of atoms or groups of atoms bonded together called molecules. At this molecular level, the inert objects in the space you are occupying are also in constant motion. Again, the higher the temperature of the object, the faster the motion of its constituent molecules and the higher its energy content.

The behavior of individual molecules is responsible for the way we experience matter on a macroscopic level. For example, if the air molecules begin to move faster in a room as a result of increasing temperature, the rate at which the molecules collide with the room's enclosing surfaces increases, leading to a higher air pressure in the space.

As we have seen in the previous chapter, buildings and cities cannot exist without the use of vast amounts of energy. Therefore, a basic understanding of the physical principles behind the conversion of energy from one form to another in buildings and cities as well as the environmental, social and economic consequences of these conversion processes is essential for those involved in the design of buildings.

In this chapter, a very simplified summary of the physics involved in the energy design of buildings and urban areas is given. Examples from real building applications are used in order to illustrate the theory. The three most important areas of physics for the field of building energy design are thermodynamics, fluid dynamics and heat transfer.

As we have seen in Chapter 1, energy exists in many different forms. **Thermodynamics** is the study of the conversion of energy from one form into another. In thermodynamics, the object or collection of objects we wish to study is called the system. This can be a region in space, such as a room, or a fixed mass, such as a concrete slab. An imaginary surface is drawn around the system which is called the system boundary. Everything outside this boundary is called the surroundings (Fig. 2.2). A system is said to be closed if the mass of the system remains constant, and open if there is mass flowing through the system boundary.

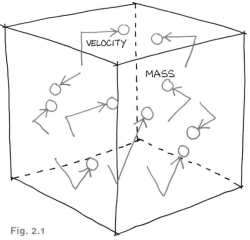

Fig. 2.1

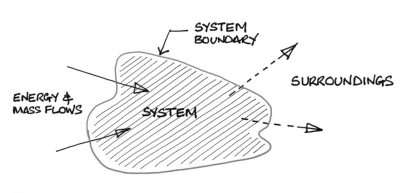

Fig. 2.2

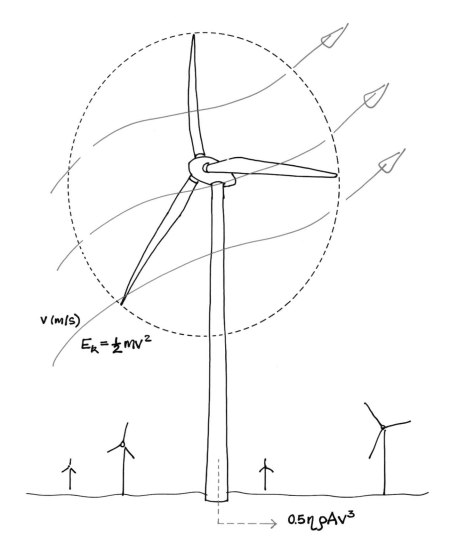

$v\ (m/s)$

$E_k = \frac{1}{2}mv^2$

Fig. 2.3

$0.5\eta \rho A v^3$

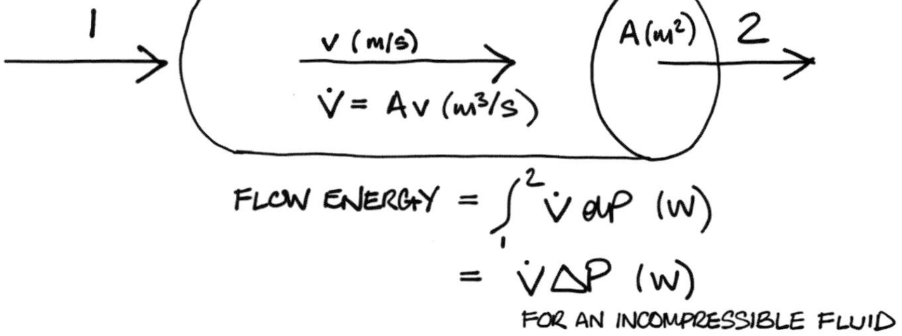

1

$v\ (m/s)$

$\dot{V} = Av\ (m^3/s)$

$A\ (m^2)$ 2

$$FLOW\ ENERGY = \int_1^2 \dot{V}\, dP\ (W)$$

$$= \dot{V}\Delta P\ (W)$$

FOR AN INCOMPRESSIBLE FLUID

Fig. 2.4

The total energy of a system is the sum of all energy forms existing in the system. These can be grouped into two categories; the energy forms on a microscopic or molecular scale, and those on a macroscopic scale. The sum of the energy forms associated with the microscopic structure of the system is called its internal energy. This is the sum of the kinetic and potential energies of all the individual molecules which make up the system.

The macroscopic forms of energy a given system has are those associated with the system as a whole, when related to some reference datum, e.g. potential energy due to height above the ground, kinetic energy due to a higher velocity compared to the surroundings etc. In the wind turbine shown in Fig. 2.3, all the molecules that make up the air stream flowing through the cross-sectional area of the wind turbine are moving at a certain velocity relative to the ground. This organized movement of all the air stream's molecules in a certain direction at a certain velocity constitutes the kinetic energy of the wind or the air stream as a whole. The disorganized movement of these molecules at a microscopic scale constitutes the internal energy of the air stream. The macroscopic energy forms, such as the kinetic energy associated with the wind or the potential energy associated with a water mass such as in a hydroelectric plant, were discussed in chapter one.

Temperature is a measure of the energy of a system associated with the kinetic energy of its molecules. As we have seen, the higher the activity of the molecules, the higher the temperature. There are various temperature scales currently in use to measure temperature. In the SI unit system, which is used practically everywhere except in the US, temperature is measured in degrees Celsius. In the British System, still in use in the US, the Fahrenheit scale is used. In science, the Kelvin scale – which is a thermodynamic temperature scale – is used universally. When converting from the Celsius to the Kelvin scale, you only need to remember that zero Kelvin (0 K) is equal to –273 °C (absolute zero, the lowest possible temperature) and 0 °C is equal to 273 K. All other values can be linearly interpolated or extrapolated from these. The internal energy of a system and the product of its pressure and volume constitute its enthalpy or total heat content. In flowing fluids, the sum of the internal energy of the fluid and the flow energy required to make it flow constitute its enthalpy. The flow energy of a moving fluid is equal to its pressure multiplied by its volume flow rate (Fig. 2.4).

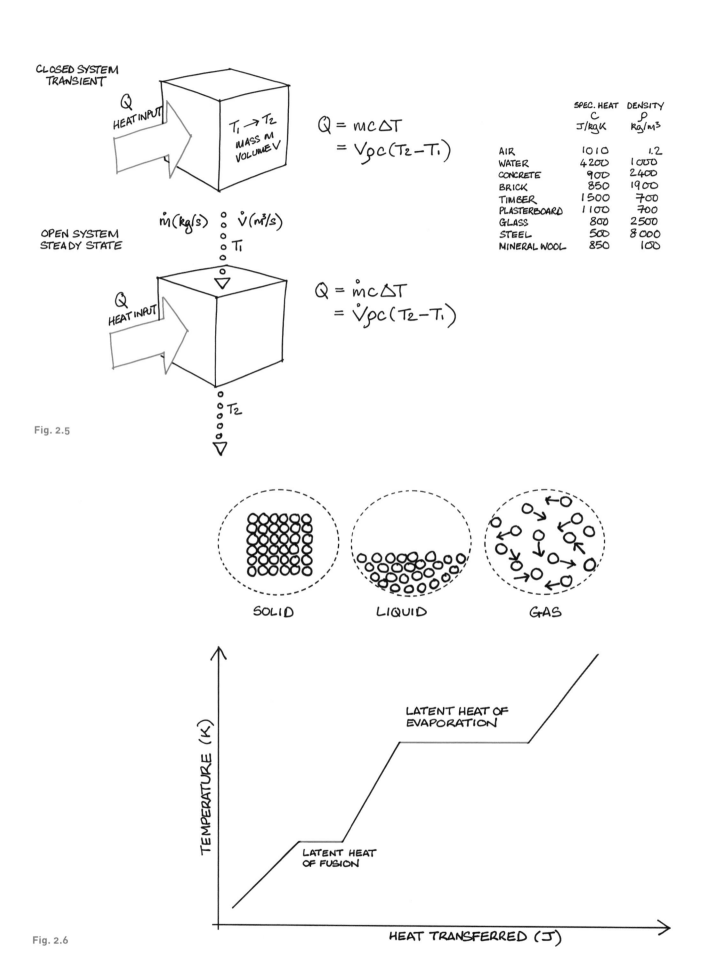

CLOSED SYSTEM
TRANSIENT

Q
HEAT INPUT

$T_1 \rightarrow T_2$
MASS M
VOLUME V

$Q = mc\Delta T$
$= V\rho c(T_2 - T_1)$

	SPEC. HEAT C J/kgK	DENSITY ρ kg/m³
AIR	1010	1.2
WATER	4200	1000
CONCRETE	900	2400
BRICK	850	1900
TIMBER	1500	700
PLASTERBOARD	1100	700
GLASS	800	2500
STEEL	500	8000
MINERAL WOOL	850	100

$\dot{m}(kg/s)$ $\dot{V}(m^3/s)$

T_1

OPEN SYSTEM
STEADY STATE

Q
HEAT INPUT

$Q = \dot{m}c\Delta T$
$= \dot{V}\rho c(T_2 - T_1)$

T_2

Fig. 2.5

SOLID   LIQUID   GAS

LATENT HEAT OF
EVAPORATION

TEMPERATURE (K)

LATENT HEAT
OF FUSION

HEAT TRANSFERRED (J)

Fig. 2.6

Fig. 2.5
Specific heat capacity

Fig. 2.6
Phase change processes

The heat necessary to raise the temperature of 1 kg of a substance by 1 K is a physical constant called the specific heat capacity of a substance. The value depends on whether the process is carried out at constant volume or at constant pressure and on the temperature during the process. In a steady state process, the conditions remain constant over the considered period of time, while in a transient process, conditions vary over time. Figure 2.5 shows typical values for materials used in building design and the method of calculation for a transient closed system; e.g., heat being absorbed in a concrete slab and for a steady state open system, e.g., a heating coil in an air handling system. If, for example, in the design of a groundwater cooling system tests have shown that the maximum amount of water which can be pumped from the ground is 25 kg/s, and the maximum allowable temperature increase of the water is 5 K, the maximum cooling capacity of the system is 525 kW.

Heat transfer to or from a substance which changes its temperature is called sensible heat transfer. Latent heat transfer occurs when heat is transferred to or from a substance without any change in the temperature of the substance, but resulting in the substance changing phase, e.g. from solid to liquid or from liquid to gas. Latent energy is the energy associated with the intermolecular forces between the molecules in a substance. Every substance can exist in one of three possible phases; solid, liquid or gas. In a solid, the molecules are arranged in a lattice structure which is repeated throughout a given mass of the substance. The distances between the molecules are small and the intermolecular forces are strong. The molecules in a solid oscillate about their fixed position in the lattice structure and the magnitude of their velocities depends on the temperature. If enough heat is added, the molecules acquire sufficient energy to overcome the intermolecular forces and break away from their fixed positions, thus beginning the melting process, in which a phase change transition from solid to liquid form takes place (Fig. 2.6). In the liquid phase, the molecules are free to move relative to one another on account of the weakened intermolecular forces and thus a liquid has no fixed shape but takes on the shape of the container in which it is held. In general, the distance between the molecules increases in liquid form (the exception being water). If sufficient heat is supplied to a substance in liquid form, the intermolecular forces weaken further, initiating the transition into the gas phase, in which the molecules are completely free to move about at random and the distances between the molecules are much greater. A gas expands in the atmosphere and does not form a free surface. On account of the fact that the forces between molecules are strongest in solids, weakest in gases and somewhere in between in liquids, a substance is in its highest energy form as a gas and its lowest as a solid. At a given temperature, the pressure at which a pure substance changes phase from liquid to vapor (a gas is called a vapor when it is close to the state of condensing to a liquid) is called the saturation pressure. For example, the saturation pressure of water at 100 °C is approx. 1 bar (atmospheric pressure). Therefore, at atmospheric pressure water boils at 100 °C.

When the atoms in a molecule of a substance combine with other atoms or when they separate from atoms to which they are attached, chemical energy – the energy binding the atoms in a molecule together in so-called atomic bonds – is involved. In a chemical reaction such as combustion, in which energy is released, the binding energy between the atoms is less in the products of the reaction than it was in the reactants. In a reaction in which energy needs to be supplied, such as photosynthesis, the atomic bonds in the products are greater.

In a nuclear reaction, thermal energy is released. This is the energy associated with the bonding forces within the nucleus of the atom itself. In nuclear fission, the nucleus is split. In fusion, two nuclei are fused together. In both cases, the mass of the products is less than the mass of the reactants and the missing mass is converted into energy in accordance with Einstein's $e = mc^2$ equation.

In the preceding discussion of the energy associated with the microscopic structure of a substance or system, we started with the kinetic energy of the molecules (sensible energy), continued with energy associated with the intermolecular forces (latent energy), continued further with the energy associated with the atomic bonds between atoms in a molecule (chemical energy) and finished with the energy associated with forces within the nucleus of an individual atom (nuclear energy).

All of the energy sources available to us on Earth are ultimately a result of the Sun's activities. Even tides are caused by gravitational forces between the Sun, Earth and Moon. Solar radiation, air temperature, biomass, the precipitation which makes hydropower possible, winds and waves all result from nuclear fusion processes in the Sun's core. Even the fossil fuels found under the Earth's surface are the results of decomposing biomass, and are therefore also products of nuclear fusion in the Sun many millions of years ago. Geothermal energy, on the other hand, is generated by radioactivity in the Earth's core.

In the design of buildings, we are primarily concerned with energy transfer processes. Energy can be transferred to a system in only three ways; by heat, work or mass. If energy is being transferred to a system and the driving force of the energy transfer is temperature difference, then en-

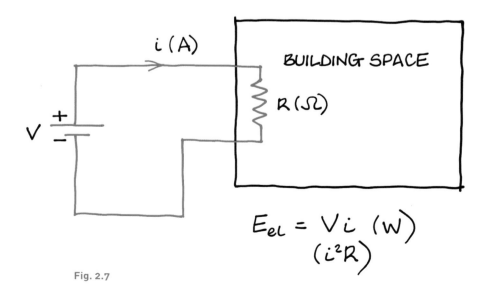

Fig. 2.7

Fig. 2.7
Electrical energy

Fig. 2.8
First law of
thermodynamics

ergy is being transferred by heat. If not, and there is no mass flow into or out of the system, then energy is being transferred by work, caused by a force acting through a distance. When electrons cross a system boundary, for example passing through a wall via a cable to equipment within a room, energy is transferred to the room in the form of work (Fig. 2.7).

The first law of thermodynamics states that in any process, energy is always conserved. Energy can be neither created nor destroyed but only transformed from one form to another (Fig. 2.8). This is a fundamental law of nature. The energy flowing into a system minus the energy flowing out of the system in a given time period is equal to the change in the total energy of the system.

The total energy of a system is, in most cases, equal to the sum of its kinetic energy, potential energy and internal energy. Therefore, according to the first law of thermodynamics, in an isolated system – a system in which neither mass nor energy are allowed to cross the system boundary – a change in any one of these three quantities must be compensated for by a change in one or both of the others. The sum of the potential and kinetic energies of a system is also called its mechanical energy – the ability of the system to do work.

The quantity of energy is conserved in any process. However, the quality of energy is never conserved and this is a simple way of stating the second law of thermodynamics. If we start the engine of a car by setting fire to the fuel, causing it to accelerate forwards, all the molecules that constitute the car move forwards in a certain direction at a certain velocity in an organized manner. On the other hand, if we set fire to the car, we increase the disorganized movement of the molecules of the car only. The organized energy in the first case does useful work, the disorganized energy in the second case increases the thermal energy of the car but performs no useful work. It is the degree of organization which determines the quality of energy. Besides the fact that the study of the second law offers a very interesting and rewarding intellectual pursuit, it is also arguably the most

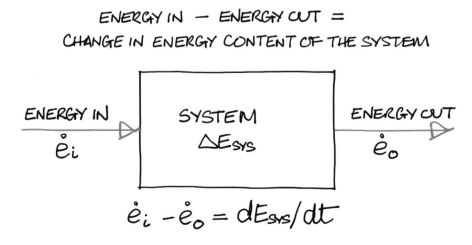

ENERGY IN — ENERGY OUT =
CHANGE IN ENERGY CONTENT OF THE SYSTEM

ENERGY IN $\dot{e}_i$ SYSTEM ΔE_{SYS} ENERGY OUT $\dot{e}_o$

$$\dot{e}_i - \dot{e}_o = dE_{SYS}/dt$$

Fig. 2.8

important physical law of nature with regard to the sustainable development of the built environment. Therefore, a basic grasp of the second law and its consequences for the design of buildings and cities is a fundamental requisite in the education of every building design professional.

The second law can be stated in several different ways. We have already met one in the last paragraph. A common way of stating it is that heat cannot be completely converted into work. We will look at this in detail below. Another way of stating it is that thermal energy always flows in the direction of decreasing temperature difference. For example, in hot weather, in the absence of a suitable natural heat sink such as the ground, a space can only be cooled by using a heat pump, which uses high quality energy to "pump" the energy in the opposite (unnatural) direction.

A fourth way of stating the second law uses the term entropy, which was introduced in chapter one. According to the second law of thermodynamics, a process in the universe can only proceed in the direction of increasing entropy. This statement implies the one-way direction of time or the "arrow of time". The second law also introduces the notion of irreversibility. All processes in the real world are irreversible and can only occur in a certain direction. Reversing such a process is only possible if energy is supplied from outside the boundary of the system under consideration. As a simple example, imagine you heat a house with a log fire. When the wood is expended, the house will be warmer and there will have been emissions from the chimney into the ambient air. While it is theoretically conceivable

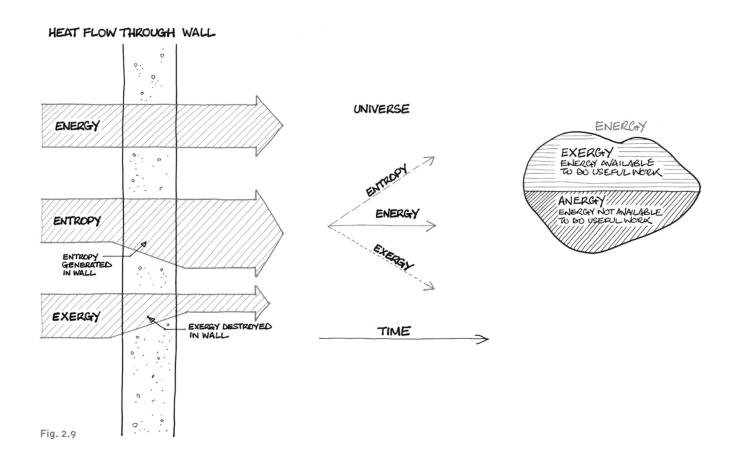

Fig. 2.9

Fig. 2.9
Energy, entropy, exergy

Fig. 2.10
Heat engine

that you could go out, find and gather together all the particles of CO_2 and other gases from the outside air and use the heat contained in the air and surfaces of the room to reconstruct the logs, this is certainly not going to happen without a major energy investment.

In the process described above, the chemical energy of the wood logs was converted into thermal energy. The binding energy between the atoms is less in the products of the reaction (CO_2 and H_2O) than it was in the reactants. The difference appeared in the form of thermal energy, which raised the temperature of the room. If we accurately measured the energy content of the whole system before and afterwards, we would find that the total amount of energy is the same, i.e. energy is conserved. The quality of energy was however degraded. High quality chemical energy, which could have theoretically been used in a heat engine to generate electrical energy, was converted to low-grade thermal energy. In a real process, the quality of energy is always degraded.

There is a hierarchy with regard to the quality of various energy forms and low temperature thermal energy is at the bottom. The judge of quality is how much useful work can be done. In our society, we depend on energy in the form of work; transportation which moves, pumps and fans which transport water and air, electrons flowing in cables to transport electricity. Mechanical energy can make things move. Chemical and nuclear energy can be converted with relatively high efficiencies to high temperature thermal energy, which in turn can cause turbines to rotate and generate electricity. All of the other forms of energy can be converted with almost 100 % efficiency to thermal energy. The reverse process however is dependent on the temperature of the source and has in all practical applications a much lower efficiency. The second law of thermodynamics is the reason why gathering all the heat from the lecture theater mentioned in chapter one will not enable us to take even one hot shower without the use of a high-quality energy source such as electricity for a heat pump to raise the temperature.

The "exergy" of a system is a measure of the quality of energy in a system. It is defined as the maximum amount of useful work which can be performed by a system if it is brought into thermodynamic equilibrium with its environment. Whereas – as we have seen – energy is conserved during a process and entropy increases, exergy decreases. Energy cannot be destroyed but exergy can and is destroyed in every irreversible process. Energy can be thought of as comprising exergy and anergy, whereby anergy is the part unavailable to do useful work. In a real process, such as heat transfer through a wall, energy is conserved, entropy increases and exergy is reduced (Fig. 2.9).

A heat engine is a device used for the conversion of heat into work (Fig. 2.10). An internal combustion engine in an automobile, or a thermal power plant to generate electricity, are two common examples. In a heat engine, heat flows from a high temperature thermal reservoir to a low temperature thermal reservoir and a fraction of this heat flow is converted into useful work. In the nineteenth century, Lord Kelvin and Rudolf Clausius showed, independently from each other, that it is impossible to eliminate the low temperature reservoir from the process; i.e. heat cannot be completely converted to work.

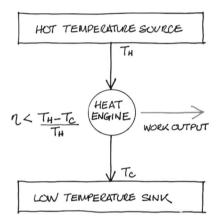

HOT TEMPERATURE SOURCE

T_H

$\eta < \dfrac{T_H - T_C}{T_H}$

HEAT ENGINE

WORK OUTPUT

T_C

LOW TEMPERATURE SINK

Fig. 2.10

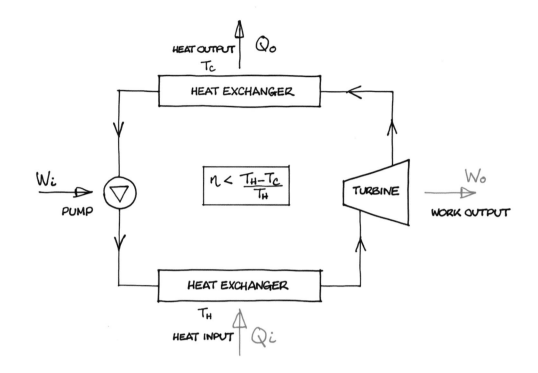

HEAT OUTPUT Q_o

T_c

HEAT EXCHANGER

$$n < \frac{T_H - T_c}{T_H}$$

W_i → PUMP

TURBINE

W_o

WORK OUTPUT

HEAT EXCHANGER

T_H

HEAT INPUT Q_i

Fig. 2.11

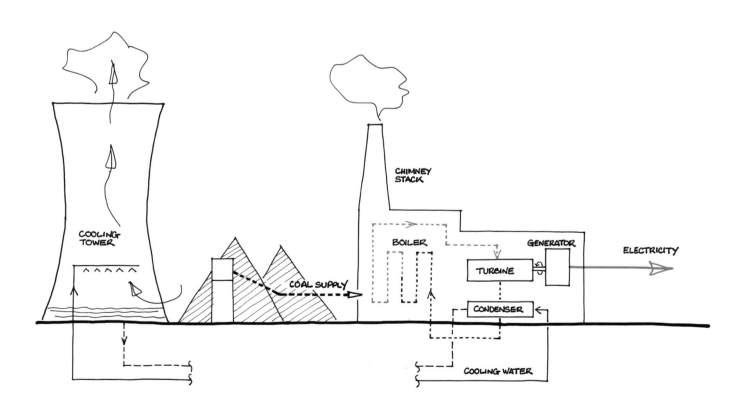

COOLING TOWER

CHIMNEY STACK

COAL SUPPLY

BOILER

GENERATOR

ELECTRICITY

TURBINE

CONDENSER

COOLING WATER

Fig. 2.12

Figure 2.11 shows a conventional power plant in schematic form. Steam is generated by heating water in a boiler and used to rotate a turbine and perform work. In the coal-fired power plant shown in Figure 2.12, the mechanical energy supplied by the turbine is converted into electrical energy in the generator. Note that the coal-fired boiler could be replaced by an oil-fired or natural-gas boiler or by a nuclear reactor. The schematic principles shown remain the same. In a wind turbine or water turbine (hydroelectricity), the turbine is turned by the kinetic energy of the moving fluid (Fig. 2.13).

The French engineer Sadi Carnot showed in the late nineteenth century that the highest possible efficiency theoretically attainable by a heat engine is set only by the temperatures of the heat source and heat sink. The consequences of the simple formula in Fig. 2.10 for the so-called Carnot efficiency are far-reaching. The temperature of the heat sink is set by the temperature of an available natural cooling source; e.g. a river, a lake or the atmosphere. The temperature of the heat source is restricted by material constraints. The highest temperature possible in steam power plants today is approx. 600 °C. Using this temperature for the heat source and assuming 20 °C for the heat sink, the maximum possible efficiency for a thermal power plant is 66 % (the temperatures in this formula must be entered in Kelvin). This is the theoretical upper limit for the efficiency of an ideal heat engine. In reality, friction and other unavoidable losses cause the actual efficiency to be roughly half of this, so 33 %. This means that for every 1 kW of electrical energy generated in a conventional power plant, roughly 2 kW must be rejected in the form of low grade heat to the atmosphere (unless some of the heat is captured and utilized in a district heating system).

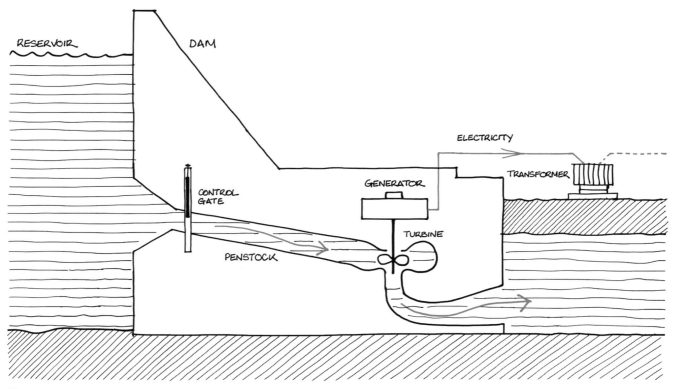

Fig. 2.13

If we reverse the operation of a heat engine, we have a heat pump (Fig. 2.14). Instead of moving thermal energy from a hot source to a cold sink and generating useful work in the process, it uses high quality energy in the form of mechanical work to move thermal energy from a cold place to a hot place. The efficiency of a heat pump system also depends on the temperature difference of the two reservoirs and is referred to in practice as the Coefficient of Performance (COP). Assuming a heating system flow temperature of 45 °C and a ground temperature of 10 °C, the highest achievable COP is less than 9. Again, the COP of a real heat pump can be expected to be about 50 % of this value.

A large portion of the heating and cooling energy demand of the new campus for the Vienna University of Economics and Business (WU campus) in Vienna – completed in 2013 in accordance with a master plan by BUS architects and with buildings designed by Zaha Hadid Architects, Hitoshi Abe, CRAB studio (Peter Cook), Estudio Carme Pinós and NO.MAD Arquitectos – is met by a heat pump installation using groundwater with an average temperature of approx. 12 °C as the heat source for heating in winter and as the heat sink for cooling in summer (Fig. 2.15). Heating and cooling is achieved by activated concrete slabs and radiant floors operating with a low temperature difference between the system and the spaces, allowing a high COP to be achieved. In summer, ground water is used directly for cooling via a heat exchanger.

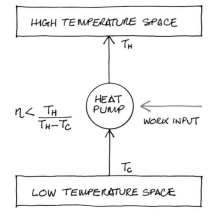

Fig. 2.14

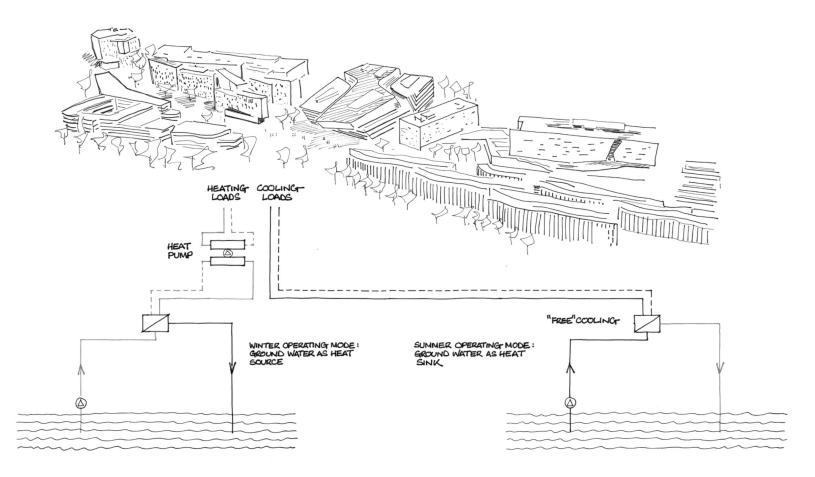

Fig. 2.15

If groundwater is not available, geothermal energy (heat stored in the ground) can be used. In fact, this has become a very popular way of heating new residential buildings. It is often thought that using "heat from the ground" in this way is 100 % renewable energy, which of course it is not. The actual effectiveness of such a system in reducing CO_2 emissions depends on the temperatures of the heat source and heat sink employed and the CO_2 emissions of the local electrical supply grid. In the case of the WU campus, for example, assuming an annual COP of 4 and CO_2 emissions of roughly 300 kg/kWh for the electrical grid in Vienna, the CO_2 emissions equate to 75 kg CO_2 per kWh for heat energy supplied. In a different context, say a heat pump system for a residential building in Berlin using external air as heat source and therefore a lower COP of 2.5, and employing electricity from a grid with CO_2 emissions of 600 kg CO_2 per kWh, we would obtain roughly 240 kg CO_2 per kWh, which is comparable to heating with a natural gas boiler.

A chiller system in a building air conditioning system (Fig. 2.16) is also a heat pump, the only difference being that the focus is on maintaining a certain temperature in the cold place. In the evaporator, heat is absorbed by the working fluid, called the refrigerant, and is caused to evaporate. The heat used to exact this phase change is removed from the building. The vapor is then compressed to a higher pressure in the compressor before being allowed to condense in the condenser. Here the heat is rejected to outside. The high-pressure liquid then flows through the expansion valve where its pressure is lowered before being returned to the evaporator to continue the process. Typical COP values for chiller plants used in buildings are in the range of 2.5 to 3.0.

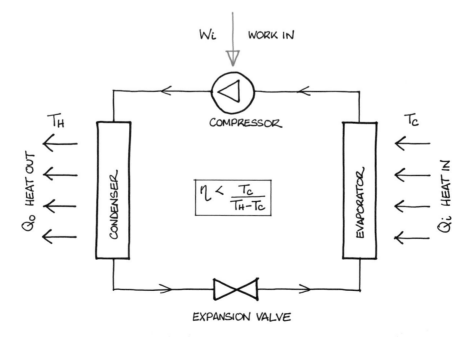

Fig. 2.16

As we shall see in the following chapter, thermal comfort in spaces depends on the humidity of the air in the space. Therefore, in order to understand the concepts behind making comfortable spaces, it is necessary to grasp the basic principles of psychrometrics, the study of humid air. The air in a building space is a mixture of dry air and moisture. In order to understand the principles, consider an indoor swimming pool (Fig. 2.17). Let us assume that at a certain starting time, we replace the air in the space above the pool with completely dry air. Now, what will happen next?

A system which is not in equilibrium, such as this, will tend towards equilibrium in the same way that a ball will roll down a hill. The driving force in this case is not gravity but the difference in concentration of water molecules per unit volume between the humid air at the pool surface (where water molecules from the pool evaporate into the air) and the dry air in the space at a distance away from the water surface. This concentration difference will cause water molecules in vapor form at the surface to drift into the dry air of the space and be replaced by more water molecules evaporating from the water surface. As we have already seen, energy must be supplied in order to allow this phase change process from liquid to vapor to take place. In this case, the energy is taken from the water body, reducing the temperature of the water. This process will continue until equilibrium is reached and the air has absorbed all the moisture it is capable of absorbing. If the water is heated, so that water and air are maintained at the same temperature, equilibrium will be attained when the air is fully saturated and its relative humidity is 100 %.

At any condition between the initial and final states, the relative humidity of the air will be between 0 % and 100 %. The relative humidity of air in a space is equal to the ratio of the actual partial vapor pressure of the moisture in the air (the pressure exerted by the molecules of the water vapor on the walls of the enclosing space) to the saturation vapor pressure (the vapor pressure of the water vapor in the air, if the air were fully saturated). It is the difference in vapor pressure between the air at the water surface and the air further away which drives the process of evaporation. The absolute humidity or the moisture content of air is the quantity of water vapor in the air and is measured in g/kg or kg/kg dry air.

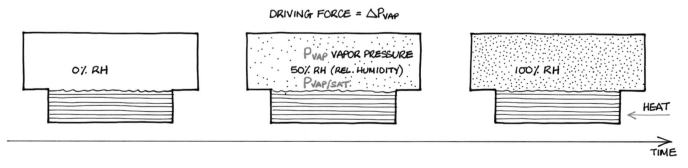

Fig. 2.17

In the design of climate control concepts, psychrometric charts are used. Air with a specific state or condition is represented by a point on this chart. The condition of a substance is fully defined when two independent properties of the substance are known, e.g. dry bulb temperature, moisture content, relative humidity, enthalpy. Figure 2.18 shows the most common processes used in air conditioning systems. In winter air is heated to near room temperature (note the drop in relative humidity) and then humidified by a steam humidifier. In summer air is cooled and dehumidified and then reheated to a suitable supply air temperature.

As we have seen above, the lower intermolecular forces in a liquid allow it to flow. **Fluid Dynamics** is the study of fluid flow. In building applications, a flowing fluid inevitably encounters solid surfaces (e.g. wind flow at a building's exterior surface, air flow in an interior space or air conditioning duct, water flow in a pipe) and an important issue in the understanding of fluid flow is the so-called no-slip condition. This assumes that the velocity of a flowing fluid at an enclosing surface is zero; i.e. the fluid "sticks" to the surface (Fig. 2.19). The no-slip condition gives rise to the characteristic velocity profile shown in the diagram. The region of the fluid which is significantly affected by the no-slip condition is called the boundary layer.

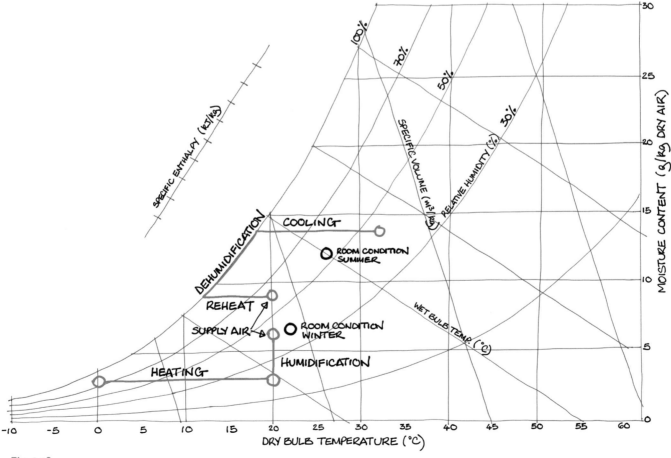

Fig. 2.18

The viscosity of a fluid is a measure of its resistance to flow caused by the frictional forces between neighboring regions of the fluid flowing at different velocities due to the no-slip condition. For example, the viscosity of toothpaste is high, that of water is low. In laminar flow the fluid flows in ordered streamlines which are parallel to each other, whereas in turbulent flow, the flow is chaotic and the flow of the fluid particles is not restricted to parallel streamlines (Fig. 2.20). The flow of a high viscosity fluid at low velocity (e.g. oil in a pipe) is laminar, while the flow of a low viscosity fluid at high velocity (e.g. air flowing through an open window) is turbulent. Whether fluid flow is laminar or turbulent can be determined by the Reynolds Number, which is the ratio of the inertial forces to the viscous forces.

An interesting application of fluid dynamics in the field of low energy building design is the development of natural ventilation concepts. In natural ventilation two types of forces are employed, thermal buoyancy and wind. Both of these give rise to pressure differences which drive air flow. First, we will consider thermal buoyancy, sometimes called the stack effect, in which air flow in building spaces is caused by temperature difference.

Pressure is force per unit area, and the pressure of a static fluid increases with depth due to the weight of the fluid layers above. The rate of change of pressure with depth depends on the density of the fluid (Fig. 2.21). Due to the increase in pressure with depth, an object submerged in a fluid experiences greater pressure at the bottom than at the top. This pressure difference results in a net upward force called buoyancy (Fig. 2.22).

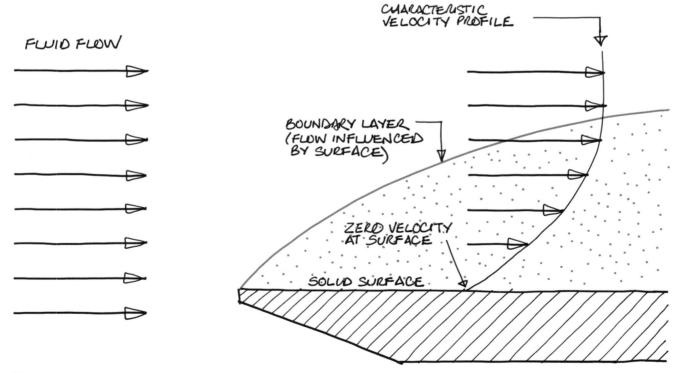

FLUID FLOW

CHARACTERISTIC VELOCITY PROFILE

BOUNDARY LAYER (FLOW INFLUENCED BY SURFACE)

ZERO VELOCITY AT SURFACE

SOLID SURFACE

Fig. 2.19

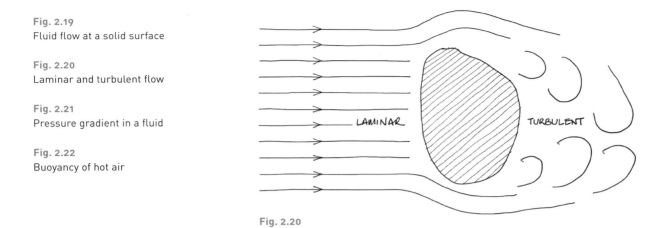

LAMINAR   TURBULENT

Fig. 2.20

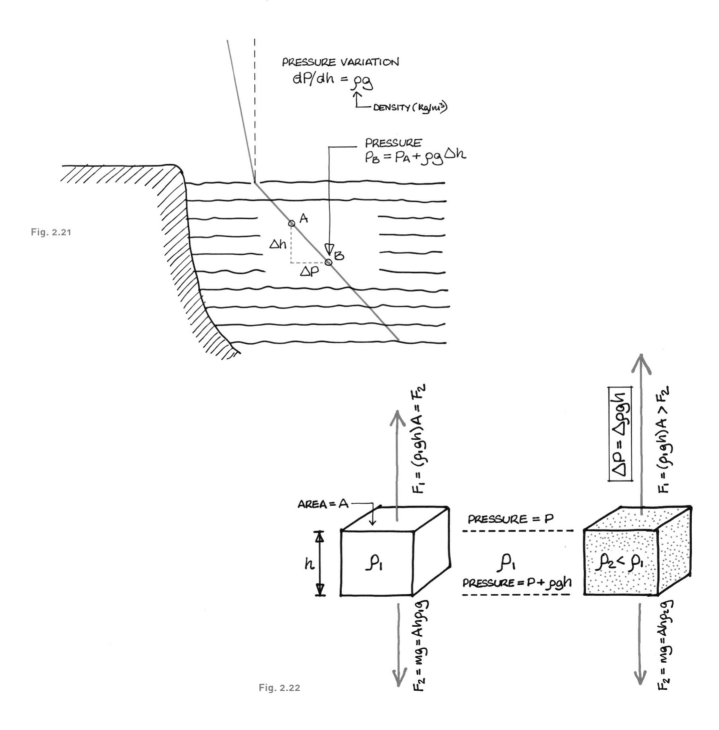

PRESSURE VARIATION

$$dP/dh = \rho g$$

DENSITY (kg/m^3)

PRESSURE
$$P_B = P_A + \rho g \Delta h$$

Fig. 2.21

A

Δh

B

ΔP

$F_1 = (\rho_1 g h) A = F_2$

AREA = A

PRESSURE = P

ρ_1

h ρ_1

PRESSURE = P + $\rho g h$

$F_2 = mg = A h \rho_1 g$

$\Delta P = \Delta \rho g h$

$F_1 = (\rho_1 g h) A > F_2$

$\rho_2 < \rho_1$

$F_2 = mg = A h \rho_2 g$

Fig. 2.22

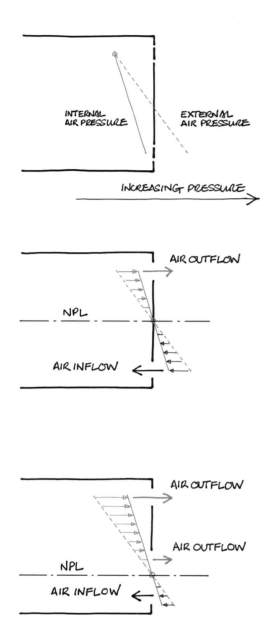

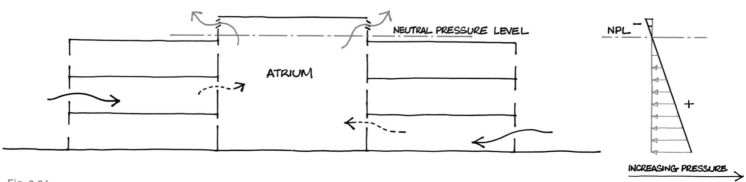

An object with a density less than the fluid in which it is submerged will tend to float. If its density is greater, it will tend to sink. If air in a space is heated, its temperature increases and it expands. As a result, its density is reduced. Just like any submerged object which is lighter than the fluid in which it is submerged, the warm air will experience a net upward force. It rises upwards and is replaced by colder air flowing into the position left by the warmer air.

Fig. 2.23 shows a sectional view of a room with two openings, one at low level and the other high. If the temperatures inside and outside are different, the pressure gradients of the internal air and the external air will also be different due to their different densities. Because the outside air is colder, it is heavier and therefore the pressure increase with depth is more pronounced due to the weight of the fluid layers above. If the openings are of equal size, the pressure gradients will meet at the centerline of the distance between the openings, so that the pressure difference between inside and outside is the same for both openings as shown in the diagram. The plane where the pressure is equal on both sides of the wall is called the neutral pressure level (NPL). Air flows into the room below the NPL and out of the room above the NPL. If the temperature relationship is inverted, e.g. in an air-conditioned space in summer, the flow directions are reversed. Increasing the area of one of the openings relative to the other will shift the NPL in the direction of the larger opening as shown. Fig. 2.24 shows a sectional view of an office building with an atrium, in which the NPL is deliberately designed to be above the last floor to prevent backflow from the atrium into the offices. This is done by adjusting the relationship between the inlet and outlet areas and increasing the height of the atrium so that the height difference between inlets and outlets is increased.

In the GSW office tower in Berlin (Fig. 2.25), designed in the 1990s by the architects Sauerbruch Hutton and completed in 1999, buoyancy forces play a major role in enabling the natural ventilation of a tall building in an urban location on a busy street intersection in Berlin for approx. 70% of the year. Air enters the building on the east side, flowing through automatically controlled windows into the office areas and from there into the double façade on the west side, which is constructed as a continuous

Fig. 2.23

Fig. 2.24

OPTIMIZED ROOF TO MAXIMIZE SUCTION

SOLAR THERMAL EXTRACT AIR FAÇADE

SOLAR CONTROL DEVICE IN CAVITY OF DOUBLE SKIN FAÇADE

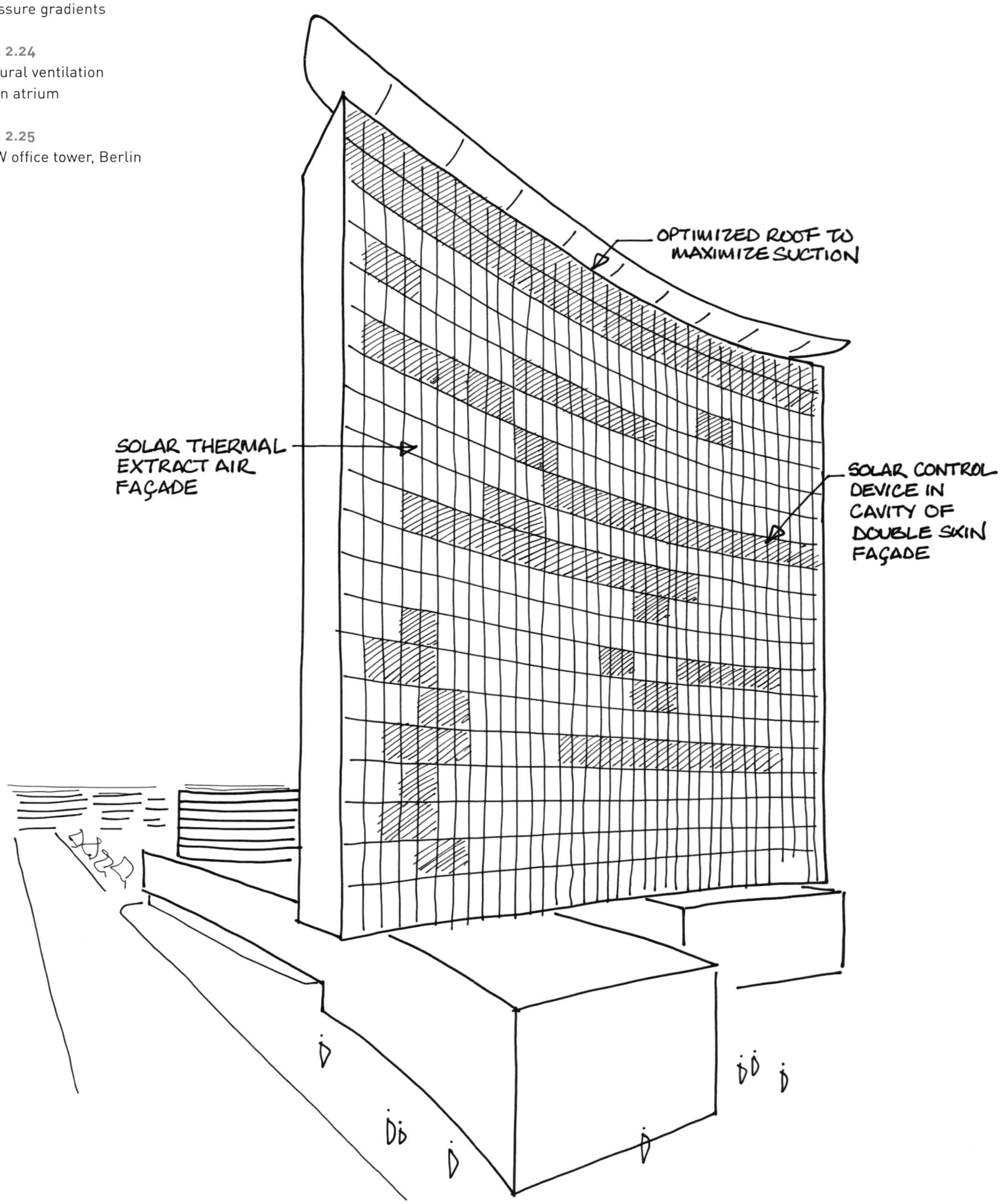

Fig. 2.25

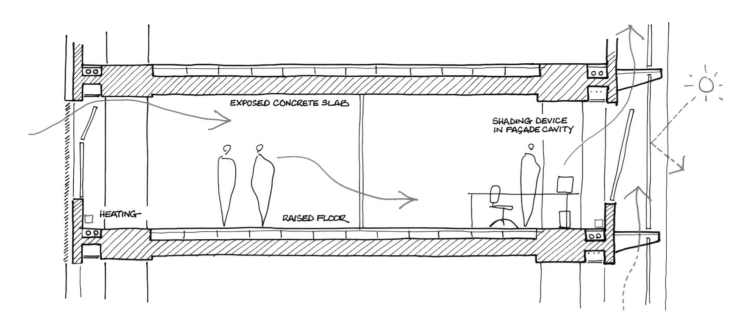

EXPOSED CONCRETE SLAB

SHADING DEVICE
IN FACADE CAVITY

HEATING

RAISED FLOOR

Fig. 2.26

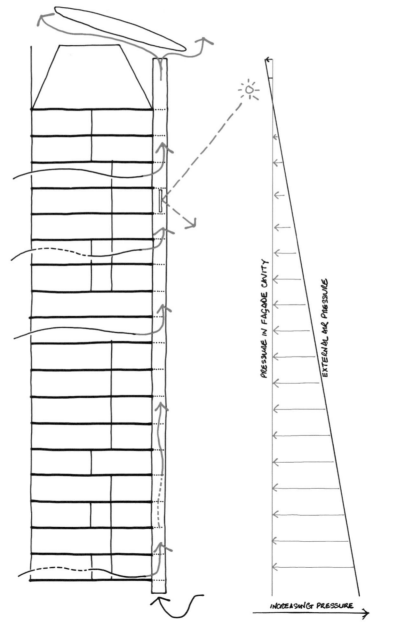

PRESSURE IN FACADE CAVITY

EXTERNAL AIR PRESSURE

INCREASING PRESSURE

Fig. 2.27

void without any horizontal or vertical separations (Fig. 2.26). Both internal heat gains in the office spaces and solar heat gains to the façade cavity increase the temperature of the air relative to the entering external air. The buoyancy force resulting from the temperature difference between the warmer air in the double façade and the colder external air is the driving force for the natural ventilation of the building. The less dense warm air rises in the vertical façade cavity and pulls air through the office floors. The blinds in the cavity of the double skin façade provide solar shading. The windows, the shading devices in the façade cavity and the dampers at the top and bottom of the façade are all automatically controlled via the building management system. The user can, however, override the control system at any time.

Figure 2.27 shows a section of the building with a simplified pressure distribution diagram. The available pressure depends on the height between air entry and exit and thus is different on each office floor, reducing incrementally with height above ground. If windows on all floors had the same opening area, there would be significantly higher air flow on the lower floors. To prevent this, the window opening areas were determined by simulations and laboratory measurements and were then set up during construction to ensure that all floors receive the correct air flow rate (Fig. 2.28). In the development of the design, the flue was extended roughly two stories above the last floor to increase the stack effect and shift the NPL upwards. The pressure distribution shown in Fig. 2.27 is very simplified and an idealized representation of the situation. In reality, pressure drop in the flue is not negligible and wind effects are nearly always present. Dampers at the bottom of the flue can be opened to lower the temperature in the flue and regulate air flow.

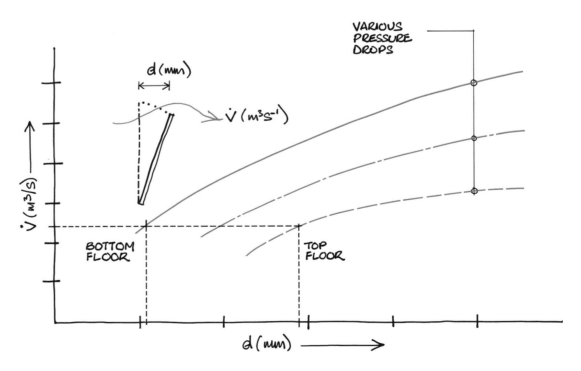

Fig. 2.28

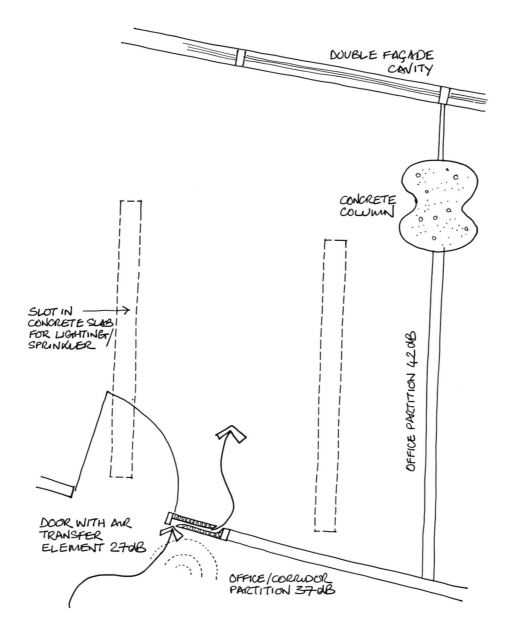

Fig. 2.29

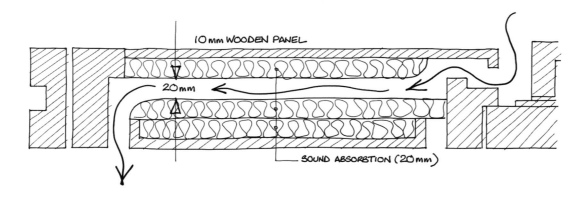

Fig. 2.30

Fig. 2.29
GSW Tower, air transfer element, typical office

Fig. 2.30
GSW Tower, air transfer element, detail

Fig. 2.31
MCUR museum, La Reunion

Fig. 2.32
MCUR museum, climate control concept

Further challenges arose on this project when the building owner introduced the need for cellular offices with associated acoustic requirements imposed on the separating wall. An air transfer element had to be designed which allowed the required air flow to take place without compromising acoustical privacy between office areas (Fig. 2.29). Due to the very low pressure available, the design of this element was involved (Fig. 2.30).

Figures 2.31 and 2.32 show the use of thermal buoyancy in another context. In this design with Coop Himmelb(l)au architects for a museum on the island of La Reunion in the Indian ocean, cooling coils at high level in combination with vertically aligned textile tubes cause the denser, cooler supply air to drop into the space by natural forces, eliminating the need for the usual fans.

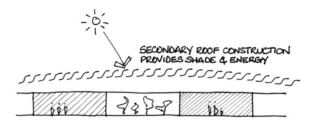

SECONDARY ROOF CONSTRUCTION
PROVIDES SHADE & ENERGY
CONDITIONED
SPACES
COURTYARDS

Fig. 2.31

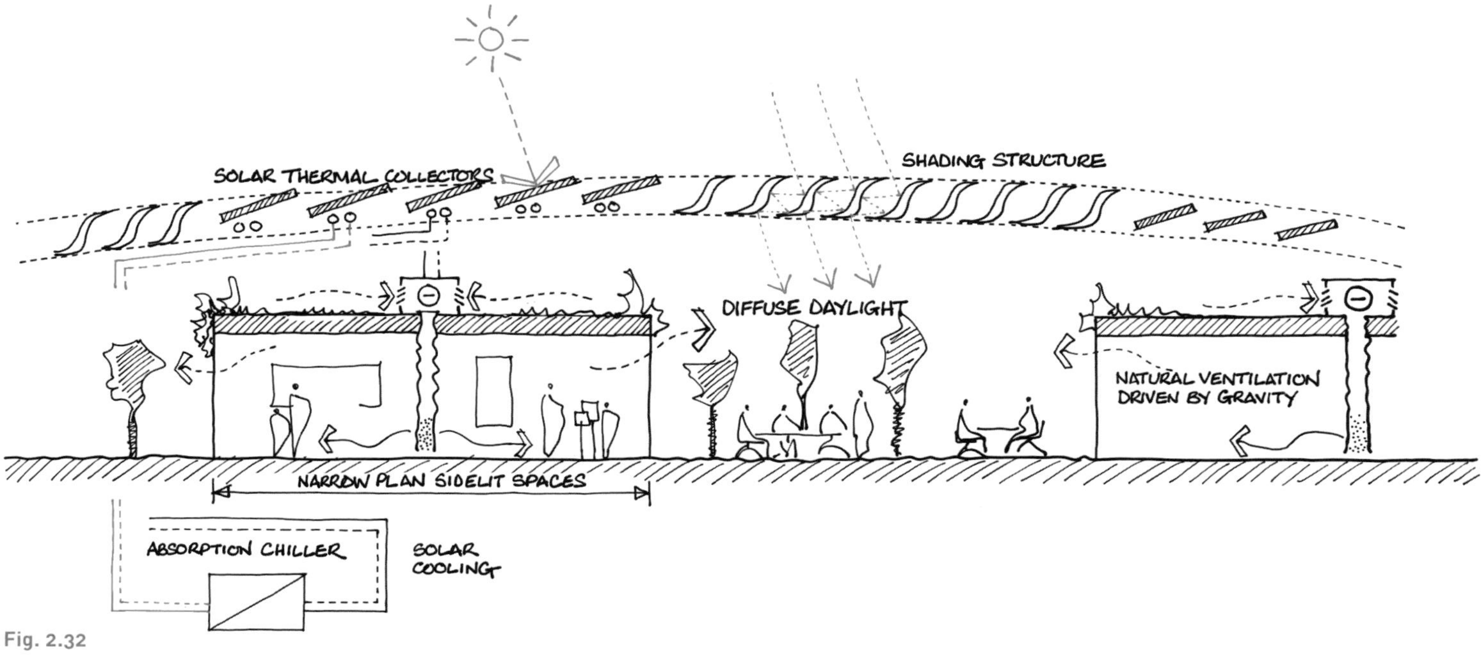

SOLAR THERMAL COLLECTORS
SHADING STRUCTURE
DIFFUSE DAYLIGHT
NATURAL VENTILATION
DRIVEN BY GRAVITY
NARROW PLAN SIDELIT SPACES
ABSORPTION CHILLER
SOLAR
COOLING

Fig. 2.32

In addition to thermal buoyancy, wind can also be used to drive air flow through a building. Fig. 2.33 and 2.34 show wind flow patterns and the resulting wind pressure distribution around some simple building shapes when viewed from above. The physics behind these patterns can be understood with the help of the Bernoulli equation, which can be derived from the first law of thermodynamics (Fig. 2.35). Total pressure comprises static pressure, dynamic pressure (due to motion) and pressure due to elevation (height above a reference datum). As energy is conserved, the total pressure remains constant (ignoring friction losses). The Bernoulli equation shows that increasing the velocity of air flow leads to a reduction in static pressure.

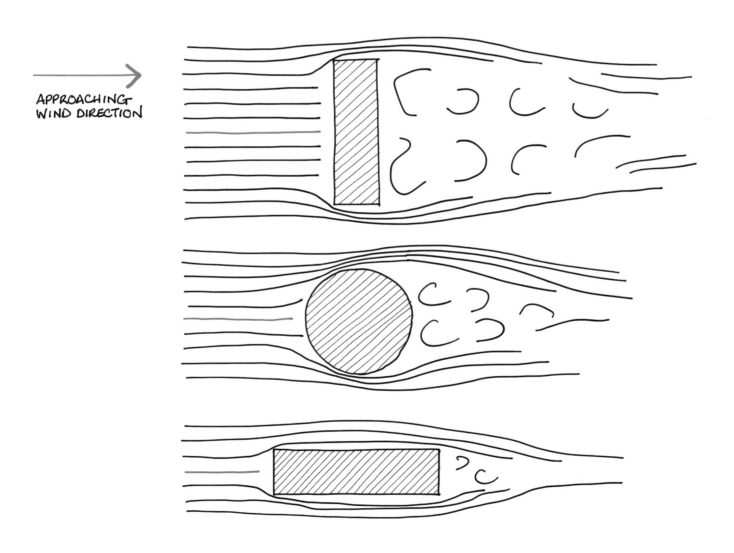

APPROACHING
WIND DIRECTION

Fig. 2.33

APPROACHING
WIND DIRECTION

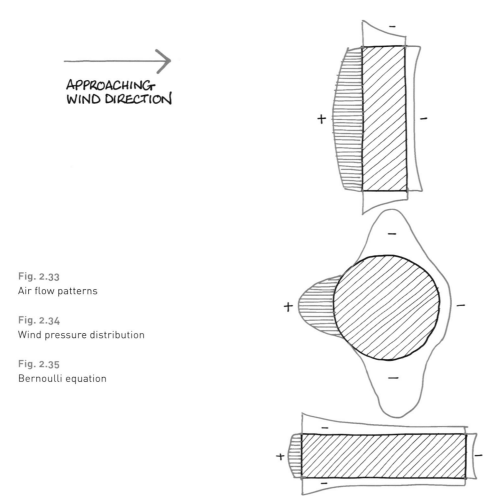

Fig. 2.33
Air flow patterns

Fig. 2.34
Wind pressure distribution

Fig. 2.35
Bernoulli equation

Fig. 2.34

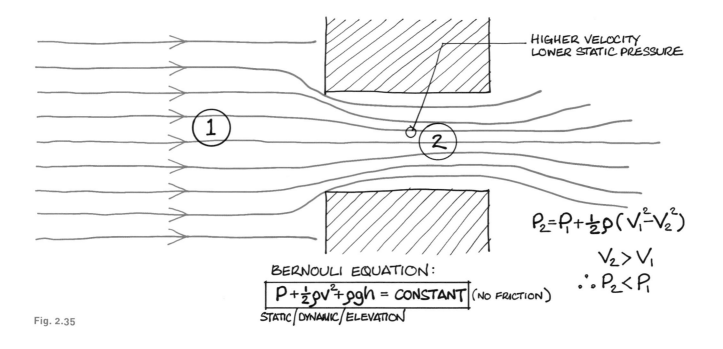

HIGHER VELOCITY
LOWER STATIC PRESSURE

BERNOULI EQUATION:

$$P + \tfrac{1}{2}\rho v^2 + \rho gh = \text{CONSTANT} \quad \text{(NO FRICTION)}$$
STATIC / DYNAMIC / ELEVATION

$$P_2 = P_1 + \tfrac{1}{2}\rho(V_1^2 - V_2^2)$$

$$V_2 > V_1$$

$$\therefore P_2 < P_1$$

Fig. 2.35

Fig. 2.36 shows the basic principles of wind flow around a building. If one side of the building is directly perpendicular to the wind, the dynamic pressure (the energy due to its motion) is converted into static pressure, causing a high positive pressure on this surface. This is called the stagnation pressure. The building presents an obstacle to the air flow, so that the wind is forced to flow through a smaller area, increasing its velocity at the building sides and at the roof and causing an increase in dynamic pressure and a drop in static pressure there.

Wind is also directed downwards and can cause turbulence and eddies at the foot of the building, which can lead to pedestrian discomfort. In practice, wind pressure coefficients (Cp values) are used. These relate the difference between the static pressure at a point measured on a building surface (or on the surface of a model in a wind tunnel) and the static pressure in the surroundings to the dynamic pressure of the wind in the surroundings. If elements in the building envelope are opened, air will flow from areas of higher pressure to areas of lower pressure (Fig. 2.37).

The GSW building was originally designed to work primarily using thermal buoyancy. Wind can either assist the air flow due to buoyancy or work in the opposite direction. To prevent the latter, a specially shaped roof over the double façade was developed to use increased air speed to create a suction effect in accordance with the Bernoulli equation described above (Fig. 2.38). This ensures that wind forces, independent of direction, assist the air flow patterns generated by buoyancy as described above.

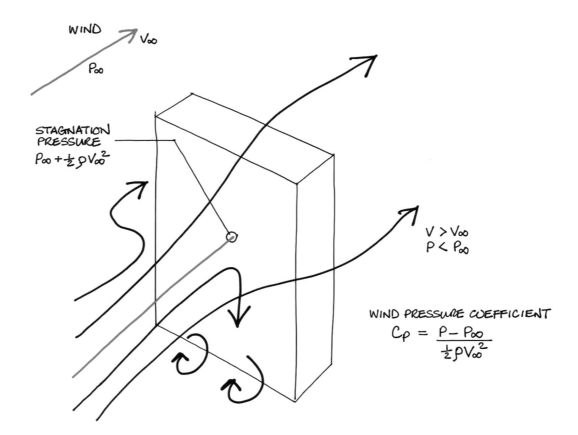

WIND V_∞

P_∞

STAGNATION PRESSURE

$P_\infty + \frac{1}{2}\rho V_\infty^2$

$V > V_\infty$
$P < P_\infty$

WIND PRESSURE COEFFICIENT

$$C_p = \frac{P - P_\infty}{\frac{1}{2}\rho V_\infty^2}$$

Fig. 2.36

In most building design situations the wind force dominates, even at relatively low wind speeds. The exception are tall buildings, in which the floors are vertically connected by an atrium or double façade. Problems can arise in winter when floors are inadvertently connected by elements such as lift shafts, which lead to unplanned excessive pressure differences and problems, particularly on the ground floor in the entrance lobby area.

For a large part of the year, the driving forces provided by buoyancy and wind are small and if they are insufficient to drive air flow through the required resistance path, fans are required. When using a system incorporating ducts, filters, heat exchangers etc., fans become essential. The pressure loss in a pipe or duct system is determined by calculating separately the pressure loss due to straight duct or pipe runs and that due to the so-called fittings (bends, valves, dampers, grilles etc.) and then taking the sum of these for the part of the system with the expected highest

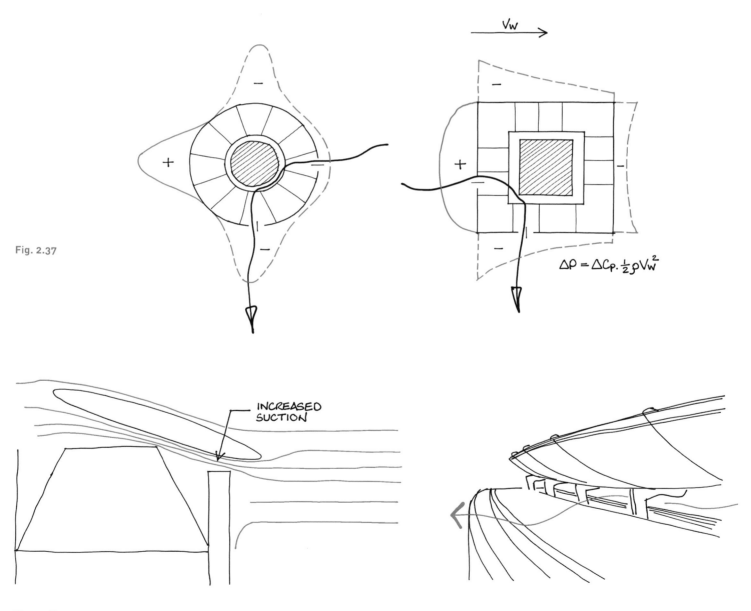

Fig. 2.37

$$\Delta P = \Delta C_P \cdot \frac{1}{2}\rho V_w^2$$

Fig. 2.38

INCREASED SUCTION

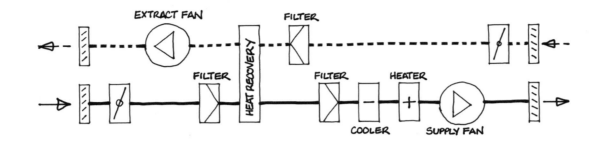

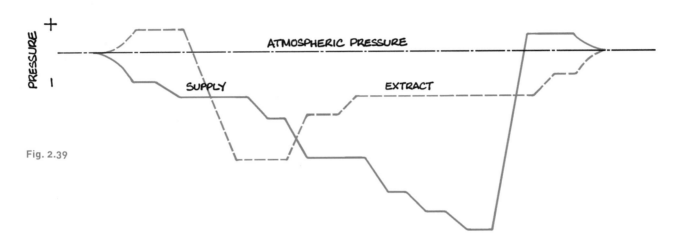

Fig. 2.39

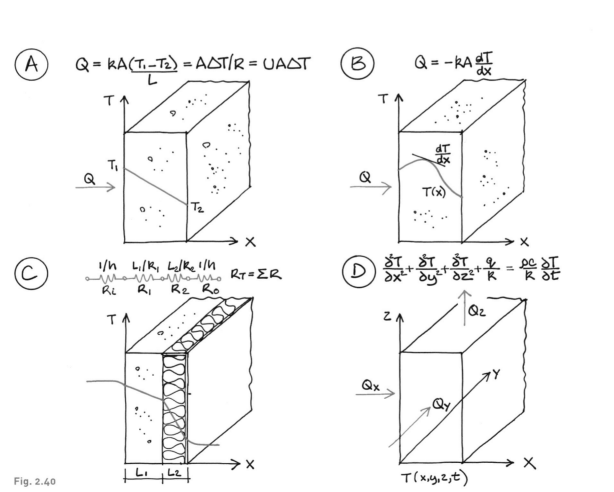

Fig. 2.40

Fig. 2.39
Pressure loss in an air
handling system

Fig. 2.40
(a) One-dimensional
steady state conduction
(b) Transient conduction
(c) Conduction through
a multilayered wall
(d) 3-D transient con-
duction with heat
generation

total pressure loss (Fig. 2.39). Typical pressure drops in an office mechanical ventilation system are between 1500 and 2000 Pa, which dwarfs the
available pressure due to the natural forces discussed above. The pressure
drop in hydraulic water heating and cooling systems is many times greater
again. The energy demand for the transport of a given amount of energy
is however many times lower than that of an air-based system. The chief
reason for this is the lower specific heat capacity of air (1.01 kJ/kg K compared with 4.2 kJ/kg K for water). The fan energy of ventilation systems is
a very significant and sometimes dominant factor in the energy consumption profiles of buildings, whereas pumps are not a major contributor. Due
to the higher volumetric flow rates involved, the physical size of air-based
systems is also much greater. On account of the much lower transportation energy demand and the lower space requirements, water and not air
should be utilized to transport energy in climate control systems where
possible. In practice, the so-called SFP value (Specific Fan Power) is used
to characterize the energy efficiency of fan systems. An SFP value of 3 kW
per m³/s, for example, means that an electrical power input of 3 kW is necessary to transport a volumetric air flow rate of 1 m³/s through the system.

As we have seen above, heat is energy transferred to or from a system as a result of temperature difference. Heat flow between a system and
its surroundings is always in the direction of decreasing temperature and
this flow will continue until both system and surroundings reach the same
temperature. There are three modes of **heat transfer**; conduction, convection and radiation. These are introduced briefly below.

In conduction, the transfer of thermal energy results from interactions between particles in a substance which are at a higher energy level
than adjacent ones. In solids, these interactions comprise contact between
adjacent molecules in the lattice structure which are vibrating about their
mean equilibrium position as well as the movement of free electrons within the structure. The latter effect is the reason for the high magnitude
of thermal conduction in materials such as metals, which are also good
conductors of electricity for the same reasons. Conduction in liquids and
gases takes place as a result of the diffusion and collisions of molecules
as they move about randomly.

The rate of heat transfer due to one-dimensional heat conduction in
a wall is directly proportional to the driving force of temperature difference
and the area normal to the direction of heat transfer and indirectly proportional to the thickness of the material in the direction of heat transfer
(Fig. 2.40a). Under steady state conditions, the driving force is simply the
difference between temperatures on either side of the wall. The constant of
proportionality k (W/mK) is the thermal conductivity of the material and is
an intrinsic property of a material. The ratio of the thickness of a material
in the direction of heat flow to its thermal conductivity is called the thermal
resistance of the structure, R (m²K/W). The larger the resistance to heat
transfer, the less heat is transferred. The U-value (W/m²K) is the inverse of
the total thermal resistance of a construction and is the value often used in
practice to describe the performance of whole building elements. The lower the U-value, the lower the heat transfer. Transient heat flow depends on
the rate of change of temperature with distance within the wall (Fig. 2.40b).

Modern building envelope constructions are generally composed of multiple layers. At steady state conditions, the heat flowing through each layer in a direction perpendicular to the construction is the same and the individual resistances can be added together to obtain the total resistance, just like with resistances in series in an electrical circuit (Fig. 2.40c). In the preliminary stages of a project, simple calculations of steady state one-dimensional heat transfer often suffice. However, in more detailed analysis, transient and sometimes multidimensional heat transfer must be considered (Fig. 2.40d). In Figure 2.41 the thermal conductivity for various materials is given as well as the length of the material required to give the same thermal resistance to heat flow. Note the different scales used in the diagram.

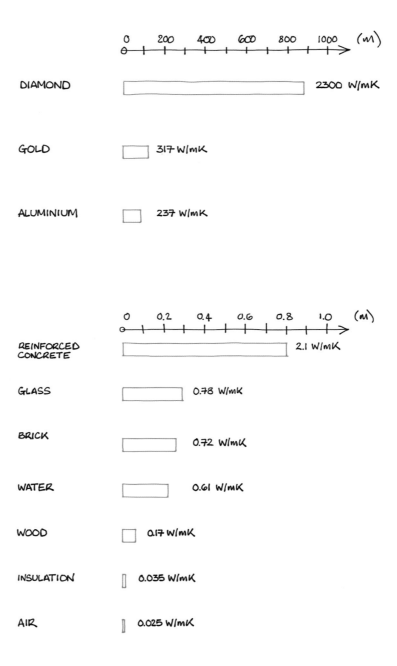

Fig. 2.41

When a fluid comes into contact with a solid surface at a different temperature, heat conduction from the solid to the fluid results in a local increase in the temperature of the fluid, which can give rise to bulk fluid movement due to buoyancy forces as described above. The degree of fluid motion is determined by the ratio of the forces due to buoyancy promoting motion and friction opposing motion. This bulk fluid motion effectively magnifies the heat transfer process due to conduction at the interface of the fluid and the solid surface, and this mode of heat transfer is called natural convection. If mechanical energy is used to promote fluid movement and enhance heat transfer by convection, this is called forced convection. Figure 2.42 shows natural convection due to a warm vertical surface such as a radiator in a space and the equation for calculating the rate of heat transfer, known as Newton's law of cooling. It is important to note that the convection heat transfer coefficient is not a property of the fluid but depends on many variables including the surface geometry, surface roughness, fluid viscosity, fluid velocity and fluid density among others. It has been determined by means of experiment and documented for many situations occurring in practical building applications.

The third mode of heat transfer is thermal radiation. All objects at temperatures greater than absolute zero (−273 °C) emit electromagnetic radiation. This comprises oscillating electric and magnetic fields, which travel perpendicular to each other and to the direction of energy propagation (Fig. 2.43). Thermal radiation comprises that portion of the electromagnetic spectrum emitted by objects due to their temperature. It includes infrared radiation, visible light (radiation in the range of percep-

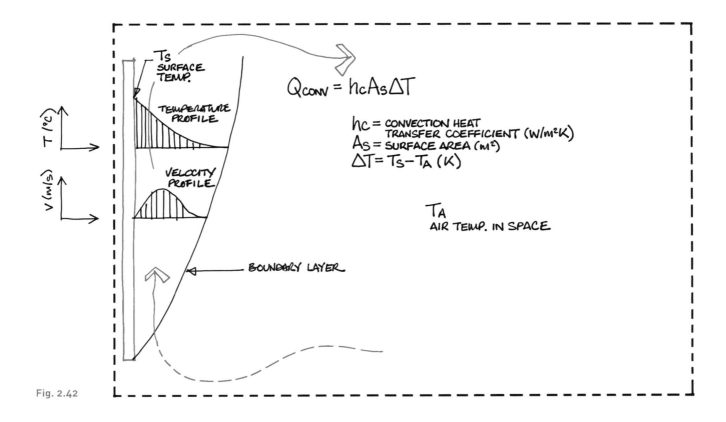

Fig. 2.42

tion of the human eye) and some of the ultraviolet light spectrum. Electromagnetic radiation does not require the presence of matter to propagate and travels in a vacuum at the speed of light (3×10^8 m/s). The product of the frequency (Hertz or 1/s) and wavelength (m) of any wave is equal to the speed of the wave. As the speed of electromagnetic waves is constant, short wave radiation is high frequency radiation and long wave radiation is low frequency radiation. According to quantum theory, radiation is propagated in discrete packets of energy called photons. The higher the frequency, the higher the energy content.

The maximum rate of thermal radiation emitted from the surface of an object is given by the Stefan-Boltzmann Law. This maximum rate of radiation is called black-body radiation. Real surfaces radiate less energy (Fig. 2.44). The emissivity of a surface is the ratio of energy radiated by a surface relative to the energy which would be radiated by a black body at the same temperature. The emissivity depends on material and surface properties and varies from around 0.02 for polished silver to over 0.9 for black

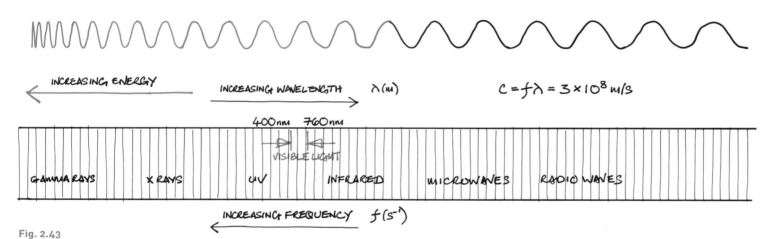

ENERGY $e = hf$ (J)
$h = 6.6 \times 10^{-34}$ (Js)
f = FREQUENCY (s^{-1})

INCREASING ENERGY

INCREASING WAVELENGTH λ (m)

$c = f\lambda = 3 \times 10^8$ m/s

400 nm   760 nm

VISIBLE LIGHT

GAMMA RAYS   X RAYS   UV   INFRARED   MICROWAVES   RADIO WAVES

INCREASING FREQUENCY f (s^{-1})

Fig. 2.43

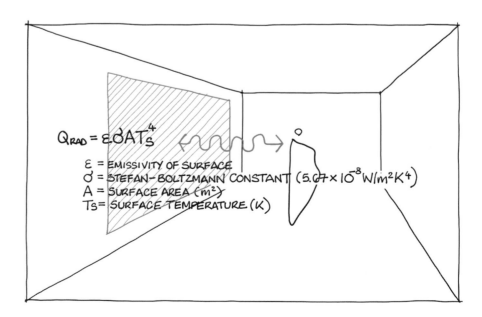

$Q_{RAD} = \varepsilon \sigma A T_s^4$

ε = EMISSIVITY OF SURFACE
σ = STEFAN-BOLTZMANN CONSTANT (5.67×10^{-8} W/m²K⁴)
A = SURFACE AREA (m²)
T_s = SURFACE TEMPERATURE (K)

Fig. 2.44

paint. Typical materials used in building construction such as concrete, brick, wood and glass have emissivities in the range of 0.85 to 0.95. Special low-e coatings used in glazing constructions are effectively metal films used to attain low levels of emissivity to reduce heat loss by long wave radiation. The absorptivity of a surface is the fraction of incident radiation which is absorbed by the surface. A black body absorbs all the radiation incident on it and thus has an absorptivity of 1. Both the emissivity and absorptivity of a real surface depend on temperature and the wavelength of the radiation.

Figure 2.45 shows the variation of blackbody radiation with wavelengths for different temperatures. The peak radiation shifts to the left with higher temperatures, so that increasing the temperature of the radiating source leads to higher frequency radiation. This is known as Wien's displacement law. Note that objects start to emit radiation in the visible range at a temperature of approx. 800 K. Conventional incandescent light bulbs with tungsten filaments (now banned in many parts of the world on account of their inefficient use of energy) need to attain a temperature of

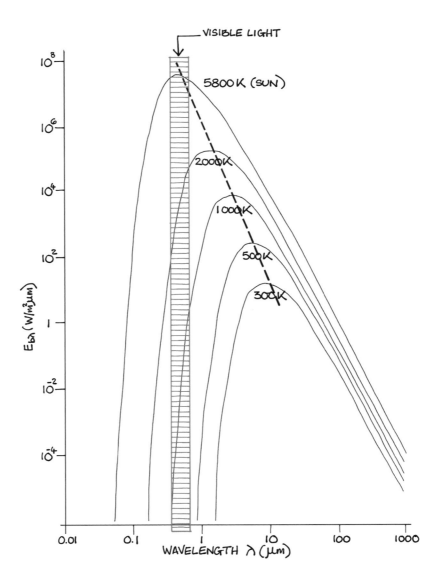

Fig. 2.45

approx. 2500 °C to fulfill their function. Even then, a large portion of the radiation is not visible and is emitted as heat in the form of infrared radiation. The sun can be considered to be a spherical black body with a temperature of approx. 6000 K which emits roughly 50 % of its radiation in the visible range. The human eye sees objects when visible radiation from a light source (an object which emits radiation in the visible range) is reflected from the observed object to the human eye. If the object reflects more light in the green part of the spectrum and less in the remaining portion, it appears green to the human eye. If it reflects the entire incident light, it appears white. Black surfaces absorb light equally across the spectrum. We see black surfaces because of the contrast with surrounding objects.

The difference between the radiation emitted by a surface and the radiation absorbed by it gives the net heat transfer by radiation. The calculation of heat transfer due to radiation is complicated due to the dependence on the spatial relationship between the surfaces, the so-called view factor (Fig. 2.46) and the properties of the surfaces. Another difficulty in calculations results from the fact that heat flow by radiation depends on the temperature of the surface to the power of four, which quickly complicates the mathematical solutions to all but the most trivial problems. To allow quick estimation of heat transfer by radiation, adjusted heat transfer coefficients are used, which when multiplied by the area and the temperature difference are found to give approximately the same heat transfer rate as the actual rate (Fig. 2.47). The heat transfer coefficients for convection and radiation can then be simply added to obtain a combined heat transfer coefficient, which allows calculation of the total heat transfer by convection and radiation in a simple way. Fig. 2.47 gives values for typical situations in building design. In most building applications, all three modes of heat transfer occur simultaneously (Fig. 2.48).

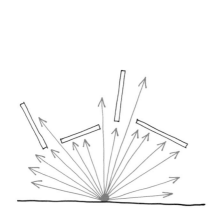

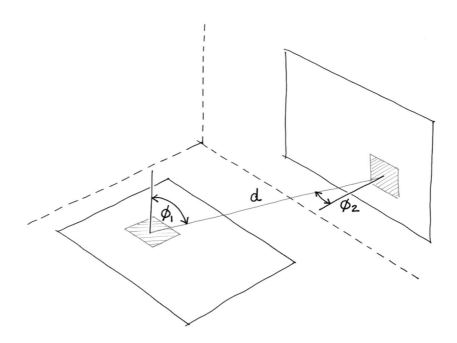

Fig. 2.46

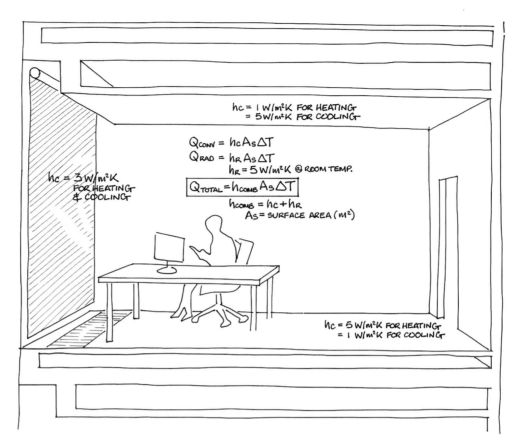

$h_c = 1 \ W/m^2K$ FOR HEATING
$= 5 \ W/m^2K$ FOR COOLING

$Q_{CONV} = h_c A_s \Delta T$
$Q_{RAD} = h_R A_s \Delta T$
$h_R = 5 \ W/m^2K$ @ ROOM TEMP.

$\boxed{Q_{TOTAL} = h_{COMB} A_s \Delta T}$

$h_{COMB} = h_c + h_R$
$A_s =$ SURFACE AREA (m^2)

$h_c = 3 \ W/m^2K$
FOR HEATING
& COOLING

$h_c = 5 \ W/m^2K$ FOR HEATING
$= 1 \ W/m^2K$ FOR COOLING

Fig. 2.47

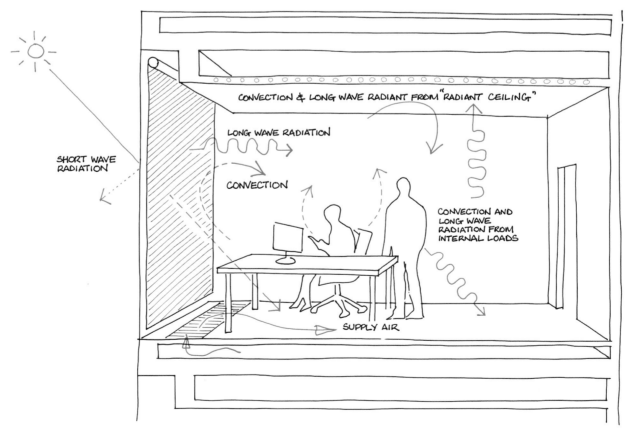

CONVECTION & LONG WAVE RADIANT FROM "RADIANT CEILING"

LONG WAVE RADIATION

SHORT WAVE
RADIATION

CONVECTION

CONVECTION AND
LONG WAVE
RADIATION FROM
INTERNAL LOADS

SUPPLY AIR

Fig. 2.48

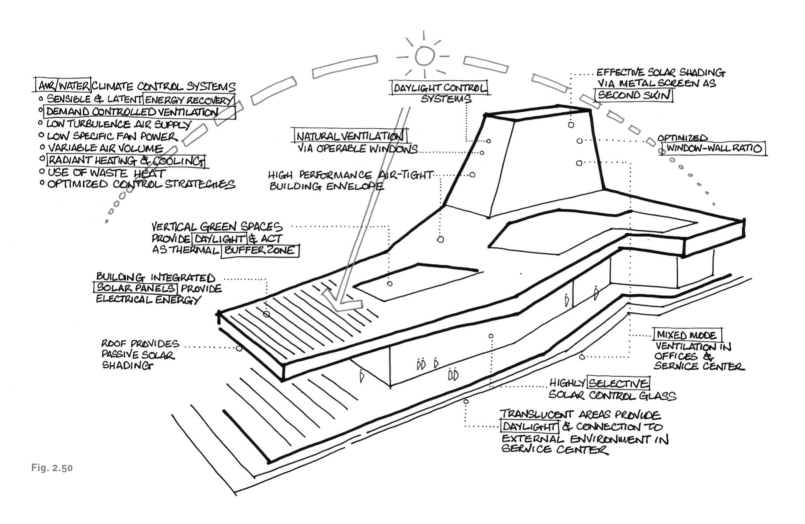

AIR/WATER CLIMATE CONTROL SYSTEMS
- SENSIBLE & LATENT ENERGY RECOVERY
- DEMAND CONTROLLED VENTILATION
- LOW TURBULENCE AIR SUPPLY
- LOW SPECIFIC FAN POWER
- VARIABLE AIR VOLUME
- RADIANT HEATING & COOLING
- USE OF WASTE HEAT
- OPTIMIZED CONTROL STRATEGIES

DAYLIGHT CONTROL SYSTEMS

EFFECTIVE SOLAR SHADING VIA METAL SCREEN AS SECOND SKIN

NATURAL VENTILATION VIA OPERABLE WINDOWS

OPTIMIZED WINDOW-WALL RATIO

HIGH PERFORMANCE AIR-TIGHT BUILDING ENVELOPE

VERTICAL GREEN SPACES PROVIDE DAYLIGHT & ACT AS THERMAL BUFFER ZONE

BUILDING INTEGRATED SOLAR PANELS PROVIDE ELECTRICAL ENERGY

ROOF PROVIDES PASSIVE SOLAR SHADING

MIXED MODE VENTILATION IN OFFICES & SERVICE CENTER

HIGHLY SELECTIVE SOLAR CONTROL GLASS

TRANSLUCENT AREAS PROVIDE DAYLIGHT & CONNECTION TO EXTERNAL ENVIRONMENT IN SERVICE CENTER

Fig. 2.50

Fig. 2.49
HVAC concept, Hyundai
Motorstudio Goyang, Seoul,
South Korea

Fig. 2.50
Energy design strategies,
Hyundai Motorstudio
Goyang, Seoul, South
Korea

Figure 2.49 shows the concept for an exhibition building in Seoul with Delugan Meissl Associated Architects (DMAA). A radiant floor is used to cool the exhibition space in summer and heat it in winter. Large-area radiant systems offer advantages both in terms of comfort (low air velocity in the occupied zone) and energy (low water temperatures for heating and high water temperatures for cooling allow the use of high-entropy energy sources). In this case, the approach is particularly effective, as during hot weather the solar radiation falling on the floor through the large areas of glazing can be directly removed by the system before becoming a load on the space. Figure 2.50 shows the energy design strategies employed in the building's design.

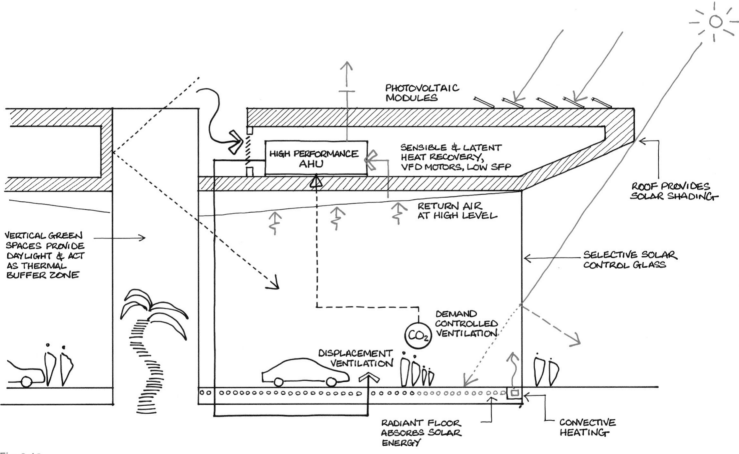

Fig. 2.49

Fig. 3.1
The Atmosphere

Fig. 3.2
Composition of
atmospheric dry
air by volume

What follows is a brief introduction to outdoor and indoor environments and their importance in the energy design of buildings. There is a vast body of literature and research into both of these topics which the reader should refer to for detailed information. In any particular design situation, it is necessary to make a detailed study of the specific parameters relating to both external and internal climate; including local microclimate, cultural context, user expectations and a host of other factors. Not making informed decisions relating to the internal design conditions during the briefing phase can mean overlooking a major opportunity to maximize energy performance. In order to be able to design buildings with high energy performance, it is important to build up an intuitive understanding based on knowledge and experience of these two important topics. In this chapter, we will look at the external climate at four different locations, to obtain insight into how the various climatic parameters affect design. We will also derive from first principles a basic understanding of what constitutes a comfortable internal environment and good air quality. Light and sound are outside the scope of this text, but are also important for the creation of a good indoor environment.

All climate phenomena which determine the **external environment** for a building design play out within the Earth's **atmosphere**, a gaseous envelope above the Earth's surface, extending roughly 1000 km beyond the Earth's surface and typically classified into zones with different vertical temperature profiles (Fig. 3.1). Weather and climate are largely determined within the troposphere zone. The composition of atmospheric air in this zone is more or less homogeneous (Fig. 3.2). The percentage of water vapor contained in the air varies depending on the climate and although it is generally very small, it can have a large influence on whether we feel comfortable or not. At sea level, the mean temperature, density and air pressure are 15 °C, 1.2 kg/m³ and 101 kPa (1 bar) respectively.

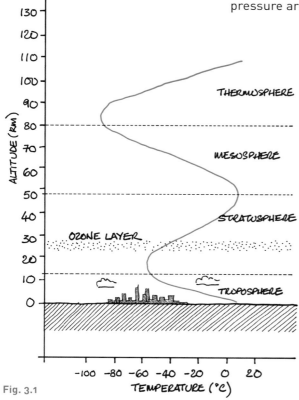

Fig. 3.1

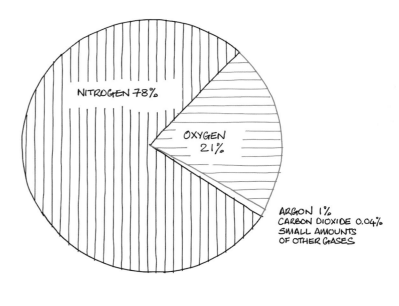

Fig. 3.2

The ozone layer, located approximately 25 km above the Earth's surface, absorbs a large portion of the ultraviolet radiation arriving from the Sun and prevents it from reaching the Earth's surface. Ozone (O_3) is an unstable form of oxygen and a very reactive and toxic gas which occurs naturally in the upper layers of the atmosphere. It can also occur at ground level in urban areas under summer fog conditions (air pollution coupled with solar radiation), causing health problems. However, higher in the atmosphere, it is an important component in reducing the risk of skin cancer and other negative health effects by reducing ultraviolet light penetration. In the 1970s, a "hole" in the ozone layer over the two poles of the earth was discovered where the ozone had been depleted. The main cause was found to be gases containing chlorine such as the chlorofluorocarbons (CFCs) used frequently in refrigeration and air conditioning systems as well as in items such as aerosol cans. When these gases are exposed to ultraviolet light, they react to release free chlorine atoms. Towards the end of the last century, governments and environmental agencies worked together to reduce CFC emissions, phasing out and eventually banning their use in air conditioning, refrigeration and other industries. The public discussion and support for the search for an appropriate solution to this problem and the fact that effective action was taken could give us hope in the search for a solution to deal with the current global warming problem. It should be recognized however that this anthropogenic interaction with the earth's climate is on a much larger scale.

Amid the billions of stars scattered across the universe, the hot ball of gases with a surface temperature of approximately 5900 K we call **the Sun** is of special importance to us, situated at the heart of our solar system and holding the solar system together by virtue of its mass via gravity. It is the cause of our climate zones, weather patterns, seasons, winds and ocean currents and, as mentioned in chapter two, the source of almost all the energy available to us on Earth; both renewable and non-renewable. The Sun is essentially a nuclear reactor, generating energy by the nuclear fusion of hydrogen nuclei into helium (Fig. 3.3). It takes over eight minutes for the Sun's radiation, travelling at the speed of light, to reach us on Earth, so that should it disappear – we would not notice until eight minutes after the event.

Fig. 3.3

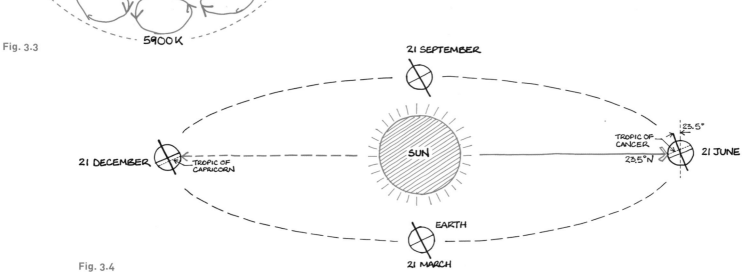

Fig. 3.4

The Earth rotates once in a counterclockwise direction around the Sun in the course of a year with the rotation axis inclined at an angle of 23.5 °, giving rise to the seasons we experience in regions not located at or near the equator. In the northern hemisphere, the maximum radiation intensity occurs on the 21st June (Fig. 3.4). Over the course of a day, the Earth rotates once about its own axis, giving rise to day and night. The diameter of the Earth is 1.3×10^7 m and the Sun 1.4×10^9 m (roughly 100 times greater). The distance between the two is approx. 1.5×10^{11} m (roughly 100 times the diameter of the Sun).

The spectrum of radiation emitted by the Sun is close to that of a black body radiator at a temperature of about 5900 K. As it passes through the atmosphere, sunlight is attenuated by scattering and absorption effects (Fig. 3.5). The longer the path through the atmosphere the more the radiation is attenuated before it falls on a surface on the Earth. Roughly 50 % of solar radiation is in the visible light range, a small amount is ultraviolet and the remainder is infrared radiation. When radiation from the Sun falls directly on the Earth's surface and creates shadow, it is said to be direct radiation. Diffuse radiation, on the other hand, has no direction, casts no shadow and is caused by the scattering and reflection of water droplets

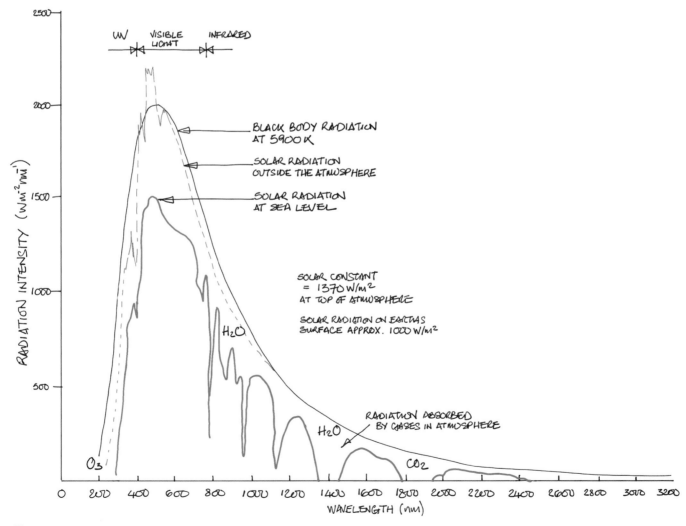

Fig. 3.5

and dust particles in the atmosphere. Global radiation is the sum of direct and diffuse radiation (Fig. 3.6). The intensity of solar radiation depends on both path length and the condition of the atmosphere.

The intensity of radiation striking the surface of an object on the Earth is dependent on solar geometry. Figure 3.7 shows the Sun's position in the sky at a central European location over the course of a year. The Sun appears to rise in the morning in the east (northeast in the summer, southeast in the winter), rises steadily higher in the sky until noon, and reaches its highest position in the south, and then descends steadily over the afternoon to set in the west (northwest in the evening in summer, southwest late afternoon in winter). The angle between true north and the horizontal component of the Sun's rays is referred to as the solar azimuth angle. Using this angle and the solar altitude angle, which gives the height of the Sun in the sky, the Sun's position in the dome of the sky can be located geometrically at any time during the year. The geometry of solar radiation's interaction with horizontal and vertical surfaces is shown in Figure 3.8 and with tilted surfaces in Fig. 3.9. Figure 3.10 shows a comparison of various tilt angles (angle between the surface and the horizontal plane) for solar energy production surfaces to be incorporated into a skyscraper project in Hong Kong. It can be seen that at this latitude, by far the best performance for solar energy production is achieved by more or less horizontal surfaces with the building façades receiving comparatively little radiation. For the same reason, people lie down on the beach to get a suntan.

The outside **air temperature** is the result of heat exchange processes between the Sun, the surface of the Earth and the atmosphere, and depends on short wave radiation from the Sun, long wave radiation from the Earth, the condition of the atmosphere, and wind and ocean current conditions. In general, the average annual temperature decreases with in-

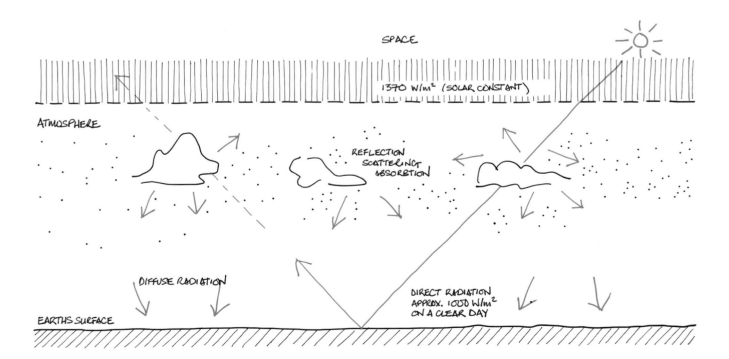

Fig. 3.6

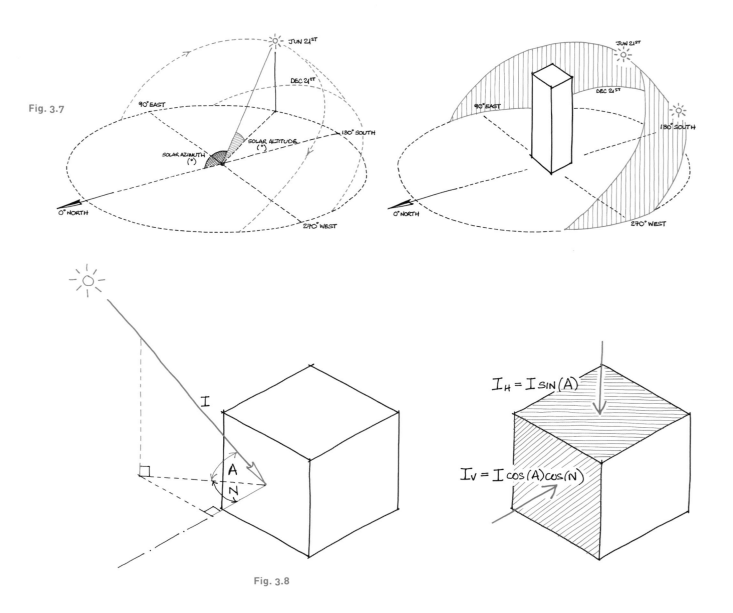

Fig. 3.7

$$I_H = I \sin(A)$$

$$I_V = I \cos(A) \cos(N)$$

Fig. 3.8

Fig. 3.6
Direct, diffuse and
global radiation

Fig. 3.7
Sun's position in sky for
central European location

Fig. 3.8
Solar radiation interaction
with horizontal and vertical
surfaces

Fig. 3.9
Solar radiation on
tilted surfaces

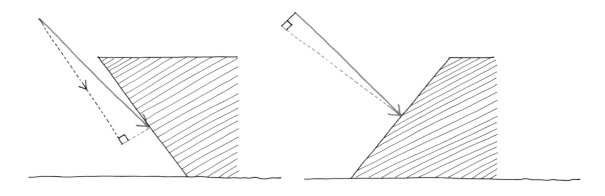

Fig. 3.9

creasing latitude and increasing altitude. In the temperate zone, both the annual and the daily variation in external air temperature can be approximated by a sine curve. Due to thermal inertia, there is a time lag between maximum solar radiation and the maximum air temperature at a location, which usually occurs 3 to 4 hours after noon on a sunny day. A similar pattern can be observed on an annual scale with the hottest month in Vienna for example occurring in July or August and not in June. The magnitude of the diurnal variation depends primarily on proximity to the sea and on the extent of cloud cover and humidity in the atmosphere at night, with the greatest variation at inland desert locations and the least variation in coastal tropical regions.

Global **wind** patterns result from the uneven heating of the Earth's surface as described above, with warmer air rising vertically upwards in convection currents at the equatorial regions to be replaced by cooler air flowing towards the equator. At high altitude in the atmosphere, moisture is condensed out of the rising warm moist air, leading to copious amounts of precipitation in the tropical regions. To complete the convection current, the dry air descends over the subtropical regions, gaining in temperature and resulting in the hot dry regions in the subtropics. A similar pattern occurs in the region near the poles which experience a negative radiation balance, with cold dense air flowing away from the poles and replacing warmer air rising upwards at the mid-latitudes. Due to the so-called Coriolis effect, explained below, air flow in the northern hemisphere is diverted towards the right, so air flowing towards the poles is diverted eastwards and towards the equator westwards (Fig. 3.11).

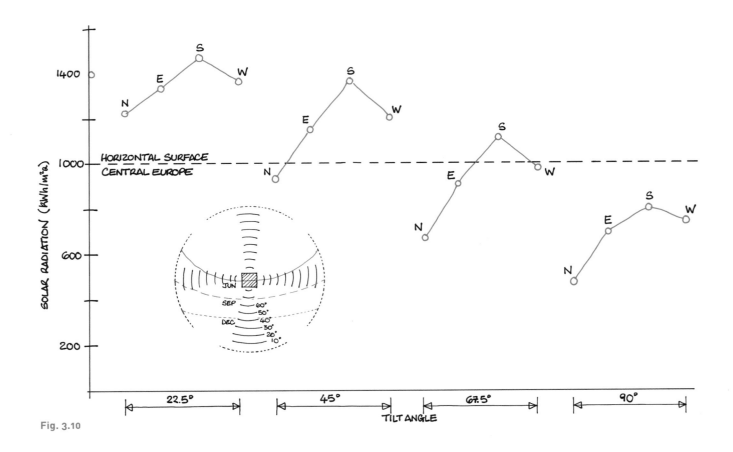

Fig. 3.10

Fig. 3.10
Solar energy production
for various tilt angles,
Hong Kong skyscraper

Fig. 3.11
Global wind patterns

Fig. 3.12
Site plan, Ecole Centrale
Paris

Owing to the rotation of the Earth around its own axis, the Earth's surface at the equator is spinning faster than at the poles (due to the greater distance to be travelled in the same time). This is also the reason why rocket take-off is located near the equator. The Earth rotates in a counterclockwise direction (when seen from the top); so in the usual depiction of maps, the direction of rotation is from left to right. To understand the Coriolis effect, imagine you are a giant standing on the north side of the equator and you throw a giant stone due north. Because the target is moving slower than the ground you are on, you miss and the stone falls to the right of it. Reverse positions and the stone falls behind the target, again to the right.

The pressure of the atmosphere at a point near the Earth's surface is due to the weight of the air layers above. Air flows from areas of high to areas of low pressure. Wind is a vector quantity with magnitude (speed) and direction. On weather maps and in building design we are concerned with the horizontal components, and the vertical components are neglected. Detailed information regarding frequency and magnitude of wind speed and direction can be obtained at most locations and is often depicted in an easy-to-read form called a wind rose diagram. Figure 3.12 shows a conceptual diagram for the Ecole Centrale Paris project with OMA architects, which shows the frequency of wind direction alongside other climatic

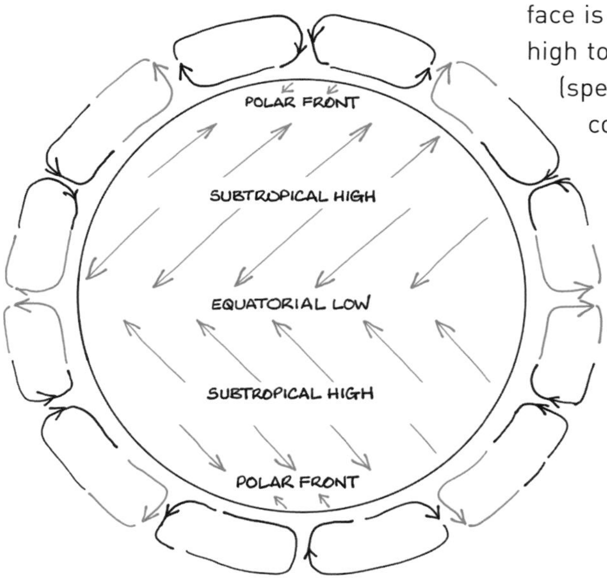

POLAR FRONT

SUBTROPICAL HIGH

EQUATORIAL LOW

SUBTROPICAL HIGH

POLAR FRONT

Fig. 3.11

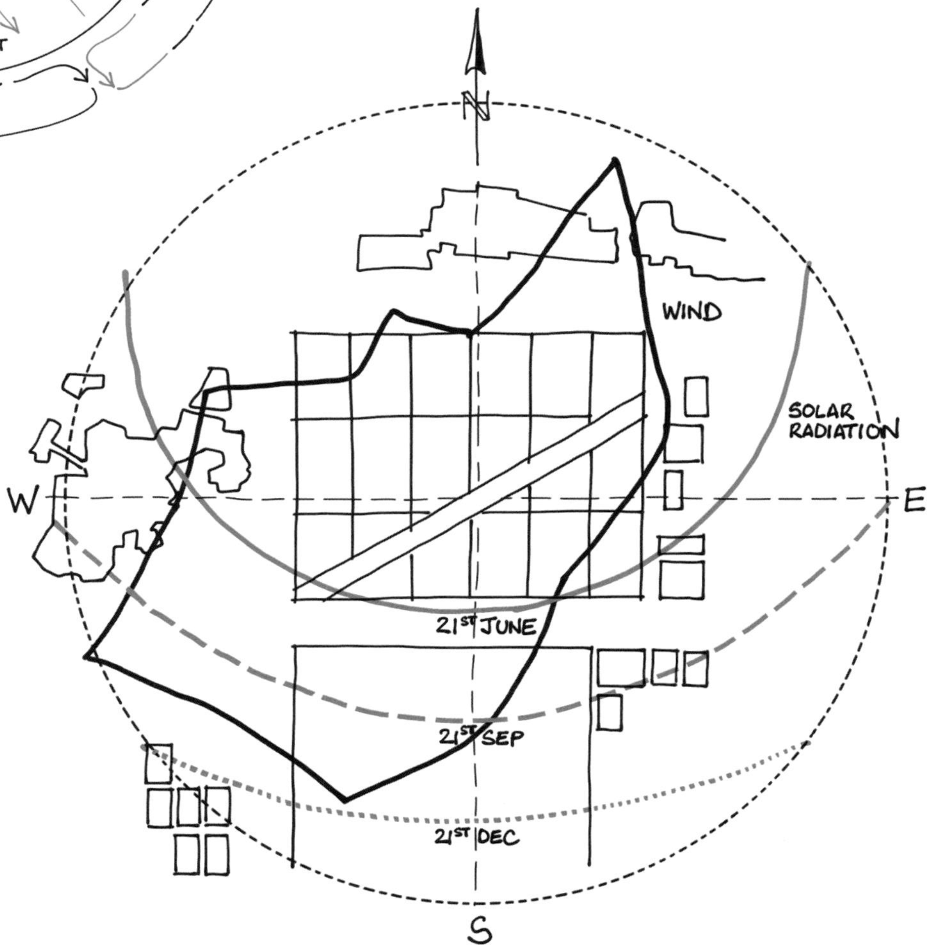

N

WIND

SOLAR
RADIATION

W

E

21ST JUNE

21ST SEP

21ST DEC

S

Fig. 3.12

factors in schematic form. Due to the no-slip condition (see chapter two) and friction at the Earth's surface, wind speed at a location increases with height. Figure 3.13 shows characteristic vertical wind speed profiles for various situations. In an urban area, the height required to achieve maximum speed is greater due to increased friction at the ground.

In the same way that the atmospheric circulation patterns discussed above arise on a global scale, similar patterns can be observed on a local scale. Local wind systems such as the land-sea wind system or the valley-hill wind system (Fig. 3.14) occur due to uneven heating of the various surfaces (a south-facing hill receives more sun during the day) and due to differences in thermal storage capacity (the ground has a lower specific heat capacity than water and thus heats up faster during the day). Local wind systems also occur on an urban scale, e.g. tall skyscrapers directing wind downwards or wind flows due to different temperatures between urban areas and the surrounding countryside. Cities in valley areas sheltered by surrounding mountains are often dependent on local wind systems such as these and therefore buildings should be designed with these in mind. The new Medical University Campus in Graz (Riegler Riewe architects) was configured so as not to disrupt the air flow patterns which are important for the ventilation of the city (Fig. 3.15).

The climate on the Earth has been classified in various systems into **climatic zones** with similar climatic conditions. Figure 3.16 shows a very simplified subdivision into four climate zones. More detailed classification systems can be found in the literature. In the tropical zone between the tropic of cancer (23.5° north) and the tropic of Capricorn (23.5° south), the sun's position in the sky varies little during the annual cycle and is almost vertically overhead at noon during the entire year. Due to the high year-

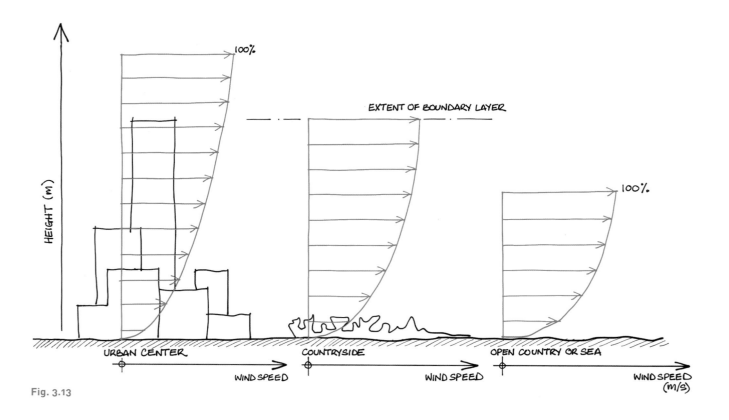

Fig. 3.13

Fig. 3.13
Wind velocity profiles

Fig. 3.14
Valley-hill wind system/
land-sea wind system

Fig. 3.15
Site plan, Med Campus
Graz

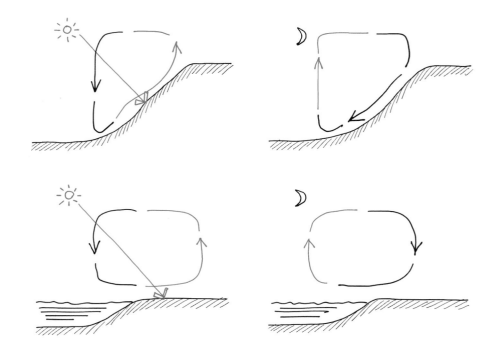

Fig. 3.14

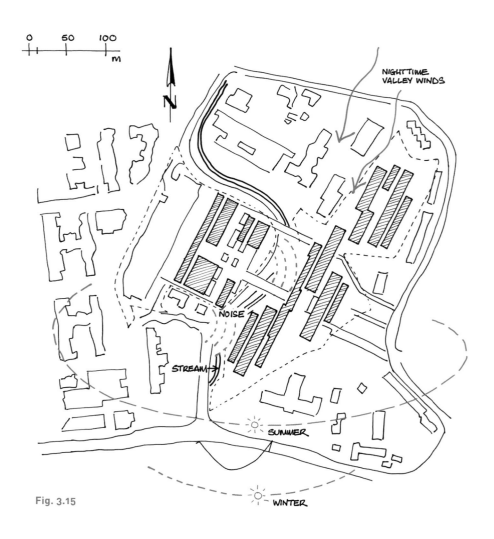

Fig. 3.15

round solar radiation, evaporation of moisture from the masses of water leads to high humidity and precipitation. Temperatures are not as high as in the subtropical zone due to frequent cloud cover. There are no seasons, high rainfall all year round and both temperature and humidity are consistently high with little variation between day and night. The climate could be considered perfect for vegetation and plants. It is however, less suitable for humans as the heat loss by evaporation necessary for the human body to achieve thermal comfort at high air temperatures is severely restricted by the humidity levels. Traditional building structures were designed to provide ample amounts of natural ventilation to cool the human body directly via air movement.

In the subtropical zone, between 23.5° and roughly 40° on both hemispheres, solar radiation and temperatures reach their peak. In the summer period, solar radiation is almost perpendicular to the earth's surface and due to the global wind patterns described above, the air is dry and there is little cloud cover. Near the coast (e.g. Dubai), summers are hot and humid, in desert zones further inland (e.g. Riyadh) hot and dry. In desert areas, the diurnal variation in temperature is high due to high solar radiation and long wave radiation at nighttime to the clear night sky. Traditional architecture in areas with hot dry climate conditions used evaporative cooling and nighttime ventilation combined with thermal mass. The winters are milder and cooler than in the tropics.

At latitudes greater than about 60° north and south, the cold zone receives less solar radiation at low angles with very short winter and very long summer days. The extreme conditions in winter result in a harsh and challenging environment for vegetation, animals and humans.

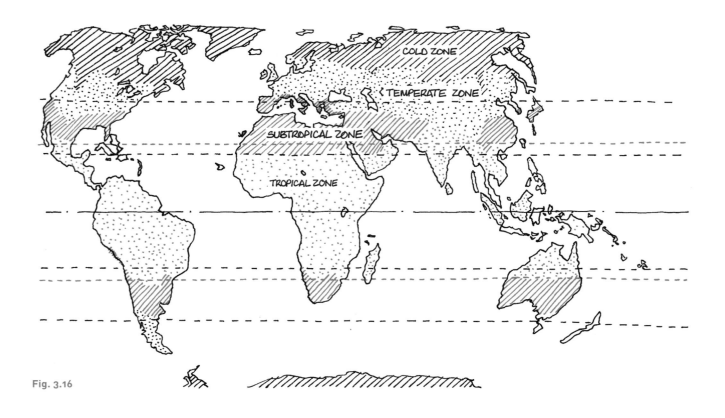

Fig. 3.16

Fig. 3.16
Climate zones of the world

The temperate zone at the mid latitudes between 40° and 60° has the most diverse range of different climatic sub-regions. Common to most is the existence of four distinct seasons. The Mediterranean climate with hot dry summers and rainy mild winters (e.g. Athens) is often thought to represent the ideal climate for humans and indeed little besides some form of shade from the sun is necessary to allow human survival in this climate. However, against the background of how we live and work today, this climate is perhaps less ideal. In traditional architecture, thermal mass and shading were employed to cope with the hot sunny summer conditions.

Inland areas, far away from large bodies of water experience a so-called continental climate, characterized by large fluctuations in temperature between winter and summer and also between day and night. Traditional buildings in many areas used timber construction, in which the cavities were filled with mud and straw to achieve a degree of thermal insulation against the cold winters.

In coastal regions, further away from the equator (e.g. Dublin), the oceans have a moderating effect on temperature due to their high thermal capacity compared to land masses. Fluctuations between winter and summer and between day and night are much less pronounced than in inland regions. These humid, cool and often windy regions with mild weather all year round do not at first sight appear ideal for humans, and necessitated the construction of sheltered accommodation from the outset of human settlement. However, for people in the twentyfirst century, who spend the majority of their time indoors, this mild climate is arguably ideal in terms of energy. Traditional buildings used straw thatched roofs to protect against wind and weather.

In mountainous regions such as the alpine area in central Europe, altitude influences climate (with a drop in temperature of approx. 10 °C for every 1000 m altitude), so that temperatures are significantly lower than in regions at sea level at the same latitude despite higher levels of solar radiation. Precipitation is often in the form of snow.

We will now look at the external climatic conditions for four cities:
- Berlin (temperate, continental)
- San Francisco (subtropical/temperate, coastal)
- Abu Dhabi (subtropical/desert, coastal)
- Singapore (tropical)

The data is taken from climatic files used on various projects for thermal simulations. Fig. 3.17 shows the location of the four cities. Sun path diagrams are shown in Figures 3.18–3.21. All four locations are located in the northern hemisphere, so that the Sun appears to rise in the east and set in the west. The distance from the center of the circle gives the solar altitude angle, while the angular distance from north gives the solar azimuth, so east is 90°, south is 180°, west is 270° etc. The resulting solar geometry leads to differing solar radiation intensities on horizontal and variously-orientated vertical surfaces. Figures 3.22–3.24 show solar radiation data for building surfaces in June, March and December for the four cities. The optimal orientation of many building types in most parts of the world is with the long axis running east-west, so that the main façades are facing north and south. The reasoning behind this becomes apparent when the variation in solar radiation intensity on the various surfaces shown in these diagrams is studied in detail. In winter, the south façade receives more solar radiation than any of the other building surfaces at locations in the temperate and cold zones, which allows passive solar heating in the cold season. The east and west façades receive comparatively little radiation in winter. In summer, the focus for all four locations is on overheating and cooling energy. Here, it can be seen that the total cumulative radiation on the north and south façades is less than on the east and west façades over the course of a day in all four cities. Also, the Sun is higher in the sky on the south side and providing shading without blocking out the necessary daylight is much easier to achieve.

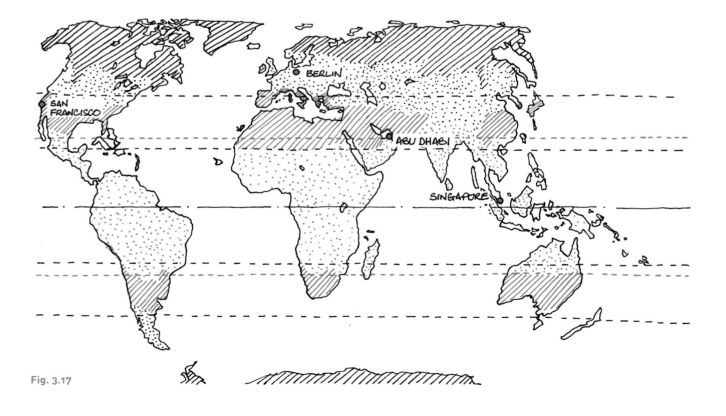

Fig. 3.17

Fig. 3.17
Locations of cities
analyzed

Fig. 3.18
Sun path, Berlin

Fig. 3.19
Sun path,
San Francisco

Fig. 3.20
Sun path, Abu Dhabi

Fig. 3.21
Sun path, Singapore

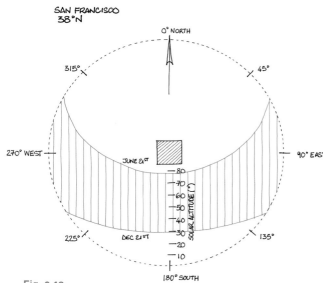

Fig. 3.19

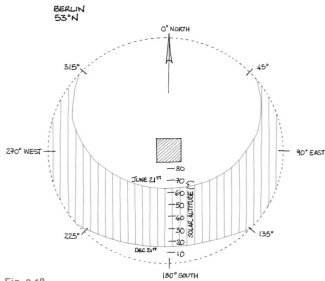

Fig. 3.18

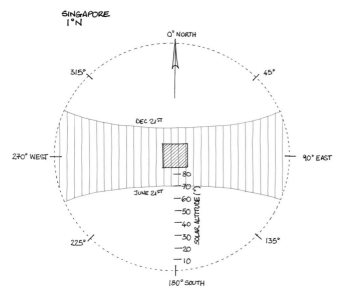

Fig. 3.21

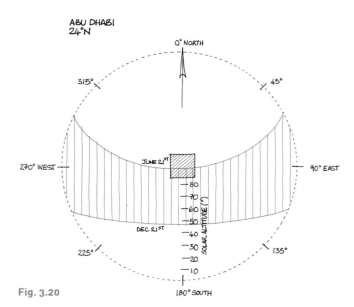

Fig. 3.20

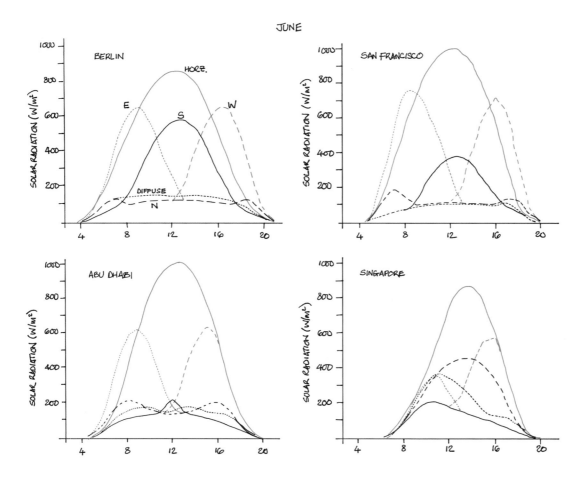

Fig. 3.22

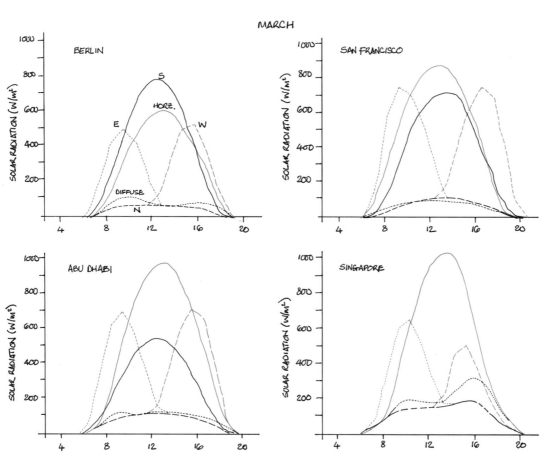

Fig. 3.23

Figure 3.25 shows the annual global radiation on a horizontal surface and the proportions of direct and diffuse solar radiation for the four locations. Annual global radiation is highest in Abu Dhabi, followed by San Francisco. The two cities also have a much higher proportion of direct radiation, meaning, for example, that the orientation of a surface to be used for solar energy production is important, and that the use of tracking, i.e. changing the orientation and tilt angle automatically, is worth considering.

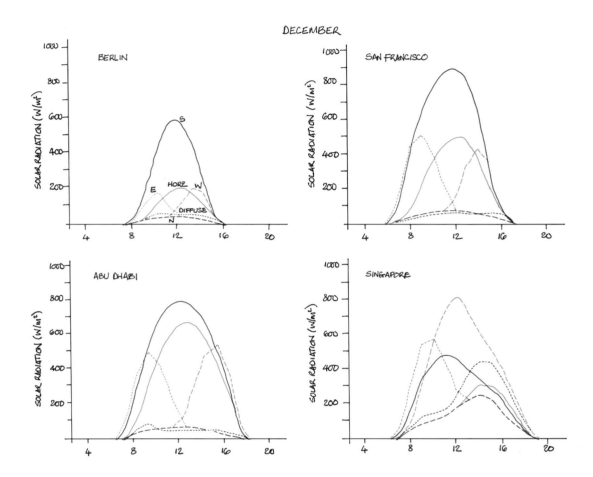

Fig. 3.24

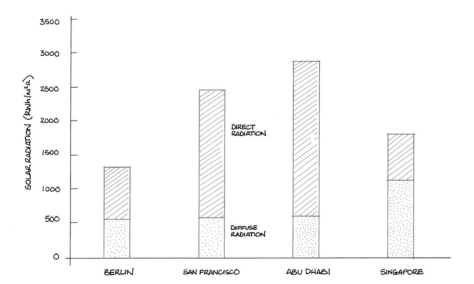

Fig. 3.25

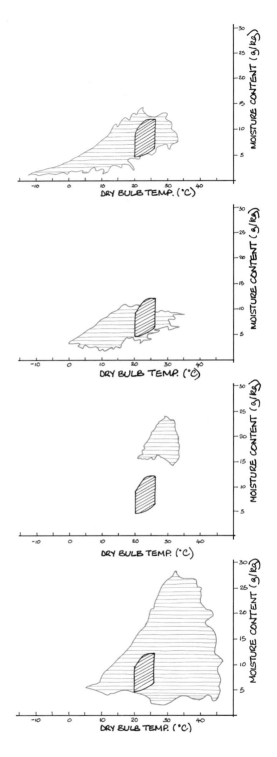

Fig. 3.26

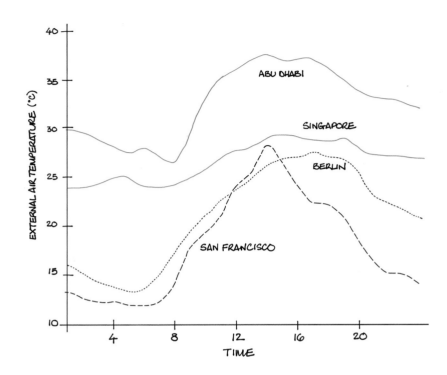

Fig. 3.27

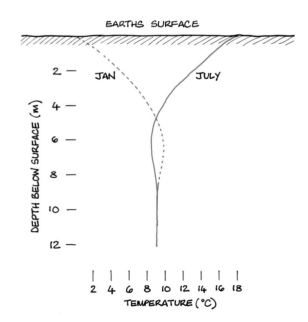

Fig. 3.29

In Singapore, diffuse radiation makes up approx. 60 % of the total global radiation, while in Berlin, direct and diffuse radiation are more or less equally distributed, which is typical for central Europe.

If the hourly values for absolute humidity are plotted against temperature for a full year, we arrive at the climate envelopes depicted in Figure 3.26. Shown for comparison is a zone typically chosen for thermal comfort in buildings. We will return to the derivation of this zone in the next section. These diagrams are a basic form of the psychrometric chart, already introduced in chapter two, and they allow the extreme values in summer and winter as well as the annual fluctuations in temperature and humidity to be read at a glance. This form of representation is very useful for comparing two climates, for example the climate at a location for a new project and a climate with which you are more familiar. The variation of temperature over a typical summer day is shown in Fig. 3.27. While the temperature at night in Berlin and San Francisco is cool enough to allow nighttime cooling, this is not the case in Dubai and Singapore.

Figure 3.28 shows average and extreme values of temperature and humidity for the four cities, again together with a typical comfort zone for the indoor environment. The degree to which heating or cooling is the dominant energy user can be readily interpreted from the diagram. It can also be seen that in Singapore, humidity levels are consistently higher than those which allow thermal comfort – as is the case for a large part of the year in Abu Dhabi – so that removing moisture from the indoor air (dehumidification) is a major energy consumer at these locations.

The ground temperature at a depth of around 10 m below the Earth's surface mirrors the average external air temperature at the location and this can be used to advantage for passive heating or cooling via underground air ducts or with ground source heat pump systems (Fig. 3.29).

To a certain extent, cities modify the climate in which they are located, creating in effect their own urban climate with, for example, different wind conditions, more clouds, fog etc. One of the observed phenomena is the so-called heat island effect, whereby the absorption and storage of

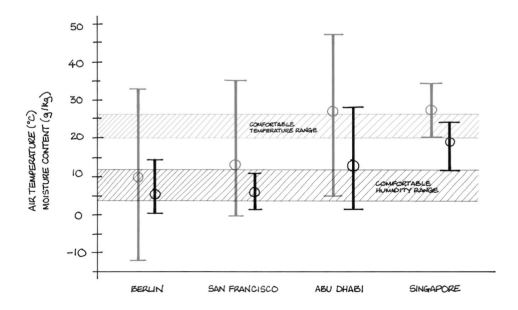

Fig. 3.28

solar radiation in urban structures and the delayed release into the ambient surroundings, coupled with lower levels of vegetation and evaporation of rainfall, leads to higher temperatures in the city; especially pronounced at nighttime (Fig. 3.30).

Humans have been modifying the landscape of the places they have occupied since the origin of the species, but especially since the agricultural and industrial revolutions. The cultivation of agricultural land (with side-effects such as deforestation, overgrazing and desertification), the use of groundwater and the building of urban areas and roads with attendant heat and substance emissions are just some of the ways we modify the natural environment and climate. Possibly the most serious way in which we have impacted on the climate is the so-called global warming phenomenon or greenhouse effect. In a greenhouse used for the cultivation of plants, short-wave radiation from the sun is transmitted through the clear glass envelope, but long-wave radiation at the much higher wavelengths of thermal radiation from the objects and surfaces contained within is not allowed to pass back out, leading to elevated indoor temperatures. In a similar way, so-called greenhouses gases in the atmosphere (the most important of which are water vapor H_2O, carbon dioxide CO_2 and methane CH_4) transmit short-wave solar radiation but do not allow the absorbed heat to escape in the form of long-wave thermal radiation from the Earth's surface, leading to higher temperatures on the Earth (Fig. 3.31). This so-called greenhouse effect is part of the natural world and is necessary to enable life on Earth, as conditions on the planet would otherwise be much too cold. However, the increased concentration of some greenhouse gases in the atmosphere, in particular CO_2 and methane CH_4, in the period since the industrial revolution has amplified this greenhouse effect, leading to increased and dangerous levels of global warming. These emissions are anthropogenic in origin, resulting mostly from energy use in buildings, transport and industry; and together with lower natural CO_2 absorption due to increased deforestation have led to an increase in concentration from less than 300 ppm (parts per million) in preindustrial times to roughly 400 ppm today with a concurrent rise in the average air temperature at the Earth's surface. Interested readers should refer to the many texts dealing with this issue.

Fig. 3.30

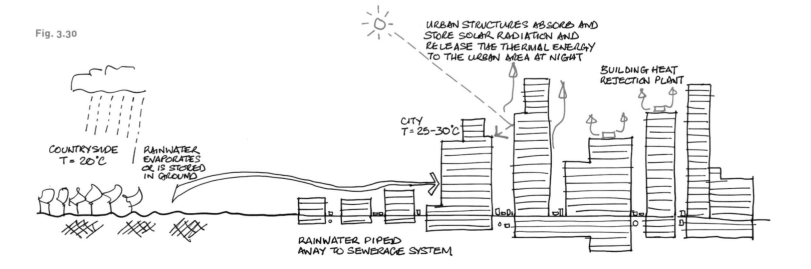

URBAN STRUCTURES ABSORB AND STORE SOLAR RADIATION AND RELEASE THE THERMAL ENERGY TO THE URBAN AREA AT NIGHT

BUILDING HEAT REJECTION PLANT

CITY
T = 25–30°C

COUNTRYSIDE
T = 20°C

RAINWATER EVAPORATES OR IS STORED IN GROUND

RAINWATER PIPED AWAY TO SEWERAGE SYSTEM

Fig. 3.30
Heat island effect

Fig. 3.31
Greenhouse effect

Most buildings, though by no means all, are designed to be used by humans. Thus, comfort conditions for humans often set the criteria for the design of the **internal environment** and humans are often the biggest source of pollutants in these buildings. In other buildings, processes, machines and products are more important and the comfort of humans is secondary or there are no humans present. In our efforts to reduce energy demand, we must be careful not to take our eyes of the important issues of thermal comfort and air quality in indoor spaces. This is the mistake we made in the aftermath of the energy crisis in the 1970s, resulting in phenomena such as sick building syndrome etc. One of the primary functions of architecture is the making of comfortable spaces for people.

What is a comfortable space? It is sometimes as simple as sitting on a bench in the shade on a sunny day and reading a newspaper. If the temperature is not too warm, not too cold, the wind speed not too high, the humidity low enough to prevent perspiration forming on the skin, the light sufficient to allow reading without strain, but not too bright as to cause glare or unwanted reflections from the page, the absence of unwanted background noise to distract. As simple as that. On the other hand, that is a lot of ifs. To help create comfortable spaces in an environment, such as outdoor seating in a restaurant or café, devices such as shading umbrellas and wind breaks are employed. Sometimes cooling systems using evaporative cooling (fans and water spray systems) or radiant heating are employed to extend the period of use. At this stage, the space being created begins to resemble a space within a building in the conventional sense.

The focus of architectural discourse, education and of course practice has long been heavily focused on visual aspects. Architecture can be treated as art, to be visually appraised and enjoyed. Our visual perception is of course the most important sense for collecting information. However, architecture needs to be more than this. Architecture is about how we experience the spaces with all our senses, both within and between buildings in our cities. It is the quality of this total experience which determines the true value and quality of our built environment.

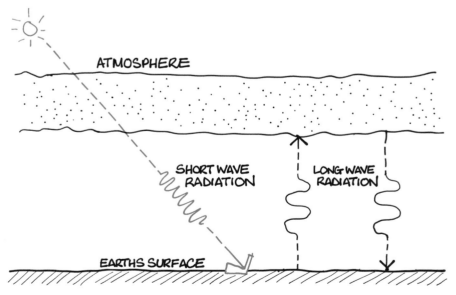

Fig. 3.31

The **human body** consists of about 100 trillion cells (Fig. 3.32). A cell is the most basic unit of structure and function in living things. Cells carry on the processes that keep organisms alive and in the human body there are many different types such as nerve cells, blood cells, and bone cells. A tissue is a group of similar cells that perform the same function. There are four basic types of tissue in the bodies of all animals; epithelial tissue such as the skin, which acts as a protective layer and interface with the environment, connective tissue to connect everything together, muscle tissue (muscles perform any external mechanical work) and nerve tissue to perceive and communicate information. Organs such as the stomach, heart, brain, and lungs are structures composed of different kinds of tissue. The heart is essentially a pump which transports blood continuously through your body and contains all four types of tissue. Each organ in your body is part of an organ system, of which there are twelve in the human body. For example, the heart is part of the circulatory system, which carries oxygen and other materials throughout the body. Foods (carbohydrates, fat and protein) are slowly combusted to enable metabolism, the physical and chemical processes within a human being necessary to maintain life. In these processes, large molecules are broken down into smaller ones and other molecules needed by the body are created. In these chemical reactions, energy is released and absorbed, while the internal core is maintained at a constant temperature of approximately 37 °C.

The human being, like all other creatures, perceives the world through a filter developed by evolution. There are wavelengths of light and frequencies of sound that other animals or insects can see and hear which we remain oblivious to. In the design of buildings, we are usually concerned with creating comfortable conditions for human beings, which means that we are dealing with the range of light and sound perceived by humans and the thermal sensation caused by temperature and humidity felt by the human body. The human being, like the vast majority of mammals and birds and unlike almost all reptiles, fish and insects, is a warm-blooded creature, and as such needs to maintain a constant internal core temperature regardless of the condition of the environment in which he finds himself (homoeostasis). This entails a balancing of heat generation within the body and heat loss to the environment. The basal metabolic rate is the metabolic rate necessary to maintain basic bodily functions on

AVERAGE VALUES

MASS	60 – 80 kg
BODY VOLUME	0.06 m³
SURFACE AREA	1.7 – 1.9 m²
PULSE RATE	60 – 100 min⁻¹
BREATHING RATE	12 – 16 min⁻¹
INHALED AIR QUANTITY	0.5 m³/h
EXHALED CO₂ (SEDENTARY)	18 – 20 L/h
CORE BODY TEMPERATURE	37 °C
AVERAGE SKIN TEMPERATURE	33 °C
METABOLIC RATE	70 – 80 W
EVAPORATION RATE	40 – 50 g/h

Fig. 3.32

Fig. 3.32
Human being

Fig. 3.33
Heat generation for
various activities

an empty stomach without performing any activity. The magnitude varies from around 4200 kJ (1000 Calories) for a light elderly female to about 8400 kJ (2000 Calories) per day for a young heavy male. This is equivalent to an energy consumption rate in the range between 50 and 100 W. A large portion of this energy is converted to thermal energy in the body and lost by heat transfer to the environment. Increased activity rate leads to increased energy generation in the body and the total heat generation is equal to the basal metabolic rate plus the metabolic rate due to the activity. This increased rate of heat production varies from around 25 % when sitting quietly to more than 1000 % for very intensive sporting activities. With increased activity level, the rate of food intake must also increase to maintain the energy balance. On the other hand, if more food than necessary is eaten, i.e. more energy than the body needs for the activities undertaken, this energy will be stored in the body in the form of fat. Heat generation as a result of metabolism is quantified directly in Watts or with the special Met unit (Fig. 3.33). One met is equal to 58 W/m² based on the outer surface skin area of the body. Human body skin area varies from roughly 1.5 to 2 m². The heat generation of an average person at rest is equal to 1 Met. Assuming an average surface area of 1.75 m² this gives a heat output of approximately 102 W (this resting metabolic rate is higher than the basal metabolic rate). Depending on the activity being undertaken, some of the energy generated is converted to work, but ultimately all of this energy is converted to thermal energy in the space.

The human body must constantly lose heat to the environment in order to maintain a constant core temperature, so that even when we heat spaces in winter to achieve thermal comfort, we are in fact concerned with reducing the cooling of the human body to a level which matches the heat generation within. If this heat is not continually removed from the body, the core temperature increases to harmful levels with potentially lethal consequences. The process of maintaining a constant internal body temperature, independent of the environmental conditions of the surroundings, is called **thermoregulation**. The control system, which regulates the heat balance in the human body, comprises local cold receptors distributed over the entire skin surface (lower set point approximately 33 °C) and central heat receptors in the brain (upper set point 37 °C). The skin, the largest organ in the human body, plays a major role in this process.

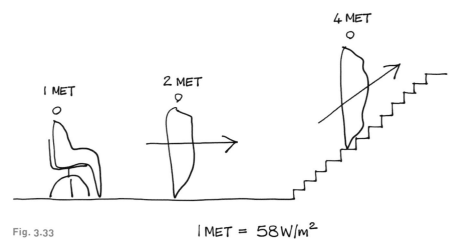

Fig. 3.33

1 MET = 58 W/m²

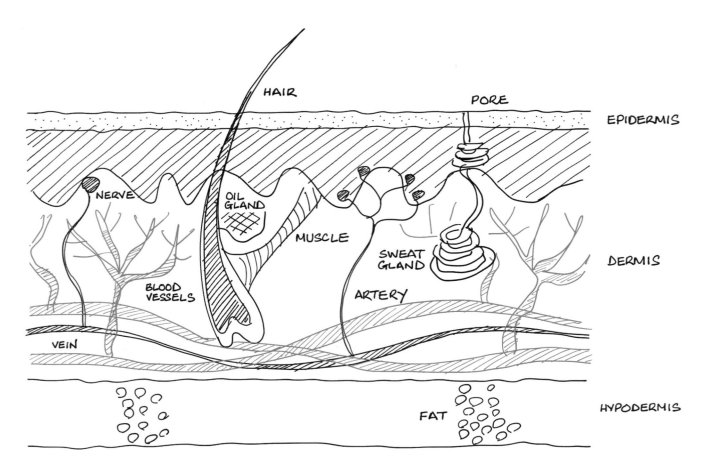

Fig. 3.34

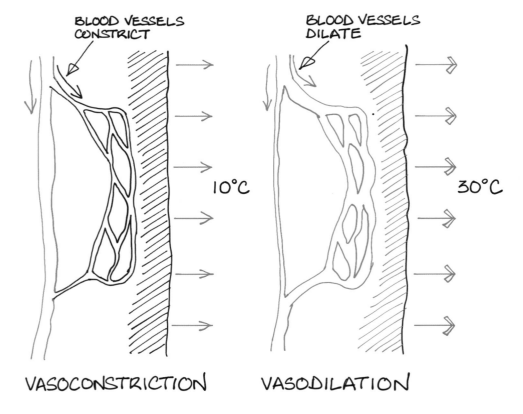

VASOCONSTRICTION   VASODILATION

Fig. 3.35

The skin, with a thickness of approximately 2.5 mm, forms the primary interface between the body and the environment (Fig. 3.34). It is also the primary source of sensation. In order to maintain a constant body temperature, heat is transported to the skin surface via blood flow and released into the environment before returning to the core of the body. Blood flow to the skin surface is regulated by the nervous system according to the requirement for heat transfer (Fig. 3.35). With increased activity, heat generation in the core increases and therefore blood flow to the external body surface is increased to balance the excess heat production with an increase in heat loss to the environment. The necessary increase in heat loss rate due to increased activity or a warmer ambient environment is effected by a process known as vasodilation. The subcutaneous vessels increase in cross sectional area to allow increased blood flow. In some people, the occurrence is clearly visible, as their skin becomes redder. In cold conditions, vasoconstriction of the subcutaneous vessels restricts the flow of blood in order to reduce heat loss and the skin becomes paler. The higher the blood flow, the higher the skin temperature and the resulting heat transfer to the environment, as long as the temperature of the surroundings is below the body temperature.

The average skin temperature of a sedentary person in a comfortable environment is between 32 and 34 °C, whereas the core temperature remains almost constant at around 37 °C. In changing conditions, the external surface of the body changes temperature in response to the surrounding environment, while the temperature in the core remains constant (Fig. 3.36). In cold conditions, blood is diverted away from the peripheral parts of the body, causing their temperature to drop.

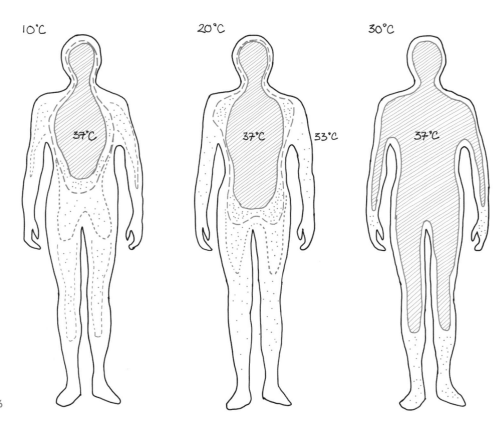

Fig. 3.36

The formation of goose bumps is a throwback to a response from the time when we had more body hair, which then stood up to form an insulating layer of still air to reduce heat loss. Shivering and perspiration are other forms of thermoregulation. When an environment is too cold, the body strives to achieve a balance by increasing involuntary muscle movement and thus heat generation. When an environment is too hot, higher rates of perspiration are employed in an effort to increase heat loss by evaporation.

The continual process of matching heat production in the body core (dependent on activity) and heat loss from the body (dependent on ambient conditions) in order to maintain constant core body temperature forms the basis of understanding **thermal comfort.** In a thermally comfortable environment, a balance between heat generation in the body and heat loss to the surroundings is maintained by regulation of the blood flow through the skin surface alone, without the body having to resort to measures such as shivering or sweating.

The body loses heat by all three modes of sensible heat transfer and also by evaporation of water vapor from the skin and lungs. Heat loss from a sedentary person at lower room temperatures is mainly by radiation and convection. At higher temperatures, the latent heat loss due to evaporation of moisture from the skin (perspiration) increases (Fig. 3.37). Therefore, thermal comfort in a space depends on the air temperature in the space (convection), the surrounding surface temperatures (radiation) and the relative humidity (evaporation) (Fig. 3.38). Increased air movement around the body influences convective heat transfer and heat loss by evaporation. These parameters largely determine what is known as global thermal comfort. Other factors influence local thermal comfort and are also important in achieving a comfortable thermal environment. These include direct solar radiation, drafts due to excessive air movement, particularly if the air is cool, asymmetric thermal radiation, direct contact with hot or cold surfaces (e.g. floors if barefoot) and vertical temperature gradients.

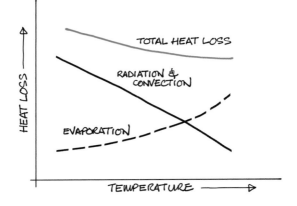

Fig. 3.37

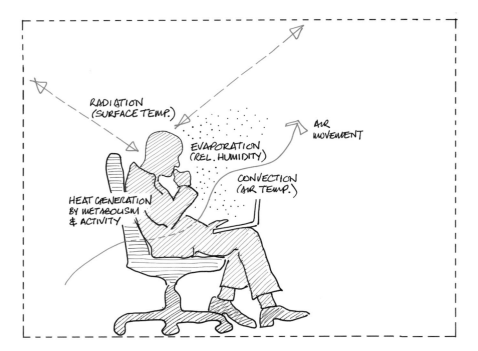

Fig. 3.38

As we shall see shortly, the air temperature and the temperatures of the surrounding surfaces are of roughly equal importance. The mean radiant temperature (MRT) is defined as the temperature of an imaginary enclosure in which the radiant heat transfer with a human body would be exactly equal to the actual radiant heat transfer in the space considered. MRT is often used to model the average temperature of the surrounding surfaces and is calculated by summing the products of all the surfaces and their temperatures and dividing by the total surface area to obtain the area weighted mean temperature of all the surfaces surrounding the body.

The operative or dry resultant temperature is defined as the temperature of an imaginary enclosure in which the heat transfer with a human body would be exactly equal to the actual heat transfer by radiation and convection in the space considered. It is therefore a much more effective measure than simply stating the air temperature, which depending on the average surface temperature of the surroundings may give a grossly incorrect evaluation of comfort, and will only be close if the MRT and the air temperature are approximately equal. If the air speed is not too high, the operative or resultant temperature can be estimated as the average of the air temperature and the MRT.

Using the principles of heat transfer discussed in the last chapter, it is possible to derive the conditions necessary for the thermal comfort of a human being in various situations. We start with the basic heat balance equation for a person in a space, e.g. in an office (Fig. 3.39). At steady

Fig. 3.39

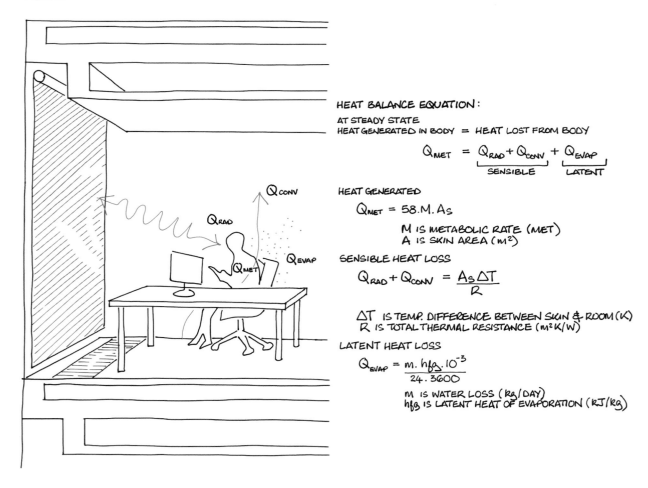

HEAT BALANCE EQUATION:

AT STEADY STATE
HEAT GENERATED IN BODY = HEAT LOST FROM BODY

$$Q_{MET} = \underbrace{Q_{RAD} + Q_{CONV}}_{SENSIBLE} + \underbrace{Q_{EVAP}}_{LATENT}$$

HEAT GENERATED

$$Q_{MET} = 58 \cdot M \cdot A_S$$

M IS METABOLIC RATE (MET)
A IS SKIN AREA (m²)

SENSIBLE HEAT LOSS

$$Q_{RAD} + Q_{CONV} = \frac{A_S \Delta T}{R}$$

ΔT IS TEMP. DIFFERENCE BETWEEN SKIN & ROOM (K)
R IS TOTAL THERMAL RESISTANCE (m²K/W)

LATENT HEAT LOSS

$$Q_{EVAP} = \frac{m \cdot h_{fg} \cdot 10^{-3}}{24 \cdot 3600}$$

m IS WATER LOSS (kg/DAY)
h_fg IS LATENT HEAT OF EVAPORATION (kJ/kg)

state conditions, the heat generated by metabolism and activity is equal to the heat lost by convection, radiation and evaporation. The thermal energy required to warm the air we breathe and the heat lost by conduction to surfaces we are in contact with is neglected, as the effect in most cases is negligible. Convection and radiation constitute the sensible heat loss, i.e. heat which causes a change in temperature.

For the sake of simplicity, we assume that room air temperature and mean radiant temperature are equal. Otherwise, we would need to calculate heat loss by radiation and convection separately. Assuming a metabolic rate of 1.2 Met for office work and a skin area of 1.75 m², the heat generated can be calculated to be 122 W.

Next, we turn to the heat losses. The sensible heat losses can be calculated in a similar way to the heat loss from a building as described in chapter two, namely as the product of external surface area and temperature difference divided by the total thermal resistance. The driving force of temperature difference in this case is the difference between the skin temperature and the temperature of the room. The area is taken to be the external skin area. The thermal resistance is due to clothes, which act as a form of thermal insulation, and the resistance of the air layer on the outer surface of the clothed body. The thermal resistance of clothes is measured in Clo, whereby one Clo is equal to a resistance of 0.155 m²K/W. Typical values are 0 Clo for a naked body, 0.5 Clo for office clothing in summer, 1 Clo for office clothing in winter and 2 Clo for outdoor clothing in cold winter weather. We will assume 1 Clo for clothing. The resistance of the air layer is the inverse of the combined heat transfer coefficient due to convection and radiation. Assuming values of 3 W/m²K and 5 W/m²K for convection and radiation respectively, the air layer resistance is calculated to be 0.125 m²K/W. This resistance is in series with the resistance due to clothes and, as seen in chapter two, the total resistance is equal to the sum of these two individual resistances, giving a value of 0.28 m²K/W.

The human body is largely composed of water, and a daily water loss of around 2 to 2.5 liters needs to be continually replenished by eating and drinking. In a thermally comfortable environment, roughly 1.2 liters or 1200 grams of this water loss is due to breathing and evaporation from the skin, whereby both processes make up a roughly equal proportion. This results in a latent heat loss due to evaporation of moisture of roughly 30 W for our person. The only unknown in the heat balance equation is therefore the temperature difference between skin and room, which can then be calculated as approximately 14.7 K. If we assume a skin temperature of 34 °C, the room temperature is approx. 19 °C.

We can repeat the calculation for other situations. Changing the thermal resistance for clothing to 0.5 Clo for office clothing in summer gives a room temperature of approximately 23 °C for the summer case. Assuming a lower metabolic rate of 1.0 Met for a resting position and no clothes gives a room temperature of approximately 29 °C, to model the situation in a swimming pool hall. These calculations are of course a very simplified approach to what is in reality a very complex situation. However, the approach does provide meaningful insight into the mechanisms involved and the importance of the various parameters. The calculated temperatures come close to the actual values used in practice and found in the relevant codes and literature. In the approach above, the heat loss from the office worker due to radiation makes up nearly half of the total heat loss, while convection accounts for less than 30 %, meaning that under the assumed conditions the temperature of the surrounding surfaces is more important than the air temperature in terms of comfort. With increased air movement in a space, on the other hand, the heat transfer due to convection increases and the air temperature becomes more important. At higher temperatures, the heat loss due to evaporation gains significance.

Low relative humidity can lead to problems with increased dust collection, electrostatic charging of surfaces and drying out of mucous membranes. Often, a lower limit of 30 % is utilized in the design of HVAC systems to avoid problems of this nature. Due to the fact that a substantial proportion of the necessary heat loss from the human body at higher air temperatures is via evaporation, high relative humidity at higher temperatures can lead to discomfort. An upper threshold of 12 g/kg is often used in HVAC design as the upper limit of humidity at higher indoor temperatures. Standard values for operative room temperature for office buildings, but also for a large number of other building types, are usually chosen in the ranges 20 °C to 22 °C (winter) and 22 °C to 26 °C (summer). In many countries, a summertime indoor temperature set point in the higher range, e.g. 25 to 26 °C, is chosen for reasons of energy efficiency. Excessive air movement can cause thermal discomfort, especially when the moving air is at a lower temperature. To avoid drafts in occupied spaces, air speed should be kept below approx. 0.15 m/s.

Fig. 3.40 shows the build-up of a simplified comfort zone on the psychrometric chart based on the above. Note that an upper limit of 60 % relative humidity is shown. In the lower temperature range (wintertime design conditions), higher relative humidity would not lead to thermal discomfort; however an upper limit of 60 % to 70 % is used in order to minimize the risk of mold growth. Further important issues with regard to the indoor environment are air quality (see next section), lighting (quantity, quality, glare control, amount of daylight) and acoustics (noise protection, room acoustics). Experience has also shown that individual control over the personal environment is important for thermal comfort. For example, operable windows provide the occupants with some control over their environment, and this means of connection to the external environment can allow a greater tolerance for a wider range of internal environmental conditions.

Thermal comfort essentially depends on perception. If we are not conscious of the thermal environment and have no desire to change it in some way, we are comfortable. As we have seen above, different levels of clothing affect heat loss from the body and therefore thermal comfort. This has implications for building design with regard to building type, cultural context etc. Alongside the environmental parameters described above and the personal physical parameters (metabolic rate and clothing), the human perception of warmth or coldness also depends on psychological factors such as expectation levels, general satisfaction level, need for concentration etc.

A vast amount of research work has been carried out in the field of thermal comfort. Work done by Ole Fanger in the US and Denmark in the 1960s, in which sophisticated mathematical heat balance models were developed to allow predictions on how comfortable a given environment is likely to be for persons dressed in a certain way and engaging in a certain activity, deserves particular mention. Because of the perceptional nature of comfort, all of this research work employs empirical studies of real people and their responses to different environmental conditions. In recent years, research advocating an "adaptive comfort model" approach has suggested that if greater personal control is made possible over some of the factors which affect thermal comfort, e.g. clothing, temperature set point etc., people can feel comfortable within a wider range of conditions than those determined by the heat balance approach currently in use.

On the one hand, it is important to understand the physiology of the human body in order to enable us to create comfortable environments for humans. On the other hand, the human body is a fascinating source of inspiration for us in the design of intelligent buildings. Figure 3.41 shows the façade concept of the Braun HQ building in Kronberg, designed in collaboration with schneider + schumacher architects. Similar to the human skin, the façade reacts to ambient conditions, the outer layer opening and closing in response to temperature and user behavior while the shading device in the façade cavity is controlled in response to solar radiation. This very effective façade design meant that the spaces could be conditioned with a very simple capillary tubing system embedded in a plaster layer on the underside of the concrete slabs, almost like the veins and arteries circulating blood throughout the human body (Fig. 3.42). In the simulation of the

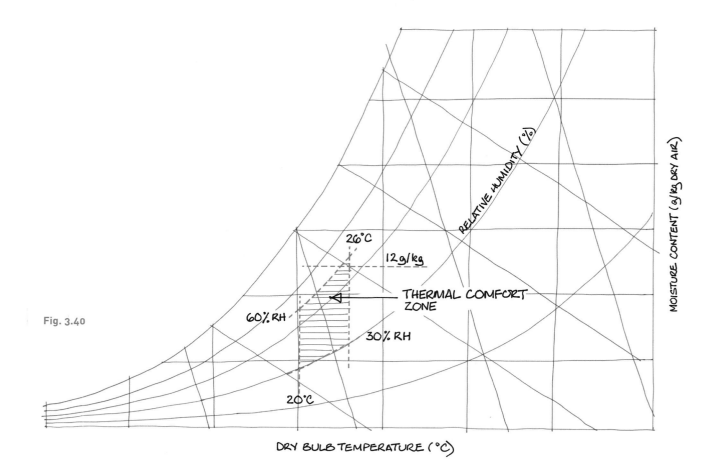

Fig. 3.40

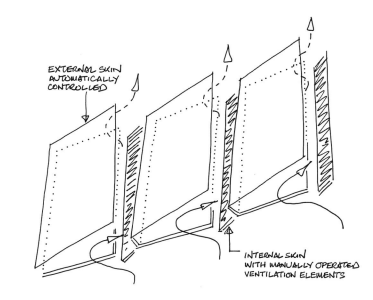

EXTERNAL SKIN
AUTOMATICALLY
CONTROLLED

INTERNAL SKIN
WITH MANUALLY OPERATED
VENTILATION ELEMENTS

Fig. 3.41

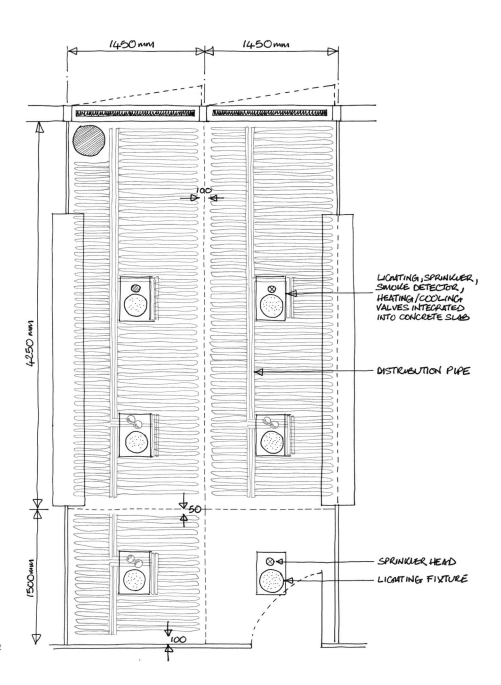

1450 mm   1450 mm

100

4250 mm

1500 mm

50

100

LIGHTING, SPRINKLER,
SMOKE DETECTOR,
HEATING/COOLING
VALVES INTEGRATED
INTO CONCRETE SLAB

DISTRIBUTION PIPE

SPRINKLER HEAD

LIGHTING FIXTURE

Fig. 3.42

internal office temperature on a hot day compared to outside (Fig. 3.43), it can be seen that the resultant temperature in the space is lower than the air temperature due to the cooler surface of the ceiling. On account of the fact that the building design combines natural ventilation with radiant ceilings, the flow water temperature in hot weather is controlled in accordance with the external humidity level in order to avoid condensation on the ceiling surface. This means that there are times when the resultant temperature is higher than the design condition. This was calculated to occur during approx. 2.5 % of operating hours and was discussed with the client and found to be acceptable. This decision, based on a dynamic appraisal of the indoor environment over the entire annual cycle, enabled the building to be completed without a mechanical ventilation system in the external zones, saving embodied energy, plant room space, capital and operating costs.

Atmospheric air, particularly in urban locations, contains both gaseous and particulate pollutants. In order to achieve acceptable levels of **indoor air quality**, these pollutants may have to be removed by filtration. Other pollutants occur in building spaces due to people, animals, processes and materials; these must be removed from the space, usually via a ventilation system using outdoor air, and less commonly via filtration or air cleaning systems. Some gaseous pollutants are perceived by humans as odors. Others, including some of those which present the greatest source of danger for human occupants, are not detected by the human nose, such as carbon monoxide, radon and infectious microorganisms. The CO_2 concentration in a building space is often used to measure the air quality. The threshold used is approx. 1000 ppm (parts per million), based on work done in the nineteenth century by Max von Pettenkofer, a pioneer in modern hygiene. CO_2 is, as we have seen, a normal byproduct of all combustion processes and thus is also present in exhaled air from humans as a result of slow combustion. At the levels which normally occur in building spaces, even in spaces with very low levels of ventilation, CO_2 is not normally harmful to humans. It is used as a suitable indicator of air quality, based on the assumptions that humans are the main source of pollutants in the space and that the level of pollutants in the space is

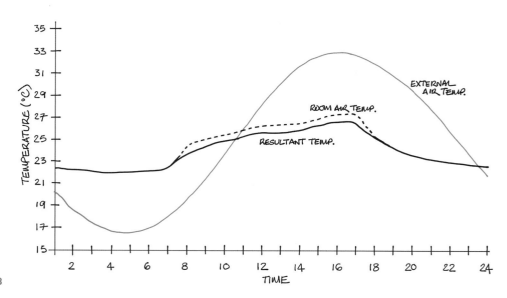

Fig. 3.43

Fig. 3.43
Braun HQ Germany,
summertime temperatures

proportional to the emissions from humans and therefore to the level of CO_2. Other sources of gaseous pollution within typical building spaces besides people are building materials, furniture and equipment, which emit so-called volatile organic compounds (VOC). These are substances which, due to their relatively low boiling points at room temperature, evaporate or sublimate from the material into the ambient room air. An area of particular interest for the future development of healthy sustainable buildings is the development and specification of materials for building construction, fittings, furniture, equipment etc. which do not employ such materials, allowing good levels of indoor air quality to be achieved in spaces with lower ventilation rates and therefore lower energy demand.

Outdoor air also contains particles resulting from emissions from traffic, building heating systems and industry. Other particles are emitted by humans, animals, processes and materials in the building spaces, including bacteria, viruses and allergens. A major source of discussion in many European cities at the present time is the mass concentration of PM10 particles or fine dust of which the allowable daily and annual levels of mass concentration are frequently exceeded. These are particles which have a diameter less than or equal to 10 micrometers and are thus small enough to be inhalable and deposited in the lungs, potentially causing serious health problems. In building spaces, particles of this dimension and smaller tend to remain suspended in air and travel with the prevailing air flow patterns through the building spaces. Larger particles tend to accumulate on surfaces in the spaces as dust. In general, devising and employing filtration systems to remove particulate pollutants is far easier than for gaseous pollutants.

The symptoms associated with poor air quality in spaces are well known; fatigue, shortness of breath, lack of concentration, headaches. You have probably experienced this at some time in your life. The sight of people falling asleep in public transport systems, airplanes, lecture halls etc. is frequently a result of bad air quality. Often you will notice that the air quality is poor only after you leave a space for a short time and return, e.g. to a meeting room. As mentioned above, the CO_2 concentration in room air does not normally rise above dangerous levels. However, because it is easily measurable and because it is a relatively good indicator of the general level of air pollution in spaces where the chief source of air pollution is humans, it is often used in practice to control the supply air quantity in concepts employing demand-controlled ventilation. This strategy is effective, as long as the rise in concentration of CO_2 and that of other odors and pollutants in the air are more or less directly proportional to each other.

CONSERVATION OF MASS:

VOL. OF CO_2 SUPPLIED $-$ VOL. OF CO_2 EXTRACTED $+$ VOL. OF CO_2 GENERATED

$=$ CHANGE IN VOL. OF CO_2 IN SPACE

IN A TIME INTERVAL Δt

$$(\dot{V}_S . C_S - \dot{V}_S . C_R + 10^6 \dot{q}_{co_2}) . \Delta t = V_R . \Delta C_R$$

$$\frac{\Delta C_R}{\Delta t} = \frac{\dot{V}_S}{V_R}(C_S - C_R) + 10^6 \frac{\dot{q}_{co_2}}{V_R}$$

$\Delta t \to 0$

$$\frac{dC_R}{dt} = n(C_S - C_R) + 10^6 \frac{\dot{q}_{co_2}}{V_R}$$

$n = \dfrac{\dot{V}_S}{V_R}$ AIR CHANGES PER HOUR

$$C_R' + n C_R = n C_S + 10^6 \frac{\dot{q}_{co_2}}{V_R}$$ GENERAL GOVERNING EQUATION

$\dot{V}_S$ SUPPLY VOLUME (m^3h^{-1})

$\dot{V}_E$ EXTRACT VOLUME (m^3h^{-1})

C_S CO_2 CONCENTRATION, SUPPLY (ppm)

C_R CO_2 CONCENTRATION, EXTRACT (ppm)

$\dot{q}_{co_2}$ CO_2 SOURCE EMISSIONS (m^3h^{-1})

C_0 INITIAL CO_2 CONCENTRATION (ppm)

$n = \dot{V}_S/V_R$ AIR CHANGES PER HOUR

t TIME (h)

SPECIAL CASE:

NO AIR CHANGE $n = 0$

$$C_R' = 10^6 \frac{\dot{q}_{co_2}}{V_R} \Rightarrow C_R = 10^6 \frac{\dot{q}_{co_2}}{V_R} t + k_1$$

INITIAL CONDITION: $C_R(0) = C_0 = k_1$

(1) $\boxed{C_R = C_0 + 10^6 \frac{\dot{q}_{co_2}}{V_R} t}$ NO AIR CHANGE

$$C_R' + n C_R = n C_S + 10^6 \frac{\dot{q}_{co_2}}{V_R} = A$$

INTEGRATING FACTOR

$$= e^{\int n dt} = e^{nt}$$

$$e^{nt} C_R' + n e^{nt} C_R = A e^{nt}$$

$$(e^{nt} C_R)' = A e^{nt}$$

$$e^{nt} C_R = \frac{A e^{nt}}{n} + k_2$$

$$C_R = \frac{A}{n} + \frac{k_2}{e^{nt}}$$

SPECIAL CASE
$t \to \infty$

(3) $\boxed{C_R = C_S + 10^6 \frac{\dot{q}_{co_2}}{\dot{V}_S}}$ STEADY STATE

INITIAL CONDITION:

$C_R(0) = C_0 = A/n + k_2 \Rightarrow k_2 = C_0 - A/n$

$$C_R = A/n + (C_0 - A/n) e^{-nt}$$

$$= C_S + 10^6 \frac{\dot{q}_{co_2}}{\dot{V}_S} (C_0 - C_S - 10^6 \frac{\dot{q}_{co_2}}{\dot{V}_S}) e^{-nt}$$

DECAYING INITIAL CONCENTRATION

(2) $\boxed{C_R = C_0 e^{-nt} + (1 - e^{-nt})(C_S + 10^6 \frac{\dot{q}_{co_2}}{\dot{V}_S})}$ GENERAL EQUATION

INCREASING CONCENTRATION DUE TO SOURCE

Fig. 3.44

In a similar manner to the way in which we determined the optimal temperatures for thermal comfort from first principles, we will now calculate the outdoor supply air rates required for ventilation. Figure 3.44 shows the derivation of the governing non-homogeneous linear first order differential equation together with its solution for a space with a ventilation system and a human as a CO_2 source. In a differential time increment, the CO_2 volume in the supply air flow, minus that in the extract air flow, plus the CO_2 emissions from the person in the space must be equal to the change in CO_2 volume in the space. As shown, a special case arises when there is no air change in the space: equation (1). Using this equation, we can calculate how long it takes for the CO_2 concentration to rise above the desired level – say 1000 ppm – if the space is not ventilated. Let us assume the initial concentration of CO_2 in a 20 m² meeting room is equal to the concentration outside, say 400 ppm, and that ten people, each emitting 20 liters of CO_2 per hour, enter the room for a short meeting. After a certain time interval, the concentration in the space will have risen to 1000 ppm. The concentration at this time must be equal to the concentration at the initial condition plus the cumulative CO_2 emissions from the people during this time interval. Solving for time gives approximately 10 minutes. So, no wonder you start to feel bad after a short time in such a space without adequate ventilation. After 1.5 hours, the level would have risen to over 5000 ppm. Even at this level, the concentration is not extremely dangerous to human health. However, the air quality is bad and you will probably perceive unpleasant odors and begin to feel drowsy.

Another special case arises in the steady state case: equation (3). Using the same upper limit for CO_2 concentration, we can determine the amount of fresh air needed to maintain good air quality in an office space. Consider a space occupied by an office worker. If the CO_2 concentration in the outside air is 400 ppm, what is the minimum outdoor air flow rate needed? Again, assuming the person emits 20 liters of CO_2 per hour and the supply air flow rate is equal to the exhaust air flow rate, the concentration of CO_2 in the air leaving the space must be equal to the concentration of CO_2 in the air entering the space plus the emissions from the person in the space. Solving for the supply air flow rate gives approximately 9 l/s per person or 33 m³/h. This value is close to the value often used in practice and given in the literature and in relevant codes.

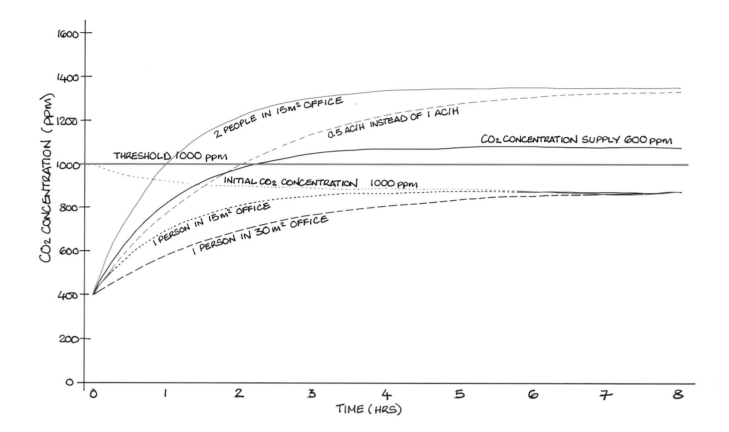

Fig. 3.45

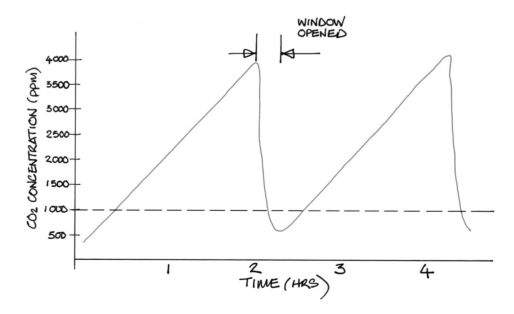

Fig. 3.46

Fig. 3.45
CO$_2$ concentration, various
scenarios for office space

Fig. 3.46
CO$_2$ concentration,
class room

Figure 3.45 shows results for various scenarios in an office building space as calculated by the general equation (2). The effect of varying occupancy density, room volume, the initial CO$_2$ concentration, the air change rate (the number of times the air is changed in one hour) and the CO$_2$ concentration of the supply air can be seen. Figure 3.46 shows a situation in a school classroom, where the only means of ventilation are operable windows in a 15 minute break between two classes. After a period of only 15 minutes, the threshold of 1000 ppm is exceeded and rises to a value of 4000 ppm at the end of the class period, even after allowing for some infiltration (air leakage through the building envelope).

Buildings provide the spaces in which we live, work and play. Some specialized buildings are used for storage and increasingly also for automated processes. They have a purpose to fulfill; namely to provide a suitable protected environment to allow some intended use to take place. Economic and other constraints (zoning laws, building codes, budget etc.) usually place severe restrictions within which solutions for providing this environment need to found. At the same time, the creativity of designers can lead to very different solutions, even within this tight framework. Beyond their functional role, well-designed buildings serve as an expression of a particular society's values and aspirations and thus provide a very important cultural contribution.

Buildings are responsible for a large proportion of global primary energy demand. Estimates lie in the range of between 35 and 50%. Alongside the practical difficulties associated with the measurement of energy consumption on this scale, there are also uncertainties associated with the question of what should be included and what not. Energy demand for lighting and HVAC (heating, ventilation and air conditioning) systems in building operation should obviously be included, but what about the energy demand of building construction and the sourcing, preparation, manufacturing and eventual disposal of all the materials involved? Should the energy demand associated with white goods in residential buildings and business equipment in office buildings be included? Ambiguity also exists with regard to the energy demand of waste disposal and water supply and also with regard to transportation; on the one hand associated with the maintenance of buildings but also with the transport of people and goods between buildings, which is influenced by the type of buildings we design and the location we set them in. In any case, the exact percentage is perhaps not so important. What is clear is that buildings and urban design are the single largest sector driving the energy consumption of modern society, followed by industry and transport. Therefore, it is obvious that the professions involved in building and urban design are in no small way connected with one of the largest issues facing humanity today; namely the energy problem outlined in chapter one. The challenge of providing solutions falls at the feet of professional building and urban designers. This in turn offers these professions the opportunity for increased relevance in society at an unprecedented level.

In building operation, energy is used for heating, cooling, ventilation and lighting as well as for various processes which occur in the building due to its use. We will now look at each of these in turn.

Heating energy demand in building spaces arises partly due to the need to counteract heat loss through the building envelope, which comprises both heat transfer through the enclosing surfaces (transmission) and heat loss associated with air leakage via cracks and openings in the building envelope (infiltration). Heating energy is also needed to increase to an acceptable level the temperature of the outdoor air, which is supplied to the space to provide the necessary ventilation. The energy demand for space heating also depends on the magnitude of internal heat gains due to building use. It can be reduced by increasing the thermal resistance of the building envelope, optimizing passive solar gains, reducing the air leakage rate of the envelope and by utilizing energy recovery systems. Strategies should, however, never be based solely on optimizing heating energy demand (or any singular energy use), but should always include the consider-

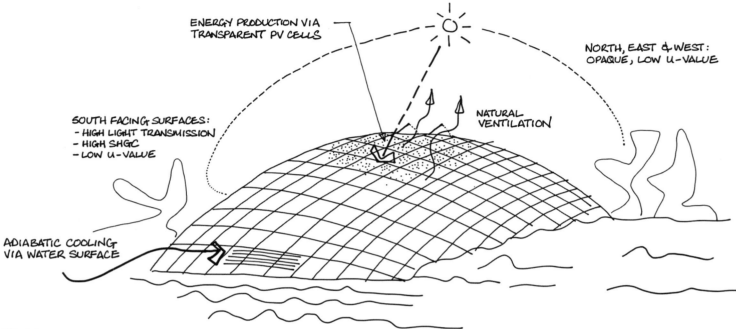

ENERGY PRODUCTION VIA
TRANSPARENT PV CELLS

NORTH, EAST & WEST:
OPAQUE, LOW U-VALUE

SOUTH FACING SURFACES:
- HIGH LIGHT TRANSMISSION
- HIGH SHGC
- LOW U-VALUE

NATURAL
VENTILATION

ADIABATIC COOLING
VIA WATER SURFACE

Fig. 4.1

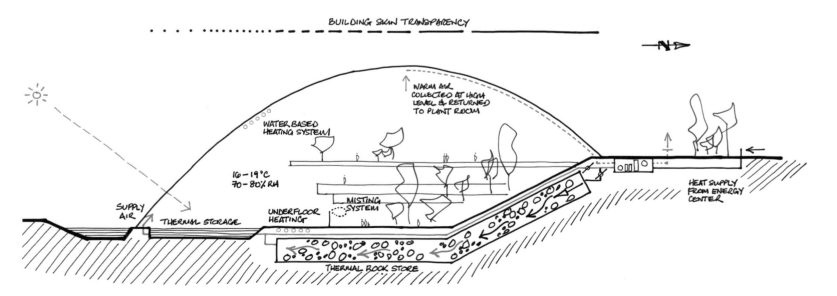

BUILDING SKIN TRANSPARENCY

N

WARM AIR
COLLECTED AT HIGH
LEVEL & RETURNED
TO PLANT ROOM

WATER BASED
HEATING SYSTEM

16-19°C
70-80% RH

MISTING
SYSTEM

SUPPLY
AIR

THERMAL STORAGE

UNDERFLOOR
HEATING

HEAT SUPPLY
FROM ENERGY
CENTER

THERMAL ROCK STORE

Fig. 4.2

ation of the total building energy performance. For instance, the embodied energy of additional thermal insulation or the increased energy demand of fans due to energy recovery systems needs to be taken into consideration.

Figure 4.1 shows the conceptual approach for the design of the tropical greenhouse for a new Botanical Garden in Taiyuan, China with Delugan Meissl Associated Architects (DMAA), currently under construction. The project comprises landscaped theme gardens with a total area of approximately 180 hectares and a variety of buildings, including tropical, desert and aquatic greenhouses, a research center with offices and laboratories, a natural museum and restaurants. Taiyuan is located at 37.5 °N and 780 m above sea level, approx. 500 km south-west from Beijing. A major challenge is achieving tropical and desert climate conditions in the greenhouses in the climatic context of Taiyuan, where wintertime temperatures fall to around -12 °C.

Figure 4.2 shows some of the strategies used to achieve this task in an energy efficient way. The locations for the greenhouses on the site were chosen to ensure maximum sunlight during the short winter days. In cold weather, ventilation is provided by a mechanical ventilation system incorporating a sensible and latent heat recovery system. A water-based heating system integrated into the façade structure is used to counteract condensation and downdrafts, and supplements the heating provided by the ventilation system and an underfloor heating system. The return air system is also integrated into the façade structure and collects warm air at high level and returns it to the plant room, where the heat is recovered and transferred to the supply air. A misting system provides humidification. To reduce heating energy demand in winter and overheating in summer, thermal storage is provided by the use of a thermal rock store, which is located beneath the greenhouse floor (Fig. 4.3). In sunny conditions in

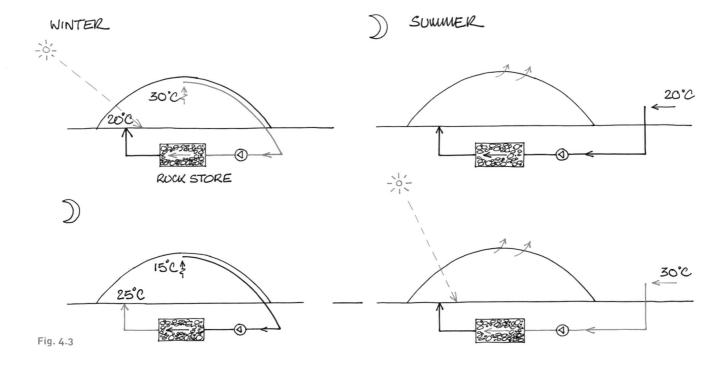

Fig. 4.3

winter, warm air from the top of the greenhouse is collected and passed through the rock store to charge the store, while at the same time ensuring better air circulation and more even temperature distribution in the greenhouse. During the night or in overcast conditions, the supply air is passed through the store to heat the air and discharge the thermal store.

In warm weather, the greenhouses are naturally ventilated. To prevent overheating in summer, large, automatically controlled operable elements are provided in the façade at the base of the building and at high level to allow natural ventilation driven by buoyancy and wind pressures. The incoming air is cooled by evaporative cooling as it flows over the water surface of the adjoining lake. Direct evaporative cooling in hot weather is provided by the misting system. If further cooling is necessary, this is provided by the water-based underfloor system and/or the mechanical ventilation system. In summer, cooler night air is used to charge the rock store. During the day, the supply air can then be cooled by passing the air through the store. The building envelope is optimized with regard to light transmission, solar gains and heat loss and is composed of individual modules, which are specified according to their specific position in the envelope, particularly regarding their orientation to the sun. The degree of transparency gradually changes along the north-south axis of the building, varying from highly transparent on the south facing areas to completely opaque on the north side and including different degrees of transparency and translucency in-between. Transparent photovoltaic modules are integrated in those parts of the dome envelopes, which face south at an appropriate angle.

In addition to the high-performance building design strategies employed throughout the project, a substantial portion of the energy required for the operation of the complex is generated by renewable sources on-site. Biomass waste generated on-site is collected and utilized as fuel in a combined heat and power plant (CHP), which provides the site with heat and electrical energy. This solution has both ecological and economic advantages compared to more conventional alternatives, but also provides a major advantage with regard to security of supply as the cogeneration plant also fulfills the function of standby power generation in the case of power failure. In addition to the waste from normal garden operations, the site includes demonstration areas for fast-growing energy plants and algae, which also provide some of the necessary biomass.

Lighting energy demand depends on the hours of building operation (absolute number of hours and time of occurrence), the use of available daylight, the efficiency of the artificial lighting system and the type of control systems for solar shading, daylight and artificial lighting systems. The available daylight depends on the climatic conditions and the specific configuration of the immediate surroundings. The use of available daylight in side-lit spaces, which constitute most of the spaces in the majority of buildings, is chiefly dependent on the room depths and the configuration of the building envelope (size, position and material of the daylight openings) and to a lesser extent on the properties of the room enclosures. Increasing the amount of space in a building design which is sufficiently close to the building perimeter to enable the use of daylight is an important factor in optimizing energy use for lighting. Besides energy-saving issues, there

Fig. 4.4
Zoning, typical floor,
ESPCI Paris

are also psychological, health and productivity benefits associated with daylighting. Daylighting and associated views of the outside are known to have significant psychological benefits for the occupants. Figure 4.4 shows a section of a typical floor of a university building, developed with OMA architects in Rotterdam in the competition for the ESPCI university project in Paris, in which offices and laboratory areas requiring daylight are located at the façades in an external zone, while other spaces, less frequently used and not requiring daylight or views, are located in the internal zone. Also shown is the ventilation concept and the resulting air pressure distribution. Glazed façade areas can be divided into a lower viewing component and an upper daylighting component, and light shelves can be used to redirect light deeper into the spaces. Light sensors and occupancy sensors can be employed, so that the electrical light output is automatically adjusted both to the availability of daylight as well as to lighting needs.

One important issue is the avoidance of the use of artificial lighting due to poorly configured solar control devices which, when operated to avoid direct solar radiation into the space, reduce the lighting level to such a degree that electric lighting is required. This can be avoided by the use of shading devices which allow sufficient daylighting while closed; e.g. louvers for vertical façades, which remain in a horizontal position in the upper section while closing in the lower section to eliminate direct radiation. Glare issues need to be considered and resolved. The use of task/ambient lighting should also be considered; e.g. a background level of 300 Lux ambient light and a task level of 500 Lux in spaces requiring this higher lighting level can work well in office areas.

Fan Energy Demand in ventilation systems for the distribution of air is one of the main components of building energy demand, particularly in public and commercial buildings in the US and Asia, where all-air systems (see below) are often used. Consequently, this area of building energy demand offers enormous potential for energy saving. For example, research

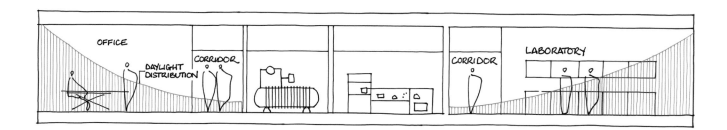

AIR PRESSURE DISTRIBUTION

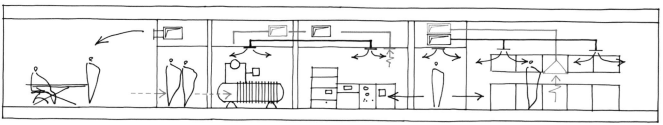

Fig. 4.4

has shown that the use of natural ventilation in tall office buildings in Central Europe can lead to significant energy savings (see chapter six). Besides savings in fan energy use, the potential for "free cooling" (cooling of the spaces using untreated outdoor air) is greater with operable windows than with mechanical systems. Figure 4.5 shows a qualitative comparison of the energy demand due to natural and mechanical ventilation. Highly efficient mechanical ventilation systems with very low specific fan power and high heat recovery efficiencies are more energy efficient than natural ventilation, whereas conventional systems (the majority of the systems in use in buildings at the present time) offer no energy advantage and often consume more energy than natural ventilation. "Ideal" natural ventilation assumes that exactly the correct amount of outdoor air is supplied to the space at all times – not more and not less – which is obviously rarely the case in practice. Therefore, in reality there is a range of energy demand associated with natural ventilation which depends on user behavior. Hybrid systems, utilizing a combination of natural and mechanical system elements e.g. mechanical extract only, can also be employed. An alternative approach which has been increasingly used in Europe in recent years is so-called mixed mode operation, in which both mechanical and natural ventilation systems are provided, with only one of these being in operation at a given time (depending on external conditions). Demand-based control of the ventilation system, whereby an automatic control system ensures air is only supplied to the space when required in order to achieve the desired air quality, is an effective strategy for reducing not only the electrical energy demand of the fans but also the demand for heating and cooling

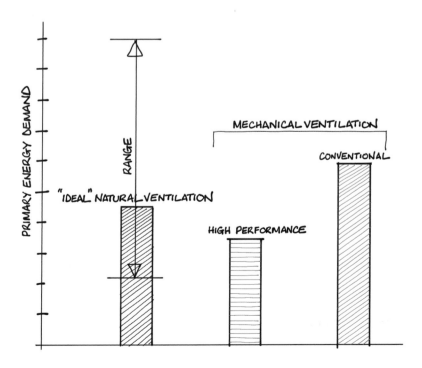

Fig. 4.5

Fig. 4.5
Natural versus
mechanical ventilation

energy. With this type of operation, the ventilation rate responds to the changing occupancy rate rather than running at a fixed rate. Air quality or CO_2 sensors are used to determine the required ventilation rate.

Since the second half of the last century, mechanical ventilation has been increasingly used in buildings, partly due to new building types and use, e.g. where certain processes impose strict requirements on internal environmental conditions or where high internal loads due to people and/ or equipment occur. In certain types of space, such as museums, swimming pools, laboratories, kitchens etc., mechanical ventilation is a necessity. Another factor is the rising expectations of users, e.g. in the office market in London, mechanical ventilation is expected to be provided. Climatic factors and other factors pertaining to the local setting in which a building is designed also play a role. Examples of these are areas with high air pollution, high external noise levels, high wind speeds or very hot, humid or cold climate conditions. On top of these factors, which result from the building's proposed use and location, other reasons may be associated with the design solution, e.g. spaces with very deep floor plans, tall building typologies or a façade design which, due to cost or architectural reasons, does not allow effective natural ventilation.

If mechanical ventilation is employed, there are two principal systems used for air distribution in the spaces; mixed ventilation and displacement ventilation. Mixed ventilation, as the name suggests, involves introducing the air with sufficient impulse to the space that the air is mixed, giving more or less the same air quality throughout the space. In displacement ventilation, supply air is introduced at low level into the occupied zone at very low air velocity and with low turbulence. The resulting air flow pattern in the space depends almost entirely on the convective loads in the space, leading to lower air velocities and lower draft risk in the occupied zone.

In recent years, there has been a development towards building envelopes which have a high degree of air-tightness and as a result there has been a corresponding increase in the use of mechanical ventilation. In residential buildings in Central Europe, two parallel developments can be observed from recent years. On the one hand, legislation in some countries such as Germany has called for the provision of ventilation systems which function independently of user interaction. In cases where such a system has not been provided, air-tight building envelopes, together with the fact that present-day residential units remain unoccupied for large portions of the day, have led to building damage through mold and rot caused by excessive humidity in cold weather. On the other hand, courts in Germany have decided in individual cases that it is not acceptable for external noise levels to be forcing residential occupants to keep windows closed while sleeping. This stipulation is independent of the provision of a mechanical ventilation system. As a result, complex window constructions allowing the opening of windows for ventilation which prevent excessive sound transmission have been developed. These parallel developments – both of which have essentially the same aim, namely building ventilation and in particular the combination of both measures – have led to increased complexity and costs. On recent projects, we have developed alternative concepts which allow some infiltration to fulfill some of the ventilation requirements and coupled this with automatically controlled natural ventilation, using CO_2 and humidity sensors to provide demand controlled ventilation via windows or other ventilation elements.

Cooling energy demand arises due to the need to counteract external loads (principally solar heat gains through transparent façade areas) and internal heat gains to the building spaces, and to cool the outdoor air supplied to the spaces via the ventilation system. In most air conditioning applications, the supply air is also cooled in order to provide dehumidification of the outdoor air, so that the relative humidity level in the spaces is lowered to acceptable levels. Cooling energy demand can be minimized through appropriate building form and orientation, effective shading, optimized use of natural daylight, demand-controlled ventilation strategies and energy recovery systems. Strategies employing nighttime ventilation with exposed thermal mass to reduce or even eliminate cooling demand can be effective, depending on the diurnal range and the nighttime temperatures at the location. The reduction of peak cooling demand by the use of exposed thermal mass can lead to reduced cooling system capital costs, better partial load operation and reduced peak electrical demand. However, these advantages need to be weighed against possible acoustical disadvantages of exposed mass (for example, in large open-plan office areas) and the expense of automatically controlled operable windows.

In many parts of the world, there is a large period of the year in which free cooling via outside air is possible. However, the use of mechanical ventilation systems to achieve adequate cooling implies high supply air rates, which carries an energy burden associated with the distribution of the air. Alternatively, operable windows can be used to cool the spaces in mild weather while at the same time increasing the temperature accepted by the occupants. However, there are user comfort issues associated with the use of operable windows in some spaces, such as open-plan office areas, which need to be considered. Experience shows that it is difficult to satisfy all occupants with one setting of the operable windows at any one time due to different personal preferences and varying conditions experienced at different positions in the space.

In regions where the occurrence of high cooling loads in buildings coincides with high solar radiation during the day, the use of heat-driven cooling processes such as desiccant cooling or absorption chillers offers the potential for saving primary energy. The use of solar heat can also be paired with the use of waste heat from a cogeneration process. On the botanical gardens project in Taiyuan described above, cooling is provided by a combination of vapor compression and absorption chillers. The absorption chiller is powered by heat from the CHP plant, allowing more efficient operation of the plant.

In many building types, even in the temperate and cold zones, cooling is required and is often more important than heating on account of the use of expansive glazing, deep floor plans and high internal heat loads due to people and equipment. In recent times, cooling has also been increasingly used on residential projects in parts of the world, e.g. Northern and Central Europe, where cooling was traditionally not provided. The reasons behind this development are first and foremost rising expectations with regard to thermal comfort from house and apartment owners, but there

Fig. 4.6
V tower, Prague,
climate control concept

are also other aspects at play; rising external temperatures, especially at night due to the heat island effect and possibly global warming, and the increased occurrence of teleworking, home offices etc. Demographic factors may also be of importance in the future. An aging, frail population in many countries may possibly be more susceptible to health risks such as heat stroke in an increasingly warmer climate. Figure 4.6 shows the proposed concept for the tallest residential building in the Czech Republic, currently under construction in Prague (Radan Hubicka Architectural Studio). Cooling is provided by chilled ceilings, making it the first building of this type to be cooled in this way.

Energy demand for **humidity control** includes the energy required to add moisture to the supply air in cold dry weather conditions and remove moisture from the supply air in hot humid weather conditions. In many cases, it is possible to set the specification for wintertime indoor relative humidity so as to avoid the need for humidification without any significant change in thermal comfort levels; and if it is possible, this should be done to achieve substantial savings in both capital and operating costs (energy and maintenance). In many parts of the world, however, the need for dehumidification in summer cannot be eliminated without making significant compromises in thermal comfort levels. The conventional use of overcooling to provide dehumidification with subsequent reheating is a waste of energy. In humid regions, the specification of air tightness levels for the building envelope is necessary to reduce latent load through infiltration. Latent heat recovery should also be considered. In climates where vapor compression chillers perform poorly, desiccants can be used to remove moisture from the air, saving electrical energy both by removing some of the air conditioning load from the chiller and by allowing it to operate with a higher COP, as overcooling of the air to remove humidity is no longer needed. The integration of vegetation and planting can have positive effects on temperature, humidity and air quality, although relatively large amounts are required to achieve an appreciable effect.

Other forms of energy use in building operation include pumps for water circulation, electronic control systems, elevators and other people-moving systems; and of course all the electrically powered equipment in buildings which is not used for heating, ventilation, cooling and lighting.

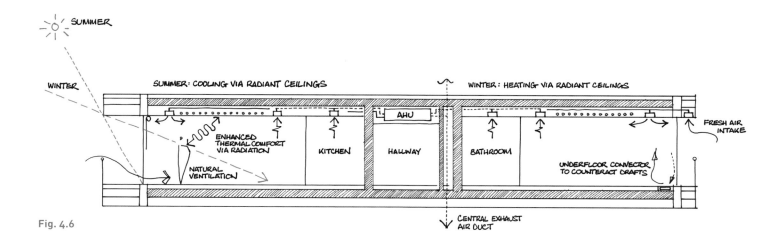

Fig. 4.6

Alongside the energy which needs to be supplied to a building to enable its operation, the construction, renovation and after-life dismantling and disposal of the building also results in an appreciable energy demand. The energy demand associated with these processes and not directly with the buildings operation is called **embodied energy.** It includes the energy used to manufacture and transport the materials used in the building as well as the energy used during the construction process itself. Key factors which determine the embodied energy of a building include building form, compactness, ratio of net usable area to gross area, and of course the materials used. It is important during the design process to consider areas where alternative design solutions could reduce the embodied energy of the building, and also to identify situations in which decreasing a building's operating energy might be associated with increased embodied energy. In recent years, strategies employed to reduce building energy use in operation, and the technologies and materials used to achieve these, have meant that the proportion of total building energy demand attributable to embodied energy has been rising steadily. Figure 4.7 shows estimated values for office buildings in 1985 and in 2015 as an example of this. The choice of building construction system and material (e.g. concrete, steel, timber) affects embodied energy, but also other factors such as thermal mass. The choice of building materials can also impact on energy performance in other ways; e.g. the use of interior finishings and fit-out materials with low VOC-emitting materials can reduce the required ventilation rate and improve indoor air quality.

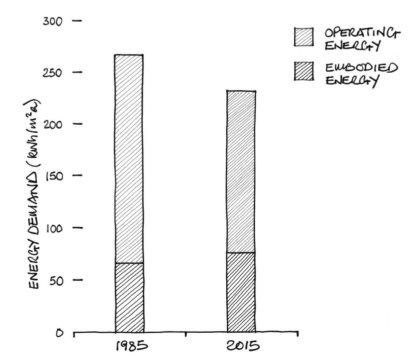

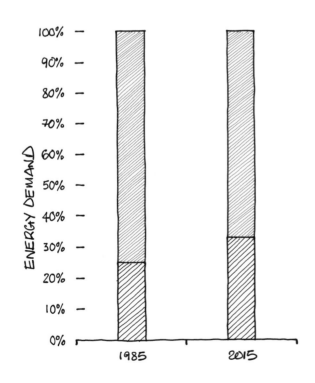

Fig. 4.7

Fig. 4.7
Embodied and operating
energy demand

Fig. 4.8
Phases in the life
cycle of a building

Figure 4.8 shows the different phases of a building's life cycle, which starts with the extraction of the necessary raw materials. These are then used in industrial production processes to manufacture building materials with which the building is constructed. Large quantities of energy are used in these phases before the building cycle proceeds to the next phase – the operation phase – in which it serves its useful purpose. This phase can last from less than a year for some special ephemeral building types to several hundred years. Typical design criteria assume a useful life of somewhere between 30 and 60 years. However, during this phase many of the components, elements and systems will be replaced many times over, so that the building after, say, 50 years may look much the same but consist of not much more than 30 % of the original material with which it was constructed. During the operational phase, substantial energy and material flows occur as a result of continued cleaning, maintenance, repairs, refurbishment and renovations as well as in providing the building with electrical and thermal energy for ventilation, lighting, heating and cooling and other processes related to the building's particular use. The final phase is the dismantling and disposal of the subsystems and elements which constitute the building. Here the aim should be to maximize the amount of those elements which can be reused or recycled, thus reducing the energy required for the construction of another building and therefore the total environmental impact. Two radically different approaches present themselves with regard to sustainability. The first approach is to build a very robust and adaptable building structure which lasts a very long time. The second is to build a structure which is deliberately designed to have a shorter life and is therefore less robust and less adaptable, but which can be constructed more efficiently and with parts that can be easily disassembled and reused on account of the reduced requirements, in order to minimize environmental impact. The first approach represents the dominant line of thinking at present, while the second approach could also present an interesting alternative model which is worthy of more detailed study.

A major driver in determining the energy demand of a building is its proposed usage. **Building type and use** is, alongside climate and location, a major factor affecting energy demand which lies outside the influence of the designer. We now look briefly at the various common building types and their characteristics.

The most ubiquitous building type is the **single-family dwelling.** Nowadays, these buildings are often occupied mostly in the evenings and at night; the occupancy density in terms of occupants per m² and the specific internal heat gains (W/m²) are relatively low. In cold and temperate climates, heating energy dominates. Recent improvements in thermal insulation standards have led to reduced transmission heat losses, to the extent that the heating energy demand due to necessary ventilation is equally significant. In recent years, there has been increased use of mechan-

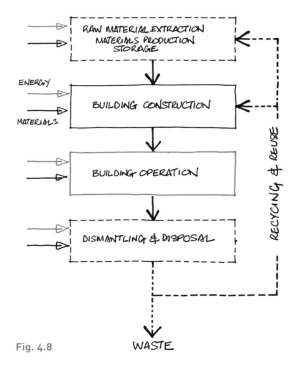

Fig. 4.8

ical ventilation systems with heat recovery. In terms of urban planning, this building type has been widely criticized for unsustainable use of land and resources.

Multiple family dwellings / apartment buildings have similar characteristics to single family dwellings, with the important difference being that due to the more compact relationship between envelope area and enclosed volume as well as the lower site area required to provide the same floor area, the energy demand for construction and operation and the required land area are substantially lower. Recent research has shown however that this difference need not be as large as it has been in the past (see next chapter).

Office buildings are mostly used during daytime, and have higher occupancy densities and internal heat gains compared to residential buildings. The requirements for lighting levels and internal environmental conditions are higher, as are the cooling loads due to greater levels of glazing and high internal loads due to people, lighting and equipment. Even in cold and temperate climates, the need for cooling is often more important than for heating in newer office buildings. Depending on the configuration of the ventilation system however, in particular on the fresh air rates employed and the type of heat recovery, heating energy demand can still be significant. Air conditioning is often provided for thermal comfort reasons (and the concurrent increase in productivity) and for preventing noise, dust and polluted air entering from outside.

Tall buildings are built to provide office, residential, hotel or other types of use. However, due to some very specific conditions pertaining to this building type, they can also be considered as a separate typology in terms of energy design. In many cases, the increase in wind speed with height creates a situation in which normal operable windows and external shading devices become impractical. Also, due to the fact that this is an inherently more expensive type of construction, the standards regarding indoor environment tend to be higher. On account of these factors, tall buildings are nearly always fully air-conditioned. This, in addition to higher energy demand for elevators, pumps and other systems leads to higher operating energy demand. The inherently less efficient relationship between usable and total floor area (due to lifts, additional stairs, technical shafts etc.) makes for increased embodied energy too. On the other hand, tall buildings can potentially be used to increase urban density and therefore make a positive contribution to the energy efficiency of a city as a whole (see next chapter).

Two important issues for commercial buildings such as **shops, department stores and shopping malls** are maximizing transparency and reducing barriers which could discourage potential customers from entering. This is particularly important at the front entrance areas. These factors lead in many cases to large glass façades and open doors. Air-lock systems, revolving doors or air curtains are used at the entrances in an attempt to maintain the impression of open doors while minimizing energy loss. On the other hand, in spite of glazed façades, extensive levels of artificial lighting are invariably used to present the merchandise "in the best light". Due to high heat loads from lighting and from people, sales areas and showrooms need to be cooled all year round, independent of the

Fig. 4.9
Hotel Tower, Shenzen Bay,
China, climate control
concept

external climate. Building systems must be flexible in order to deal with frequent changes in the way goods are displayed or the way spaces are organized and subdivided.

In **hotel buildings,** the changing conditions regarding occupancy of the rooms, which is inherent with this building type, have led to the use of quick-reacting decentralized HVAC systems that can be individually controlled by the visitors. The standard system comprises a centralized mechanical ventilation system with supply at high level in a suspended ceiling coffer at the room's entrance, an extract system in the bathroom and a fan-coil unit (a device comprising a small fan and a heating/cooling coil). This is an almost universal design, employed in hotels throughout the world. The advantage is the fast reaction time of the fan-coil units. However, this system is far from perfect and is often not particularly well-liked by visitors due to high noise levels. Figure 4.9 shows an alternative concept to this conventional model, which was proposed for a hotel tower in Shenzen Bay, China in a competition proposal developed with DMAA architects. Activated concrete slabs provide background climate control, primarily by radiation, while a fast-acting convective system deals with peak loads. This second system uses thermal buoyancy to move air through the

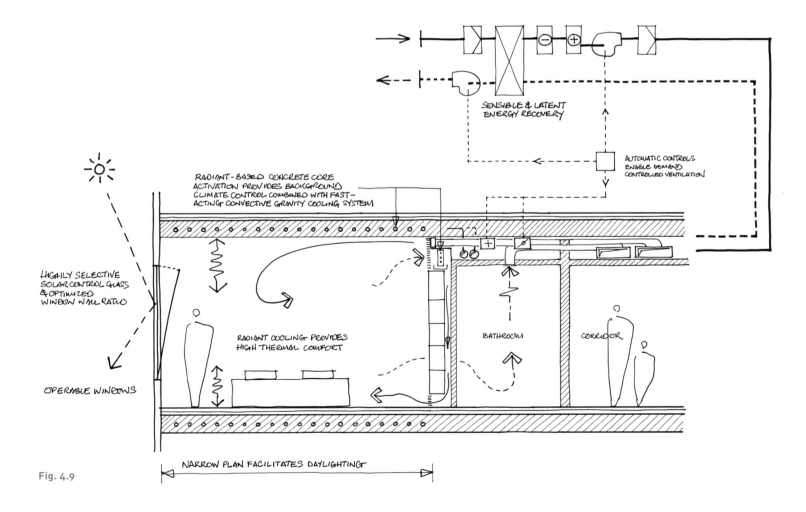

Fig. 4.9

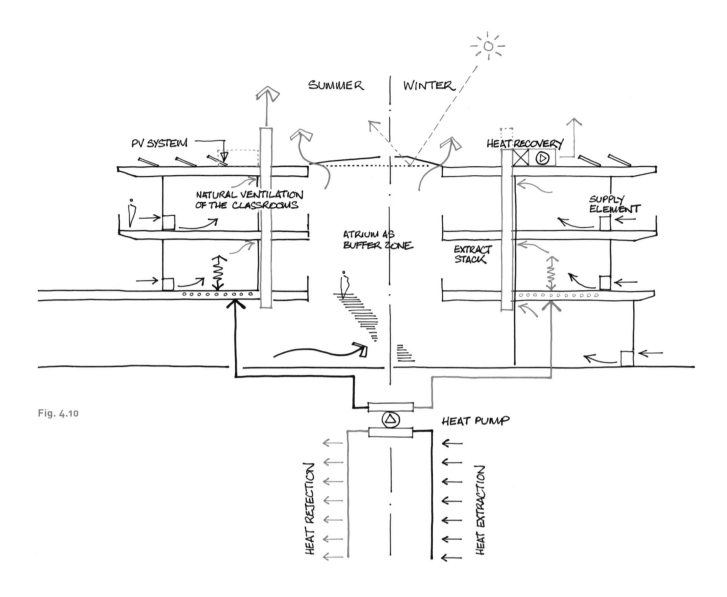

Fig. 4.10

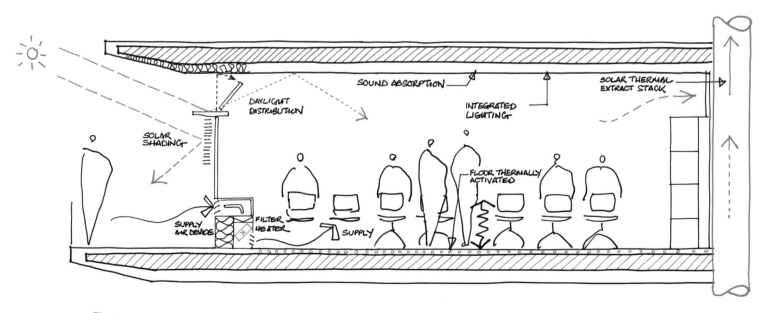

Fig. 4.11

Fig. 4.10
School building, Berlin,
energy concept

Fig. 4.11
School building, Berlin,
climate control concept

system, obviating the need for fans. Warm air from the room enters a grille at high level and is cooled and dehumidified by a cooling coil. The cooler, denser air drops by gravity in a vertical shaft behind a built-in wardrobe and enters the space at low level. The supply air is thus distributed at very low velocity into the space by natural buoyancy-driven circulation without the use of any moving parts, thus eliminating the usual source of noise in traditional HVAC systems. If the space temperature is high, e.g. when an occupant returns to the room at the end of a sunny afternoon, the natural buoyancy effect is enhanced due to the greater temperature difference, so that the space cooling effect is greater. As the temperature in the room falls, so too does the air flow in the system and thus the cooling performance, thus providing a useful self-regulation effect.

High occupancy density and intensive odors in **restaurants and dining areas** mean that they are almost always mechanically ventilated and often air-conditioned. The associated **kitchen areas** are mechanically ventilated. High air change rates are required due to odors and high heat and moisture gains.

The high occupancy densities in the classrooms of **school buildings** would suggest the use of mechanical ventilation. However due to cost reasons, often the only means of ventilation are operable windows, which usually present a far from optimal solution as windows often remain closed during class hours due to external noise levels, the necessary lowering of light levels during digital presentations or to avoid drafts in cold weather conditions, leading to very poor air quality. Experience shows that opening windows during pauses does not give adequate air quality. The basic calculations carried out in chapter three show why this is so. While mechanical ventilation may seem to be the only appropriate solution, consideration should be given to solutions employing automatically controlled natural ventilation or a hybrid system, not least on account of the costs associated with the operation and maintenance of mechanical ventilation systems and the consequences of poor maintenance. Figures 4.10 and 4.11 show a concept developed in a competition proposal for a school building in Berlin with Behnisch Architects in 2014, in which a system of controlled ventilation is designed to be largely driven by the natural forces of thermal buoyancy and wind, using low pressure supply elements incorporating sound attenuation, filters and heating coils, and solar thermal chimneys to extract air. The system is a hybrid ventilation system, employing extract fans to assist when the natural forces are not powerful enough. Energy is supplied by a large photovoltaic system on the roof in combination with a ground source heat pump installation.

University Buildings comprise many spaces with different uses and requirements such as classrooms, lecture theaters, laboratories and computer labs. Lecture theaters, with their high-occupancy densities and the frequent need to lower light levels during digital presentations, are usually mechanically ventilated or air-conditioned. Seminar rooms present a similar situation to that discussed above in the context of classrooms in school buildings. Computer laboratories are usually air-conditioned due to high heat loads and occupancy densities. Offices are often naturally ventilated, whereas laboratories and workshops are mechanically ventilated or air-conditioned depending on the purpose and activities carried out.

Figure 4.12 shows the ventilation concept for the lecture theatres in the new medical university campus in Graz (Riegler Riewe architects).

In **laboratory buildings,** mechanical ventilation is employed to remove dangerous and sometimes toxic gases and vapors, viruses, bacteria and radioactive aerosols. Cooling loads can be substantial due to the high heat loads associated with equipment. Commonly used configurations employ vertical risers in a regular grid to serve the individual laboratories or centralized shafts with horizontal distribution on the floors. In the Richards Medical Research Laboratories designed by Louis Kahn and completed in 1960, the extensive mechanical and electrical systems required by this building type found architectural expression in the form of external brick risers and shafts to give the building volume an unusual appearance. Although not the first time the volumes required for mechanical services found architectural articulation on the exterior of a building (Frank Lloyd Wright's Larkin building was completed in 1906), this is arguably the precursor for the Centre Pompidou and Lloyds of London buildings, which later exposed the naked mechanical systems on the buildings' exteriors, in the so-called high-tech style. Access for allowing the regular cleaning of the duct systems is an important issue. Floor-to-floor height of labs and offices can be different, and this can be used to minimize the building volume required. However, often the preferred arrangement from the point of view of the users is to locate offices directly adjacent to the laboratory spaces and use the same height to ensure future adaptability.

Clean rooms are used in the electronic, optical and pharmaceutical industries, where protection of the products in a dust- and particle-free environment takes priority over the comfort of occupants. Typical systems employ low-turbulence displacement ventilation with laminar flow and air cleaning with high-performance filters, often with the whole ceiling or wall areas configured as a filter system. Depending on the particle concentration allowed (clean room classification), the air change rate can be as high as 600 air changes per hour, leading to very high energy demand.

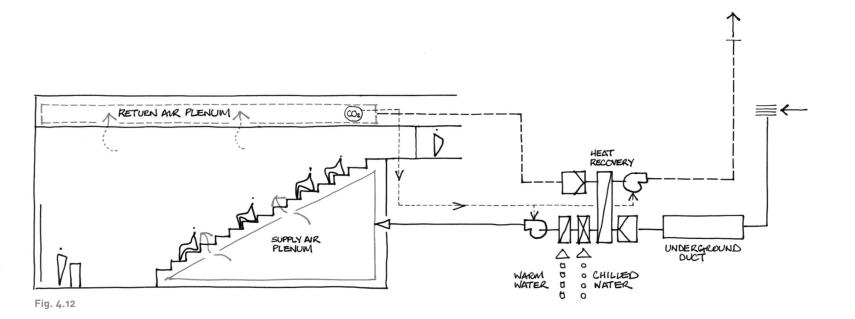

Fig. 4.12

Fig. 4.12
Lecture theater concept,
Med Campus Graz

In **factories and production facilities**, internal environmental conditions depend on the industrial process, and optimal conditions for the product or the production process are usually the main goal with the thermal comfort of occupants being secondary. Air conditioning was originally invented for use in factories, and many facilities with high product or process-specific requirements (e.g. in the chemical, tobacco, textile, paper and electronic industries) today employ air conditioning. Where products or processes lead to emissions of contaminants, pollutants or hazardous substances, air movement is designed to be in the direction of the product. Contaminants should be removed at source, if possible. In cases of products with high requirements regarding cleanliness or purity, air movement is from the products towards the occupants, as long as there are no harmful emissions involved. Production facilities with high room heights and large heat loads lend themselves to the use of displacement ventilation systems.

In **hospitals**, an important issue is the reduction to an acceptable level of the number of pathogenic microorganisms; particularly important in operation theaters where patients with open wounds are present or in areas for patients with weak immune systems. Ventilation systems are configured so that air movement is from areas with higher hygienic requirements to areas with lower requirements. Air distribution systems must be designed to allow easy access for cleaning and disinfection.

The high rate of evaporation from the pool surface in indoor **swimming pools** and the high air temperatures required (28–30 °C) make mechanical ventilation in winter necessary in cold and temperate climate zones. The evaporation rate is dependent on the difference in water and air temperatures and the degree of movement of the water surface. Water temperature is often maintained lower than air temperature to minimize evaporation (26–28 °C). Maximum relative humidity is held at around 60 % in winter, when prevention of condensation on cold surfaces is a priority. All materials used should be resistant to corrosion. In competition pools, glare control is an issue.

Museums are built to house and exhibit valuable artefacts and exhibition pieces which are often hygroscopic and therefore susceptible to damage by shrinking and swelling when exposed to rapidly changing relative humidity levels. Lighting levels often lead to very high internal heat gains. The requirements for air quality are also high and this building type is often located in urban areas suffering from air pollution. On account of these factors, some form of air conditioning is invariably provided.

In **libraries** too, short term fluctuations in temperature and particularly humidity, as well as excessive direct solar radiation, are to be avoided. Requirements for lighting levels are high and, depending on the location, requirements for air filtering can be high.

On account of the high occupancy density in **cultural and event venues,** air conditioning is usually provided. These large-volume spaces with high floor-to-ceiling heights lend themselves to displacement ventilation concepts. The occupied zone does not take up the complete volume, so the whole volume does not need to be conditioned to the same level. There is often a diverse mix of ancillary spaces with varying requirements, so many different types of systems are employed in this building type. Figure 4.13 shows the conceptual approach for the air conditioning of the concert hall at the new House of Music complex in Aalborg, completed in 2014 (Coop Himmelb(l)au architects). Supply air is introduced via the seating to the occupied zones and air movement in the space is driven primarily by thermal buoyancy. Air is extracted at high level, allowing a vertical temperature gradient to be established in the space. Convective heat gains from the lighting are directly removed by the extracted air before they become a thermal load in the space. The nearby fjord is used as an indirect cooling source.

Historically important and listed buildings can be considered as a separate typology. The integration of the necessary technical systems into the historical fabric of the existing building in order to allow these buildings to continue to serve their intended purpose is often a major challenge. Figure 4.14 shows a conceptual diagram for the Neues Museum project in Berlin, with David Chipperfield architects, in which an important element of the approach was to use the new atrium spaces as the path for the return air, thus reducing the amount of conventional ductwork systems required.

It is interesting to note that most of the above discussion on the various typologies applies independently of the climate zone in which the building is situated, showing that while the climate zone in which a building is located is important, the intended use of the building – in terms of energy performance and design – is at the very least of equal importance. Designing a concert hall in Dubai has arguably more in common in terms of energy design with designing a concert hall in Dublin than with a residential apartment building in Dubai. The cultural, social, economic and even political context into which a building is placed is also important. For example, the effects of typical clothing, customs, expectations etc. should be considered in the design.

Figure 4.15 shows a representative breakdown of the typical primary energy demand for four different building types in Central Europe and for four sectors of energy use; heating, cooling, lighting and ventilation. The energy demand attributable to the equipment and processes in

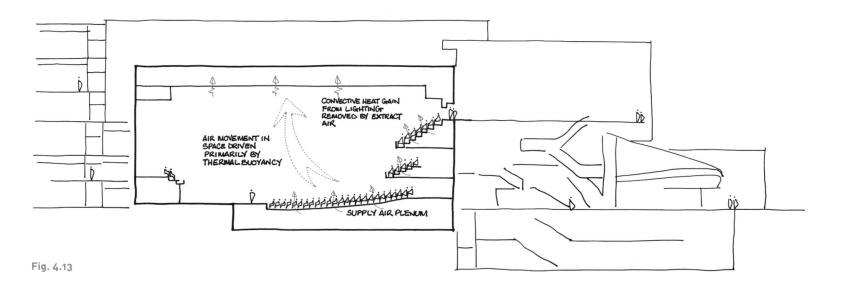

Fig. 4.13

Fig. 4.13
House of Music Aalborg,
Denmark, concert hall
ventilation

Fig. 4.14
Neues Museum, Berlin,
climate control concept

Fig. 4.15
Energy demand breakdown
for various typologies

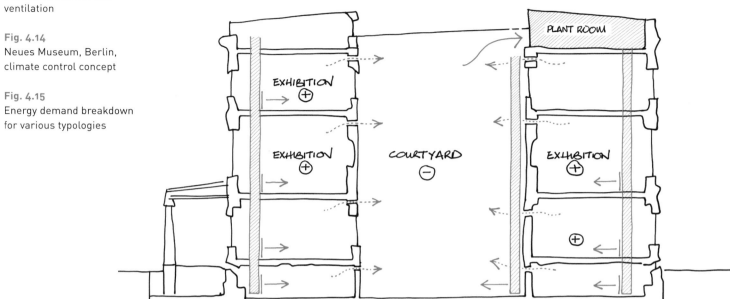

Fig. 4.14

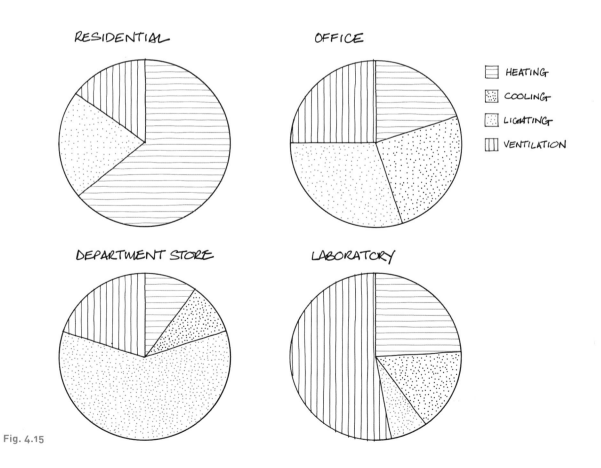

Fig. 4.15

the building that are independent of the building design is not included. In the residential building, heating energy demand dominates. In the office building, the energy demand is distributed more or less equally among all four sectors. Lighting is dominant in the department store, whereas the energy demand due to fans for ventilation is of greatest importance in the laboratory building type.

An interesting question poses itself with regard to **climate change and its impact on energy demand**. In particular, how should the anticipated change in climate affect the design of our buildings? In a research project, we examined the influence of climate change on the heating and cooling demand for buildings in Austrian cities[4]. The results of the study show that with a rise in external temperature total energy demand can be expected to remain constant. There will be however a shift from heating to cooling demand (Fig. 4.16). If, as is presently the case, the heating demand is primarily met with thermal energy and the cooling demand with electrical, this will mean a shift from thermal to electrical energy supply in our energy supply systems. This implies an unfavorable shift from a low-quality form of energy to a high quality one which is more difficult and expensive to produce. On the other hand, it is possible to use renewable heat-driven cooling processes, which are an interesting alternative, as the correlation of supply and demand is much more favorable than when using solar energy for heating. One aspect related to an increase in external temperature could however be of particular importance and deserves further attention. Many of our buildings today in parts of the world such as Northern and Central Europe are designed without any active cooling systems. Passive measures are sufficient to maintain acceptable temperatures for a reasonable portion of the warmer period of the year. At a cer-

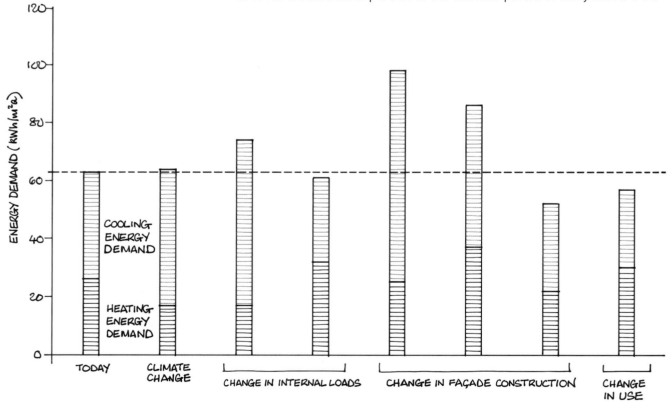

Fig. 4.16

Fig. 4.16
Climate change and
building energy demand

tain value of external temperature rise, a turning point can be expected at which the maintenance of an acceptable internal environment is achievable only through cooling. This would give rise to a paradigm shift in the mechanical systems provided in buildings in these regions and thus also to their energy demand. Another issue is the increased optimization of building design. If one considers the many examples in building design practice whereby it is stated that an upper limit for the internal condition (e.g. 27 °C) is not expected to be exceeded for a given number of hours in a year (e.g. 50 hours), the risks associated with such highly optimized concepts become apparent.

We also studied the effect of other changes related to building use, such as higher or lower internal heat gains, a change in façade construction (e.g. after a renovation) or a change in use from an office to a residential building. Perhaps the most interesting result of this study was the fact that, while the influence of climate change on the total energy demand for the heating and cooling of buildings is relatively small, the influence of changes related to building use – which are much more likely to occur over the lifetime of a building – can be much larger. If buildings are designed to be adaptable in order to cope with future variations in user parameters, a rise in external temperature due to climate change can also be accommodated.

This demonstrates that **flexibility and adaptability** with respect to changes in future use over the life cycle of a building is a key component of sustainable building design. An interesting potential area for the future is the development of concepts for usage-neutral buildings which enable adaptation for varied uses during the lifetime of a building. Buildings from former centuries, which were constructed as residential buildings, also serve well in the present time as office buildings. Should the construction of new residential apartment blocks, which on account of their design (floor-to-floor height, structure, façade, circulation systems) are destined to remain residential apartment blocks, become a thing of the past? In the design of usage-neutral buildings, key design issues include floor-to-floor height, circulation systems, core and shaft design, structural system, mechanical and electrical systems infrastructure, façade design and connection to outdoors in the form of balconies etc.

Flexibility and adaptability can however lead to monotony. Should buildings have identifying qualities in their appearance which signal their use? There is also a certain contradiction between providing flexibility and adaptability in a building design, which should lead to better sustainability, and designing an optimal building, which solves perfectly the specific challenges associated with its usage in a specific climate at a specific location. The more specific the solution, the less flexible/adaptable the building is. The more flexible it is, the less suitable for the specific function for which it is designed. Neutral does not have positive connotations in architecture. Usage-open architecture is better; at least semantically. Yet, the danger of creating neutral structures – in the worst sense of the word – is real. How can buildings retain a sense of character, of expression and emotion and still be flexible and/or adaptable? Another issue is the degree of utilization of our building stock. One look at a typical city in the western world quickly reveals that the percentage of time that any particular building is in use is very low. If we begin to think about buildings in this way, building design parameters will also radically change. One small example of this is the fact that the 24/7 use of buildings may mean that concepts employing thermal mass no longer make so much sense.

The design of energy-efficient buildings essentially boils down to the masterful manipulation of the manifold interactions between the building, its occupants, its systems and the external environment. The building should operate as an optimal filter between its planned use and the external environment (Fig. 4.17).

The following four parameters determine **Building Energy Performance** and lie within the sphere of influence of building designers:

- building form
- building skin
- climate control systems
- energy supply systems

Both during design work in the office and also when analyzing completed buildings or building designs, I find it very useful to organize and structure the thinking according to these four parameters.

The following factors usually lie outside the control of the designers but, as discussed above, have a major influence on energy demand:

- location and site
- climate
- building use
- choice of internal environmental conditions

Of course, the designer can and should advise the owner with regard to these aspects. A vital element in the design of any good building is the importance of good design criteria, which often means intensive discussion with the building owners or developers at the outset of the design process. It is particularly important to agree suitable design conditions with regard to the indoor environment. A dynamic approach, employing adaptive comfort models and accepting a certain portion of hours outside the desired range of conditions, can sometimes allow a quantum jump in terms of the necessary systems. On the other hand, we need to be wary of designing buildings which include no flexibility for future changes. With regard to

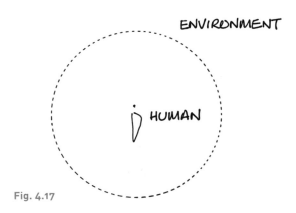
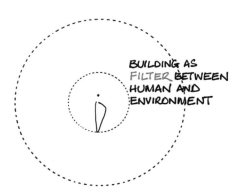
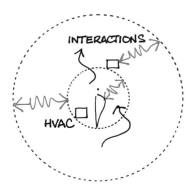

Fig. 4.17

Fig. 4.17
Building as filter

Fig. 4.18
Energy design

legislation, performance based design – where a certain performance is to be achieved by whichever measures the design team finds appropriate – should be the aim, not a decree of prescriptive measures to be followed.

As mentioned in the previous chapter, the external climate can often be approximated on a daily or annual cycle basis in the form of a sine curve. The first step in the design of an energy-efficient building is to implement adaptive comfort models and allow the internal condition to "float" with the seasons. The next steps are to develop form and skin to create a building design which achieves an internal design condition by passive means, which lies close to the desired condition[5]. The climate control systems can then be selected to achieve the final condition required with the minimum amount of energy input (Fig. 4.18). It is important to realize that "normal"

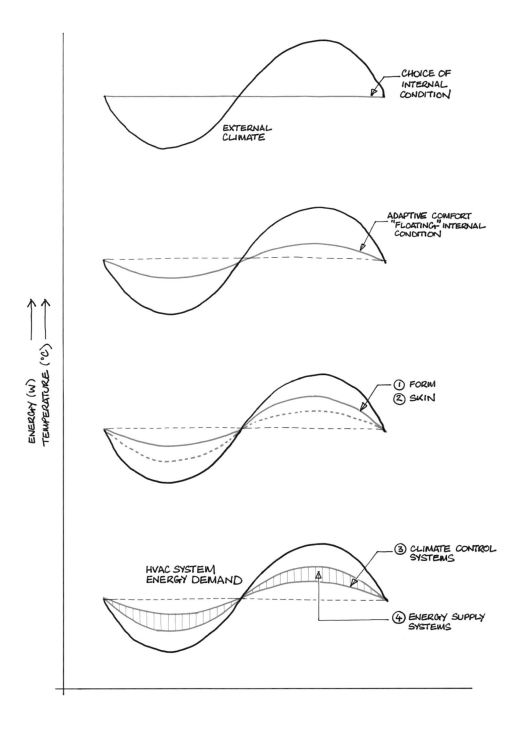

Fig. 4.18

or conventional buildings often respond in quite a different way. Figure 4.19 shows qualitatively the response in internal environment due to form, skin and construction in a less optimal conventional building.

Figure 4.20 shows some of the many interactions and relationships which arise as a result of placing a building in a particular context or setting. Every building design is to be understood as part of a whole system, and designed as such. The aim should be to maximize the positive and minimize the negative interactions with the building's environment. At the outset of any building design, a good site plan showing the particular conditions of the site including wind, sun, external noise levels and other relevant parameters is an essential part of the design process.

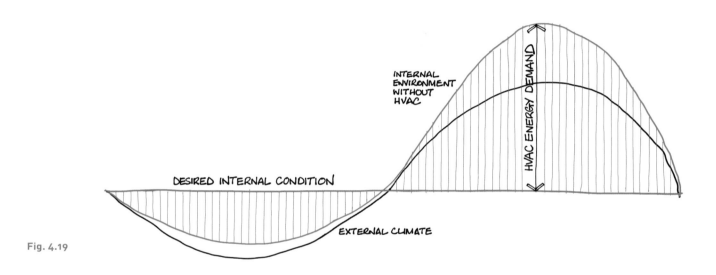

Fig. 4.19

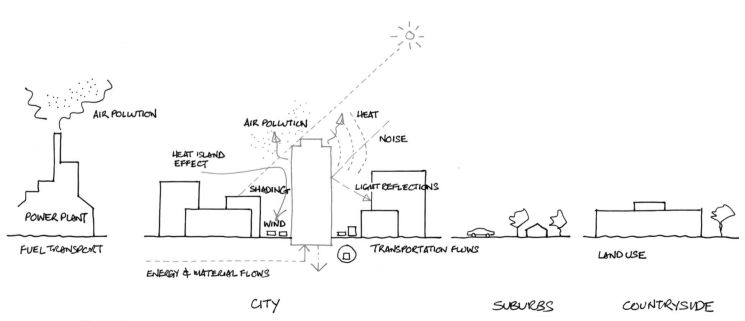

Fig. 4.20

A building is part of a continuum in a spatial but also in a temporal sense. While we are drawing lines to represent the architectural intention for a structure, we should be thinking not only of the "final product" which is to be constructed, but also about the implications of decades and sometimes centuries of associated energy and material flows which we are setting up (Fig. 4.21). Time is the fourth dimension of architecture.

Almost every building design project comes with a cost budget which is more or less fixed, if not at the start, then at some later time. Economics and ecology are often seen as conflicting objectives. While conflicts undoubtedly exist, these tend in my experience to be exaggerated. High-performing buildings need not necessarily cost more, even in terms of capital cost. Doing more with less is a strategy which often leads to better results, both in economical as well as in ecological terms. It is important to realize that we cannot continue to add more elements and systems to the total system of a building. Figure 4.22 shows a very rough breakdown of building costs. As we shall see in chapter six, designing buildings which achieve high performance through cost-intensive façade systems means that other systems, such as the MEP (mechanical, electrical and plumbing) systems, must be simplified. We need to design elements to perform as many functions as possible. The slabs in the Braun HQ building, briefly introduced in chapter three and described in more detail in chapter six, are structural elements, but also act as thermal heat emitting and absorbing surfaces. Figure 4.23 shows the conceptual approach developed for the Dutch embassy in Berlin with OMA architects, in which the architectural element of the trajectory is used as the fresh air path, to bring the required outdoor air to

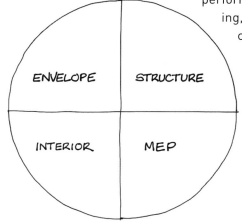

Fig. 4.22

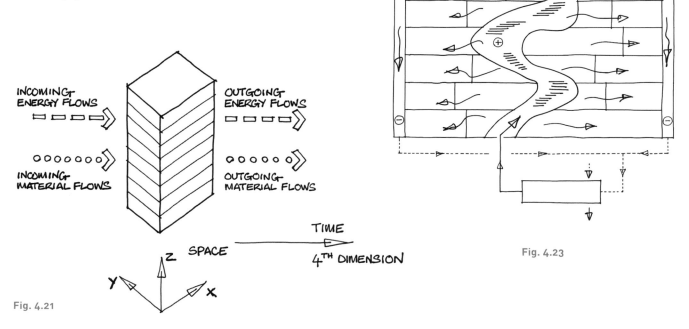

Fig. 4.21

Fig. 4.23

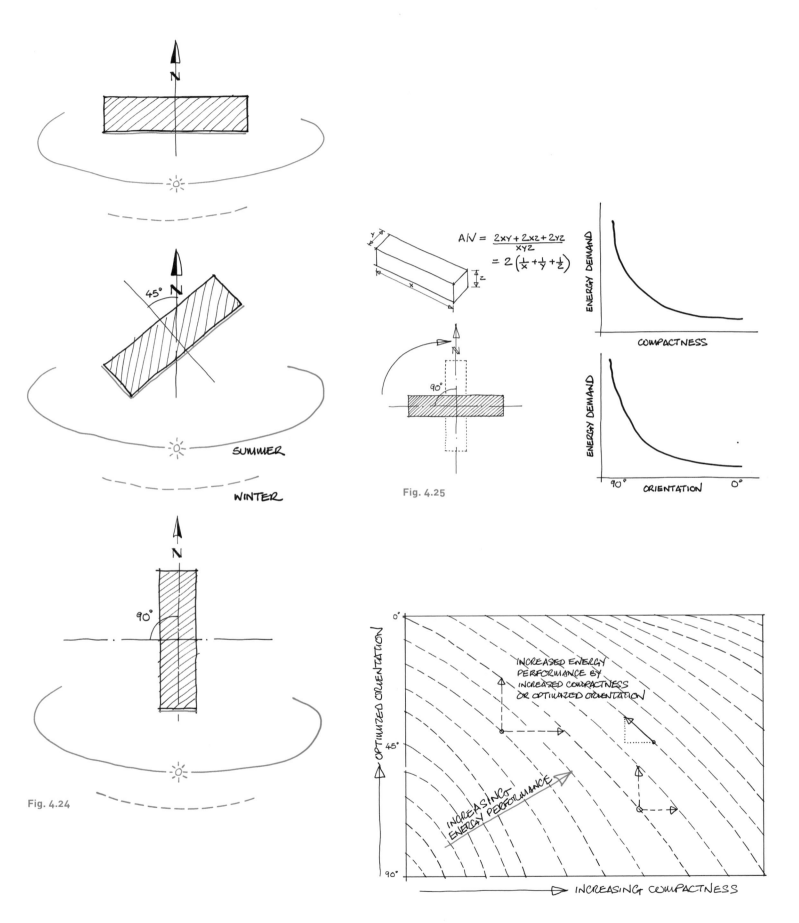

$$A/V = \frac{2xy + 2xz + 2yz}{xyz}$$

$$= 2\left(\frac{1}{x} + \frac{1}{y} + \frac{1}{z}\right)$$

Fig. 4.25

SUMMER

WINTER

Fig. 4.24

Fig. 4.26

the various spaces. In the Schloss Oberhausen museum project described below, the atrium acts as a central circulation space and thermal buffer zone, but also as the path for return air, eliminating the need for return air ductwork systems which would have been difficult to integrate into the historical building fabric.

Building Form

The degree of compactness of a given building structure is often used to judge its energy efficiency and can be measured by the so-called A/V factor, the relationship of the external surface of a building structure (A) to its enclosed volume (V). The higher this factor is, the greater the heat exchange between inside and outside. A brief look at a typical Manhattan high-rise commercial building, however, shows how the invention of air conditioning has led to a very compact form which is not very energy efficient. Therefore, this indicator needs to be considered in connection with other aspects. The most important of these are orientation, which is discussed below, the building depth, which exerts an important influence on the possibilities of natural ventilation and daylighting, and thermal zoning strategies.

As we have seen in chapter three, in many parts of the world, particularly in the temperate, subtropical and tropical zones, and for many building types, the optimal orientation for energy performance is with the long axis running in the east-west direction so that the façades with the largest areas are facing north and south. This also applies to some extent to the cold zone, although here the optimal form may tend towards a squarer form for reasons of compactness. This orientation allows optimal passive solar gains in winter, which are important in regions with cold winters, and lower cooling loads due to less solar radiation on the east and west façades in summer. Rotating the building form through 90° gives the worst orientation by the same logic (Fig. 4.24). The less effective the thermodynamic performance of the building skin, the more important the orientation becomes.

Both the relationship between compactness and energy performance and that between orientation and energy performance show a lower rate of change as the optimum is approached, so small changes in orientation near the point of worst orientation and small increases in compactness when the compactness is very low lead to larger improvements (Fig. 4.25). Energy performance can be maximized by increasing compactness or optimizing orientation (Fig. 4.26). Of course, these aspects have to be matched with considerations relating to typology (circulation systems, cores etc.), the suitability of orientations for particular room uses, urban design factors etc. Zoning strategies offer further potential, e.g. grouping together spaces with similar needs and requirements, exploiting symbiotic relationships between spaces with different needs or introducing thermal buffer zones.

Finally, optimizing the relationship between usable space and the total building volume required to provide this offers a simple but very effective means of improving energy performance. Total building volume comprises the usable building space, circulation space, space for MEP (plant rooms, shafts for vertical distribution of services, suspended ceilings and raised floors for horizontal distribution) and the space taken up by the construction elements of the building such as walls, floors etc.

(Fig. 4.27). If the space required for building services systems and the construction elements can be reduced, the building volume and therefore the external surface area will also be reduced, resulting in lower embodied energy and usually lower energy demand in operation. This should not be understood as a suggestion to squeeze MEP systems into tighter spaces, which would impact negatively on the buildings total performance, but rather to design the building so that fewer or smaller systems are required in the first place. Reducing the volume required by circulation and access systems can also lead to greater efficiency. It should be borne in mind, however, that circulation spaces can also be designed to fulfill communication and other functions so that they effectively become part of the usable space.

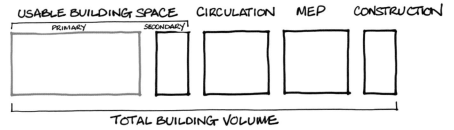

Fig. 4.27

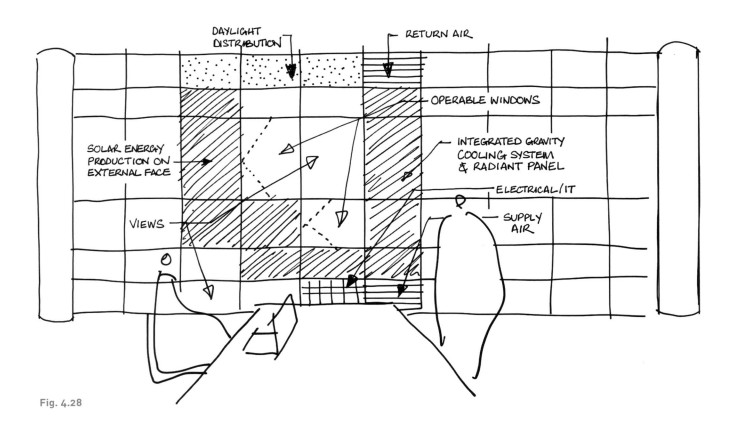

Fig. 4.28

Fig. 4.27
Distribution of total
building volume

Fig. 4.28
Office tower for Vienna,
façade concept

Building Skin

As the main interface between the external climate and the indoor environment, the building envelope, in a similar way to the human skin, needs to fulfill many functions. The most basic of these are wind and weather protection and thermal insulation. Others are solar control, daylight, glare control, natural ventilation, sound protection, communication with outside, views out, possibly transparency and views in, as well as aesthetic considerations. The harvesting of passive solar energy, active energy production and perhaps the integration of systems for heating, cooling and building services distribution systems are further possible functions.

With the competition entry for a high-rise building in Vienna with Elsa Prochazka architects in 2005, the intention was to develop a façade system which incorporated as many functions as possible; views, transparency, controllable daylight, solar control, thermal insulation, protection against wind and weather, noise protection, integration with the structure and planning module grid but also active energy production and HVAC services (distribution and terminal devices). The various elements needed to achieve this were spatially arranged to optimize their functionality, so that a heterogeneous pixel-like façade appearance was arrived at both internally and externally (Fig. 4.28).

The energy performance of a façade can be summarized with the following three technical values:
- thermal transmittance or U-value (see chapter two)
- visible light transmittance
- solar heat gain coefficient (SHGC) or g-value

The solar heat gain coefficient expresses the total amount of solar heat transmitted through a transparent façade construction, comprising both directly transmitted short-wave radiation as well as the heat energy absorbed by the construction and transferred by long-wave radiation and convection to the space. External shading devices are most effective and the best performance is achieved with automatically controlled movable devices. In terms of an optimal balance between good solar control, daylight use and views, horizontally aligned louvers work best on south-facing façades, while vertically aligned systems perform better on east and west facing façades where the sun angle is lower.

Two very important properties which should be provided by an energy-efficient façade for most building types and in most regions are selectivity and adaptability. Figure 4.29 shows the transmission of solar radiation through clear float glass. Visible light energy is largely transmitted, while some of the incident UV light passes through. A large portion of the transmitted energy is long-wave infrared radiation, contributing no visible light but containing substantial amounts of energy which is absorbed as heat by the rooms' surfaces. This may be desirable in residential buildings in the temperate climate zone and for almost all types in the cold zone. However, in other climate zones and for other building types, where the avoidance of overheating takes priority over passive solar gains to reduce heating demand, this is far from ideal. Also shown in the diagram is an idealized performance in which maximum transmittance in the visible light portion and little or no transmittance in the long wave (infrared) part of the spectrum occurs. The ability to allow certain portions of the spectrum to pass through, while others are denied access, is called selectivity.

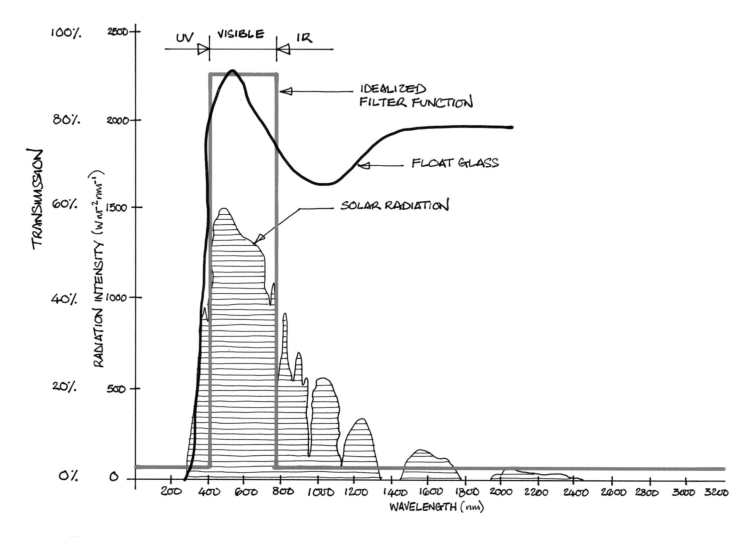

Fig. 4.29

Fig. 4.29
Glass as perfect filter

Fig. 4.30
Selectivity

Fig. 4.31
Analogy, human being
and building

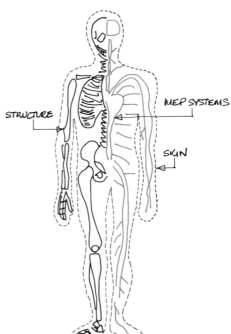

Fig. 4.31

Glazing systems currently available on the market approximate this ideal-ized performance to a certain degree, achieving a maximum selectivity of approximately two, meaning that the visible light transmittance is twice as high as the solar heat gain coefficient (Fig. 4.30). Adaptability refers to the ability to adjust the performance according to the varying requirements imposed by changing external and internal conditions and is discussed in detail in chapter six.

Climate Control Systems

The climate control systems are the heating, cooling, ventilation and air conditioning systems which are used in a building in order to ensure the desired internal conditions with regard to temperature, humidity and air quality. An analogy can be drawn between the human body and a building (Fig. 4.31) with the structural system representing the skeleton and the building envelope the human skin, as already discussed in chapter three. In this analogy, the mechanical and electrical services represent the systems which bring the body to life. The ventilation system can be compared to the respiratory system, the heating system to the circulation system, the electrical systems to the sensory nervous system etc. In a similar manner to looking at a human body on an operating table, if you remove the suspended ceiling in a modern complex building such as an airport and look up you will see the life sustaining systems in all their complexity. The MEP systems are an important part of every modern-day building. Without them, buildings are basically unusable. Besides the energy demand associated with these systems, both embodied and operational, they are

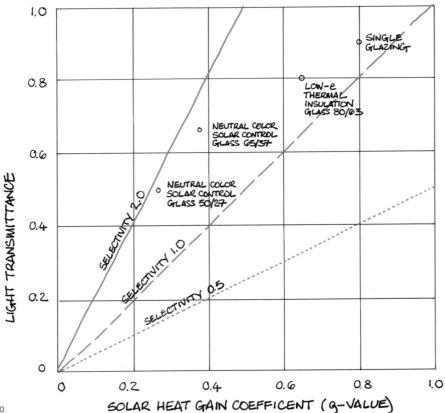

Fig. 4.30

responsible for large portions of the capital cost, operating costs and total building volume. Today, for roughly every m³ of usable building volume we build there is another 0.5 m³ of building volume taken up by the systems used to condition and make the usable space inhabitable. This is what I have called the "invisible architecture" of our buildings and is an aspect which merits more detailed study in future research. Every m³ of building volume needs to be constructed, operated and maintained and therefore translates directly into energy consumption.

Climate control systems can be divided into two broad categories, all-air systems and air/water systems. As discussed in chapter two, thermal energy transport within buildings should be carried out using water and not air wherever possible. In air/water systems, the ventilation system is designed to meet outdoor air requirements and satisfy air quality criteria in the spaces. Further thermal conditioning is accomplished with water-based systems. In all-air systems, the air system is employed for both the ventilation and the heating or cooling of the spaces, with the result that the air quantities to be moved through the building are much larger.

The necessary heat transfer for heating and cooling can occur by radiation or convection. Figure 4.32 shows a typical configuration of the climate control systems for an office space in Central Europe. This is an air/water system with the air distribution system delivering the required amount of outdoor air to the spaces, cooling via a chilled ceiling and heating via a perimeter heating system. To achieve high thermodynamic performance, the lowest possible temperature should be used for heating and the highest possible temperature should be used for cooling systems as this reduces distribution losses, allows greater use of low-grade waste heat and renewable energy as well as more efficient use of heat pumps.

Automatic control systems are an important part of the systems. Poor control leads to increased energy use. If the desired temperature in a space can be held precisely to the desired value at a given time, energy performance can be greatly improved. The same applies to lighting and ventilation. Sufficient space must be provided to allow regular maintenance of the systems, including cleaning of the air distribution ducts, and this is an aspect which is often overlooked in the design of contemporary buildings, with potentially adverse effects on the health of occupants.

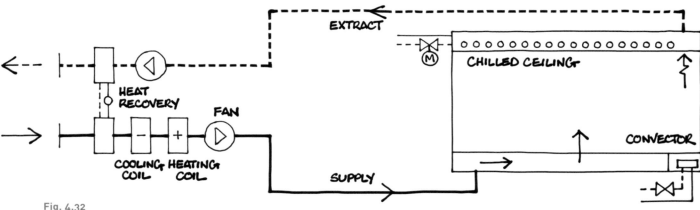

Fig. 4.32

Fig. 4.32
Typical HVAC configuration,
office building

Fig. 4.33
Range of energy supply
systems

Energy supply systems

Figure 4.33 shows the range of energy supply options which generally present themselves in the design of buildings today. Heat can be generated on-site by the combustion of natural gas supplied by a piped network operated by an energy supply utility or of fuel delivered to and stored on the site in the form of conventional heating oil or biomass. Combustion on-site always leads to local emissions. A further option presents itself if district heating is available.

A combined heat and power plant (CHP) can be employed instead of a conventional boiler to generate both power and heat on-site. From a thermodynamic point of view, if fuel is combusted on-site it is more efficient to use a CHP plant instead of a boiler and employ the electricity to power a heat pump or to supply other electrical loads. Both boiler and CHP systems require a flue to remove the combustion gases and release them to the atmosphere at a safe place.

Electricity can also be used to supply heat, either directly in the form of resistance heating (which is a very wasteful form of electricity from a thermodynamic point of view) or to power heat pumps. Heat pumps can use thermal energy from the ground, from ground water or from the external air as the heat source. The latter leads to poor energy performance if used as the sole heating system in cold climates. A particular challenge with regard to heat pump installations in residential apartment buildings is presented by the hygienic regulations related to legionella infection. Current regulations in many locations require a relatively high hot water

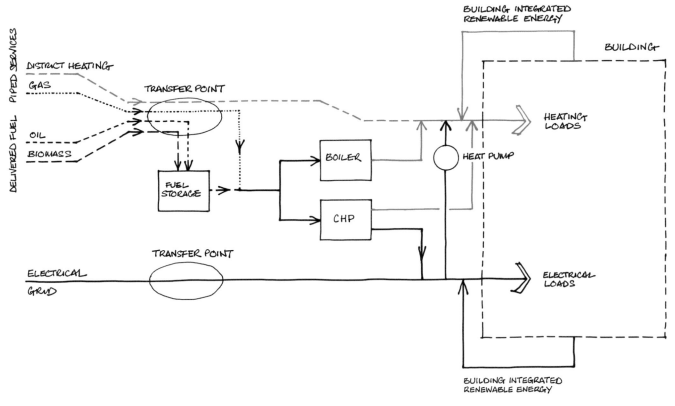

Fig. 4.33

storage temperature of about 60 °C, which leads to a low heat pump COP. Technical solutions with heat exchangers in the apartments are possible but require complicated central distribution systems with integrated storage vessels in order to cope with peak demand.

Building-integrated renewable energy systems include photovoltaic modules or wind turbines to generate electricity and solar thermal collectors to generate hot water. The electricity-generating systems can store electricity on-site or, as is more normally the case, be connected into the local grid so that excess generated energy is exported to the local network. In the majority of buildings today, most of the electrical energy is drawn from the grid. Increasingly, there is the possibility of choosing the supplier from a variety of options, thus indirectly influencing CO_2 emissions. Biomass, under certain conditions, can be considered a renewable energy source (not, for example, if it is the result of energy-intensive agriculture using fertilizers made from fossil fuels). In most cases, it needs to be imported to the site and the combustion process leads to emissions, including fine dust particles, which can present a health hazard. The sources used to generate the heat distributed in district heating systems determine the degree to which the use of district heating can be considered a renewable source.

In some regions, the best option for renewable cooling energy is given by the use of geothermal energy from the ground or by the thermal use of flowing ground water. Figure 4.34 shows the cooling system for the Schloss Oberhausen museum in Oberhausen, Germany, which was installed as part of the renovation of the complex, completed in 2000. Groundwater is extracted from the ground and used to cool the supply air,

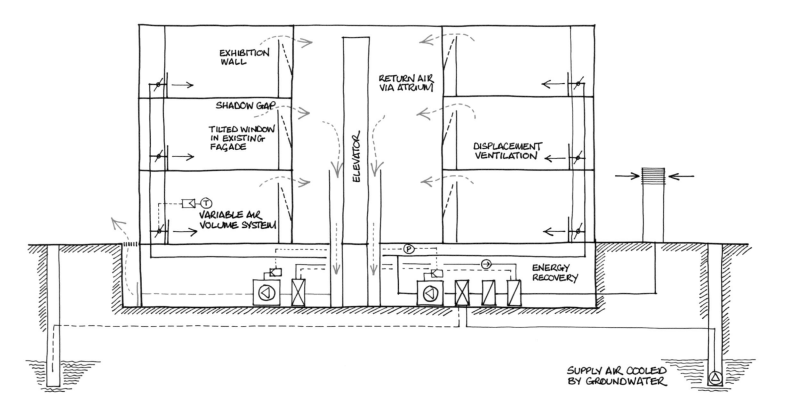

Fig. 4.34

Fig. 4.34
Museum Schloss
Oberhausen, Germany,
energy concept

Fig. 4.35
Fronius building, Austria,
energy concept

which is supplied to the exhibition spaces by a displacement ventilation system that was integrated into the historical fabric of the old castle. It was agreed with the local authorities that the groundwater would not be heated by more than 5 K before being returned to the ground, in order to avoid possible hygiene problems.

When comparing the various energy supply options for a building design, the following factors are to be considered: primary energy demand, CO_2-emissions, atmospheric pollution and noise emissions, capital cost, operating costs, space requirements and required maintenance.

Figure 4.35 shows the energy supply for the new Fronius office and laboratory building in Wels, designed with the largest borehole (vertical loop) geothermal system in Central Europe at the time. In this system, waste heat from electrical processes carried out in the buildings laboratories is transferred to the ground during the summer and stored for use as heat supply in the colder months. The nearby river is used as the main cooling source.

When the decision is between the on-site combustion of oil or gas and the use of electricity to power a heat pump, it is not only the average efficiencies, CO_2-emissions etc. of the options that need to be considered, but also temporal dependencies, i.e. seasonal efficiencies, differences between day and night etc. The type of power plant which generates the additional or avoided electrical energy, and its part-load efficiency, which depends on the time of the day, need to be considered. For example, if during cold weather – when the contribution from renewable energy sources is often lower – the source of additional electrical energy that supplies the

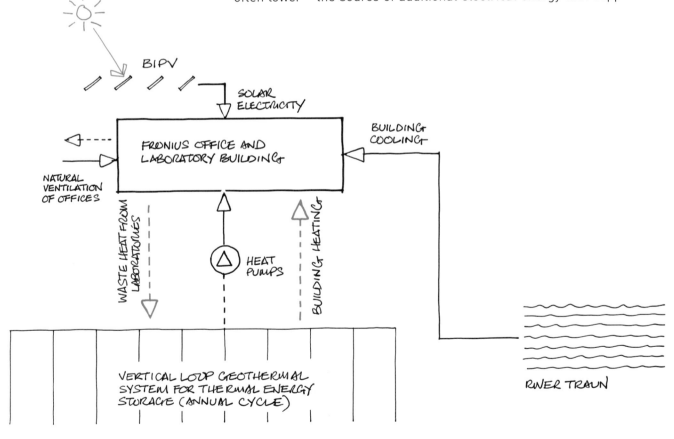

Fig. 4.35

Fig. 4.36
Plus energy buildings

increasing number of heat pump installations is fossil-fuel-powered thermal power plants, then the actual CO_2-emissions associated with the use of electrical energy might be less favorable than is suggested by the average annual CO_2-emissions of the electrical grid.

Zero-energy buildings or plus-energy buildings are a much-discussed topic at present. These terms are not precisely defined, and it is often not clear which energy demand is being met by the integrated renewable sources used to generate energy. To be considered truly zero-energy, a building would have to supply not only the energy to satisfy heating and cooling energy demand and for lighting and ventilation but also the energy demand for equipment and processes which take place within the building to allow its intended use, as well as the embodied energy of the building required for its construction and final disposal, which would be recouped over the building's lifetime. It could be argued that, depending on the buildings location, the energy demand associated with the mobility requirements of the building's occupants should also be met by renewable sources. Generating an amount of renewable energy on-site which equals the magnitude of energy consumed over the course of a typical year is just the start. A means of storing the energy must also be found in order to balance supply and demand, as the energy production and building energy load profiles are obviously usually different. In the majority of realized examples to date, this function is met by the electricity supply network, with a grid connection allowing energy export and import. This approach works quite well as long as relatively few buildings use this technology. However, as the use of renewable energy technologies proliferates, the grid system in many areas is coming under pressure to cope with the wide variations of supply and demand by the many producers and consumers connecting to the grid. In zero-energy buildings in Central Europe, for example, there are large discrepancies between energy demand and renewable energy production, with surplus energy production in summer and a deficit in winter (Fig. 4.36).

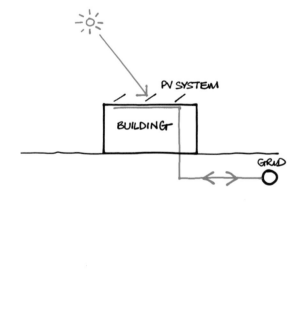

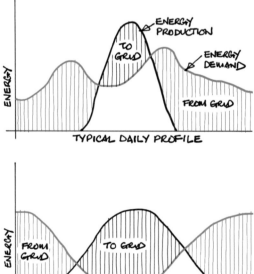

Fig. 4.36

Every building is a fragment of an urban design. Buildings should not be conceived and designed as solitary objects, but seen as part of the existing and future spatial urban fabric. Of particular importance in the energy design of urban areas are solar and daylight access for both buildings and outdoor spaces and the generation of pleasant microclimates for the urban area in terms of wind patterns, temperature, humidity and air quality. The development of energy master plans for both new and existing cities is a key component in the creation of a sustainable future.

A vast array of **infrastructural networks and systems** is necessary to make possible the urban life that many of us in cities around the world enjoy. Most of the time, we take these systems for granted. However, if you stop to think about the various infrastructural systems which have made your day possible so far, you will realize just how dependent you are on this infrastructure. Buildings tap into a lot of these systems to allow us to enjoy them in a sheltered and controlled environment. Drinking water is piped to various outlets within buildings. Water used for cleaning and other purposes is piped away after use. Electricity provides the power for a whole host of machines and equipment used for climate control, lighting, elevators and other systems, which make the buildings inhabitable as well as for food preparation, household tasks, work and entertainment. Energy for heating is piped to buildings or delivered to building storage tanks via truck. Our communication with others far beyond the immediate area is made possible via data and telephone networks.

Transport systems allow the efficient passage of people and goods from one building to another. We depend on goods delivered to our cities every day in enormous quantities by train, truck, ship and plane. Our cities today comprise a grid of streets with buildings located in the interstitial spaces within this grid network. The vast array of infrastructural systems which makes urban life possible is located within this street network, either under the streets or overhead. The street network also provides the necessary distance between buildings which allows their natural lighting and ventilation. There are many subtle interactions between buildings and transportation systems which affect building energy performance, particularly the need for mechanical ventilation in many cities due to noise and pollution emissions from the transportation systems in the streets. Added to the fuel consumption of the vehicles is the embodied energy of the infrastructure and the necessary periodic maintenance. Most cities are organized such that, at an arranged time – usually between 7 and 9 a.m. – almost everybody needs to move through the city; adults to work, children to school etc. and at the same time, goods are delivered to shops and garbage is collected, resulting in congestion. Other peaks occur at later times during the day. During peak usage times, infrastructure is often hopelessly overloaded, while at the times in-between, operation is well below full-load capacity. There would seem to be much potential to achieve more efficient use of infrastructure by the reorganization of the temporal regimes which are in place in cities today.

From the days of smoke signals and other early **communication systems**, conveying messages between people located at a distance has consumed energy. Today, energy use for our communication systems, including the internet system, data centers, the manufacture of the necessary personal devices to enable communication etc. amounts to a significant share of global energy consumption. **Water supply** is intrinsically linked to energy demand. On the one hand, the energy demand associated with preparing water for consumption, pumping it to buildings and removing and treating the associated sewage is significant. On the other hand, energy production systems frequently use large quantities of water for cooling. Energy is also consumed by the systems for collection, transport, treatment and disposal of **waste**, at least a third of which is attributable to construction. Waste can also be seen as a resource, which when combusted through incineration (waste to energy) can release thermal energy for the city. Of course, while more efficient than other options, this practice can hardly be considered sustainable and we should strive through the use of recycling and other strategies to minimize waste in the first place. There is also a significant amount of embodied energy associated with the **goods** we consume and eventually discard, whether produced by local industry or far away. The food we eat, whether produced on small local farms or by large-scale commercial **agriculture**, is also the result of intensive (fossil fuel-based) energy use.

A key element in the sustainable development of our cities is of course the **energy supply system.** As we have seen in chapter two, typical thermal power plants (both fossil fuel-powered and nuclear), employed throughout the world today to generate electricity, have an average efficiency of around 35 %. A further loss of 5–10 % is incurred during the transmission and distribution of the electricity to the final consumers. The mining, refining and transportation of fossil fuels such as coal, oil and natural gas account for further losses, resulting in an average conversion efficiency from primary to final energy at the point of use of less than 30 %. This means that for every kWh of electrical energy consumed in a building, roughly 2 further kWh of primary energy are wasted. If combined heat and power plant (CHP) is employed, some of these losses are recovered in the form of useful heat. It makes sense to use district heating networks for the heating needs of buildings in cities, if the heat is a waste product of electricity generation. If we assume that biomass will be an element of our future energy supply system and that combustion in a CHP plant represents the most efficient use of this fuel, then district heating supply in our cities will also be a part of the future energy supply system. Waste heat from industry, wastewater treatment and other processes can also be used. In the summer, district heat can be utilized to power absorption chillers or other heat-driven cooling technologies in buildings to meet cooling demand.

As discussed in chapter four, energy storage presents a formidable challenge for the energy supply system of the future, due to the large fluctuations in energy supply caused by the increasing integration of renewable energy sources, principally solar and wind, into the national grid systems. An interesting aspect of future building design is the role of buildings as energy storage systems to alleviate the pressure on the grid. Besides the challenge of energy storage, a further aspect to be considered is the very low **energy yield density** of the renewable energy sources, especially compared to the current fossil fuel-based energy system, and the consequences for land use in the future. Assuming an electricity yield of roughly 100 kWh/m²a for a PV system in Central Europe and a factor of

Fig. 5.1
Land area requirements,
renewable energy

two in order to avoid mutual shading and allow access for maintenance and cleaning gives an energy yield density of roughly 50 kWh/m²a. A calculation for wind energy gives a lower energy yield density of less than 20 kWh/m²a but in the same order of magnitude. If we compare these densities to the energy yield densities of conventional fossil fuel power plants of somewhere between 2000 and 3000 kWh/m²a (if the land area for fuel storage and handling is included), we are looking at a factor of about 50 times more land area required for energy production. In this comparison, the land area for mining and extraction of the fossil fuels is not included, as this is usually not located within the city boundaries. For this reason and because renewable energy is essentially available in quantities which far exceed the anticipated demand but at very low energy yield densities, the "currency" used for comparing various future scenarios in recent research has been land use, as we will see shortly. Figure 5.1 shows a comparison of the land area required for energy production based on biomass as fuel compared to solar electricity and solar thermal collectors. Owing to the low photosynthetic efficiency of converting sunlight to biomass of approx. 0.5 %, approx. 20 times more land is required to produce the same

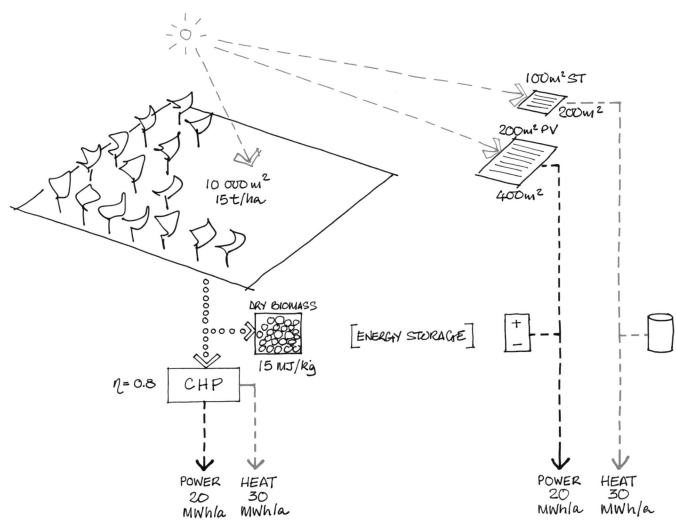

Fig. 5.1

amount of energy (or 1000 times more than for fossil fuel power plants), even when high efficiency CHP is utilized. There is however a major advantage associated with the biomass option, and that is that biomass fuel can be easily stored, avoiding the enormous problems of energy storage associated with other renewable energy sources discussed above. On the other hand, issues such as competition with food production and the energy consumption due to harvesting and transporting the biomass fuel remain to be resolved. One advantage of wind energy use, on the other hand, is that it can be integrated into farm land or into a solar energy farm without significantly affecting the yield of either. The issue of the visual impact of these vast areas required for energy production on the environment is an important one for future urban design. A portion of this energy production land can be incorporated into building complexes. Figures 5.2 and 5.3 show proposals for projects in Vienna and Prague respectively, where renewable energy technologies are integrated into the roof landscape, which also provides space for leisure and sport activities and urban farming.

A key factor in the design and performance of our cities and their future development is **urban density**. This can be defined in various ways but is essentially the amount of land required to host a given population and provide them with space to live and work. This can then be extended to include the land required to supply this population with water, food, energy and waste disposal services. Optimizing urban density is a key component of any strategy to maximize energy performance and sustainability.

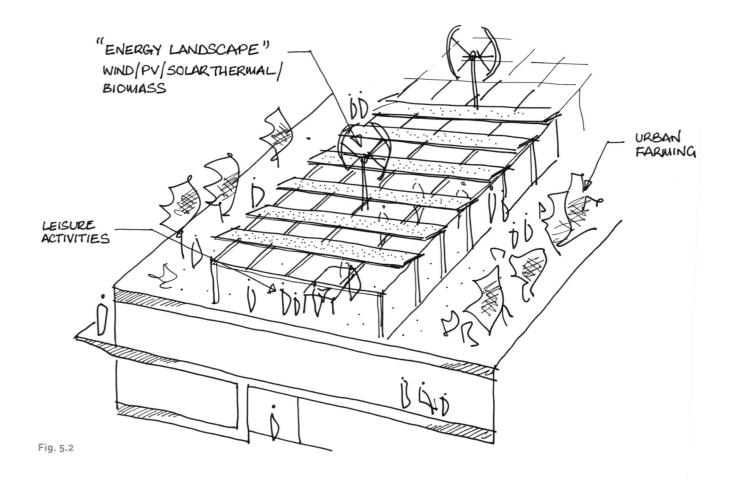

"ENERGY LANDSCAPE"
WIND/PV/SOLAR THERMAL/
BIOMASS

URBAN FARMING

LEISURE ACTIVITIES

Fig. 5.2

Increasing density can potentially lower the consumption of resources and energy through transportation by reducing the overall distances travelled and the resources required for infrastructure.

In any attempt to achieve high urban density, the **high-rise building** typology is obviously a likely candidate. The question is whether high-rise development really leads to higher density. Wall Street in Manhattan is certainly high density, yet the canyon-like street spaces and the daylighting situation in the lower floors of the buildings cannot be regarded as optimal. High-rise housing developments in the 1960 and 70s such as "Gropiusstadt" in Berlin, on the other hand, are often less dense than typical European perimeter block structures with a central courtyard. A key question then is whether it is possible to develop high-rise, high-density urban environments with attractive street spaces and squares without compromising day lighting and solar access on the lower floors of the buildings.

The chief reasons to date for building tall buildings in cities have been status-related or economical due to high land prices (Fig. 5.4). High-rise buildings have not been used to increase urban density in a sustain-

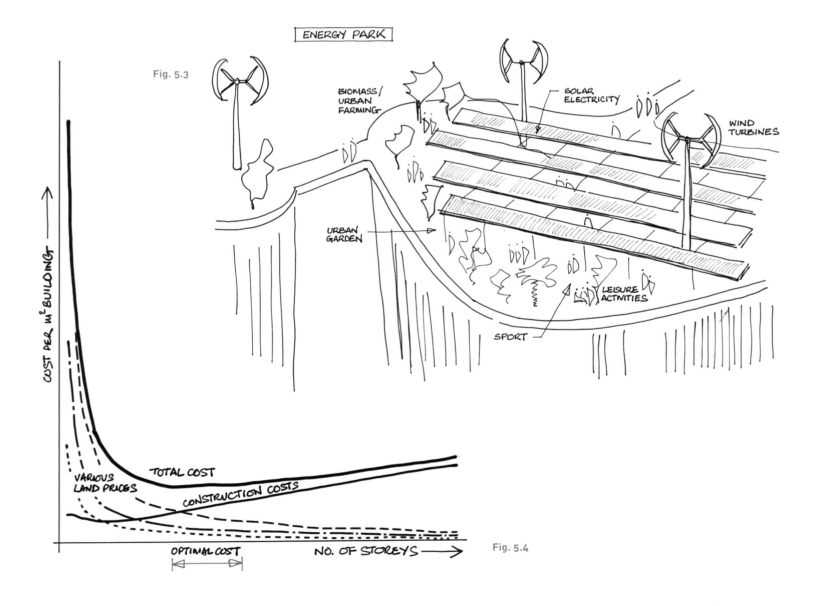

Fig. 5.3

Fig. 5.4

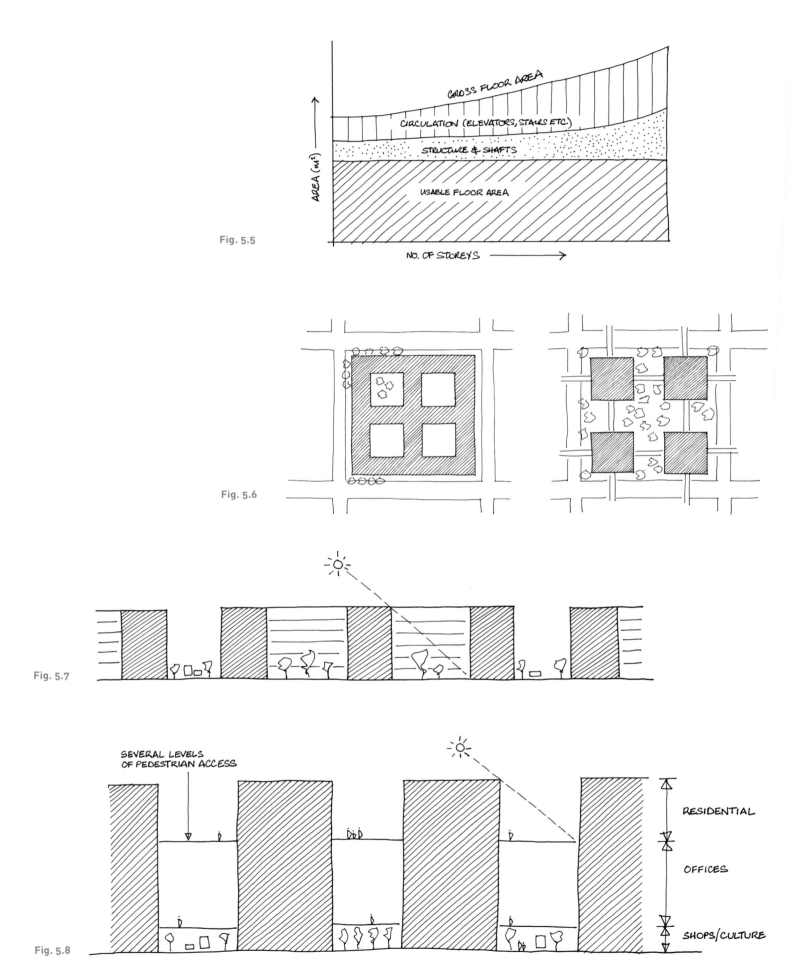

Fig. 5.5

Fig. 5.6

Fig. 5.7

Fig. 5.8

able context; at least not in a significant way. There are also two issues related to tall buildings which work against the achievement of high density. Firstly, with increasing height, the distance between buildings needs to increase in order to achieve lighting and solar access of a similar level to that provided by buildings of lower height. Secondly, the space taken up by the building core for lifts, shafts etc. also increases in a non-linear way with increasing height, making the relationship between usable and gross floor area increasingly unfavorable (Fig. 5.5).

In research at my institute, a typical 6-storey European perimeter block development, 100 m by 100 m, with a central courtyard was compared to a 15-storey high-rise development (Fig. 5.6). The increase in density achieved by the high-rise option was found to be approximately 70 percent, even when the lower net-to-gross floor area ratio of the high-rise development is taken into account. By stacking the various mixed uses vertically, it is possible to provide similar access to daylight and sunlight for the residential units as in the 6-storey block development (Fig. 5.7 und 5.8). The offices with their lesser need for passive solar gains are located below. By superimposing a 3-storey block development onto this structure, the density can be increased further. The lower stories could accommodate uses such as commercial, cultural and production facilities which require less daylight and are best accessed at ground level. As the core area needed for lifts and shafts decreases with height, the building can be tapered with increasing height to improve daylight access at the lower floors (Fig. 5.9).

In order to reduce energy consumption due to transportation, increasing density alone is of course not enough. A second necessary step, in order to reduce the amount of travel necessary, is to ensure a hetero-

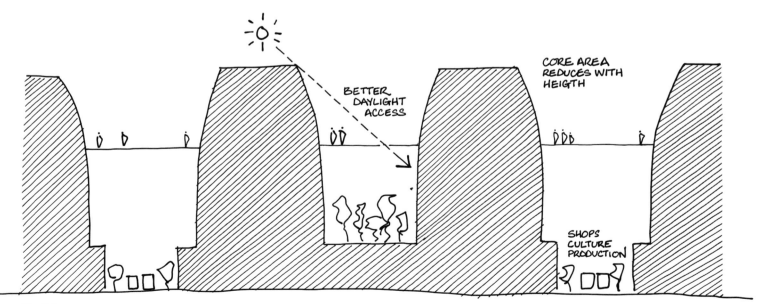

Fig. 5.9

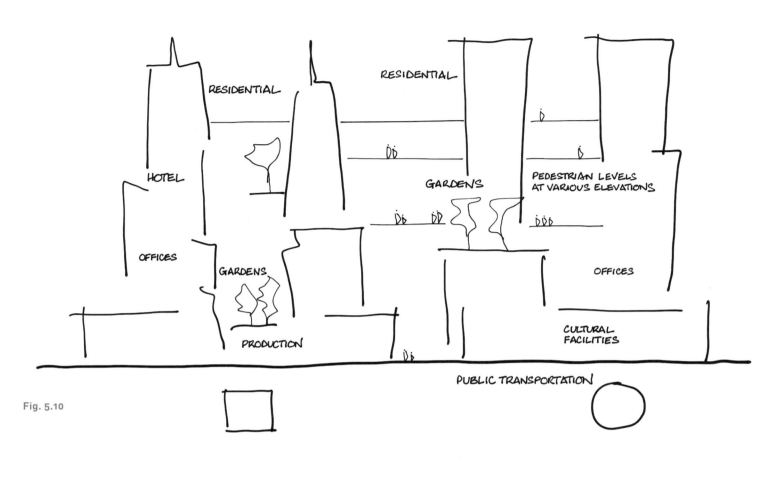

RESIDENTIAL

RESIDENTIAL

HOTEL

GARDENS

PEDESTRIAN LEVELS
AT VARIOUS ELEVATIONS

OFFICES

GARDENS

OFFICES

PRODUCTION

CULTURAL
FACILITIES

PUBLIC TRANSPORTATION

Fig. 5.10

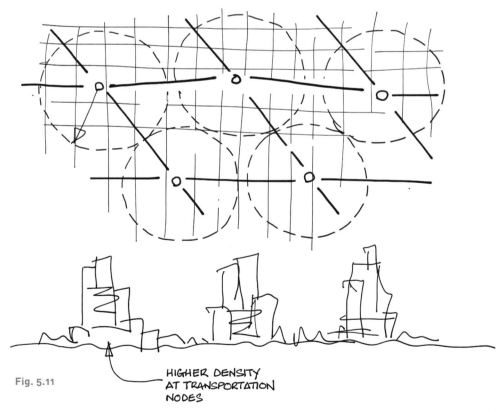

Fig. 5.11

HIGHER DENSITY
AT TRANSPORTATION
NODES

Fig. 5.10
Vertical City with
mixed use

Fig. 5.11
Increased density at
transportation nodes

geneous mix of uses and provide optimal connections to the city's public transportation system (Fig. 5.10). The density can be intensified at transportation nodes (Fig. 5.11). As already noted, the tall building typology is inherently less energy-efficient than that of low or medium height buildings due to the lower ratio of usable floor area to total floor area (resulting in higher embodied energy demand) and the higher operating energy demand, which is primarily related to higher wind pressures and the ensuing need for mechanical ventilation and air conditioning due to the lack of operable windows and efficient external solar shading devices. Therefore, if tall buildings are to make a contribution to the sustainability of future cities, strategies and concepts to improve the energy performance of this typology need to be developed (see chapter six).

While for many cities an increase in urban density is unquestionably desirable from a sustainability point of view, an interesting question is the **optimal degree of density** when viewed from an energy perspective. A research project at my institute aims to gain a deeper understanding of the role of urban density in the energy efficiency of cities. The hypothesis of the project is that, if the total energy demand for buildings and transportation is considered and the land needed for renewable energy production is also taken into account, there is an optimal degree of urban density. The approach is unconventional for two reasons: Firstly, the focus is on the usable floor area of the buildings instead of on the more conventional total floor area. The reasoning behind this is that it is the usable floor area which determines the number of people which can be accommodated in a given urban area. Secondly, the land area, which is required to generate sufficient energy to meet the demand of the city, is also included in the total area of the city. This area is significant, as it is based on the assumption that energy supply in the future will be completely from renewable sources, which will require large areas on account of their low energy yield density. These areas can be incorporated into the external surfaces of the buildings and other urban infrastructure, or located on dedicated land plots in or around the city. In this project, urban density is defined as the ratio of usable floor area to the total land area occupied by the city, including all necessary urban infrastructure but not including agricultural land.

As explained above, energy use due to transportation is expected to reduce as density increases. On the other hand, the building energy demand, both for construction and operation, can be expected to increase if density is achieved via the use of taller and deeper building structures. Renewable energy production per unit usable floor area will also decrease due to mutual shading, a lower net-to-gross floor area ratio and the lower ratio of suitable energy-producing surfaces to usable floor area. Increasing density is expected to increase energy efficiency until the point of optimal urban density is reached (Fig. 5.12). Beyond this point, increasing density further is expected to lead to a reduction in energy efficiency.

A major portion of any city is occupied by the residential building stock and an important part of the research comprises the evaluation of the energy performance of various residential building types. Three very different typologies were selected for suitability in achieving urban density and compared in terms of their energy performance in operation. Two of the typologies studied were apartment buildings (a high-rise tower development and a medium-height perimeter block development with courtyards, both configured to allow a 45° daylight access angle on a skewed grid to improve solar access), while the third typology comprised single family homes located on small plots. This third typology may seem an unusual choice. It was chosen for investigation as numerous studies have shown that this is the preferred housing type for the vast majority of the population in many different parts of the world, and it was felt that research should not ignore this fact. In an attempt to investigate whether

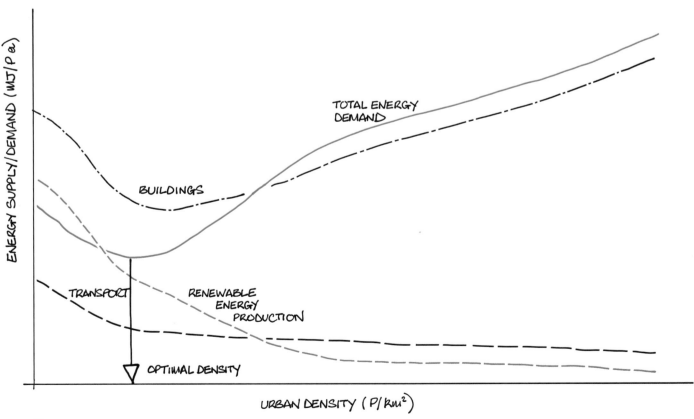

Fig. 5.12

Fig. 5.12
Optimal urban density

Fig. 5.13
Mutual shading,
3 urban models

this desire could hypothetically be accommodated without the excessive use of resources, an optimized single family home model was developed. It should be noted that this model does not represent the majority of single family dwelling typologies today, with the major difference being the much smaller plot size. Nevertheless, it is arguably able to provide its occupants with the attributes responsible for this building type being preferred.

An important factor under consideration was the integration of the studied building typology into the respective urban design configuration so that mutual shading of the buildings and the ensuing impact on energy performance is evaluated (Fig. 5.13). Operating energy demand for thermal conditioning (heating, cooling, dehumidification and humidification) as well as embodied energy over the entire life cycle of the buildings were calculated for the three building types. Dynamic thermal simulations were carried out for four locations in Europe: Helsinki, Finland at latitude 60° N having a maritime continental climate and – due to its northerly location – very long summer days and very short winter days; Dublin, Ireland at latitude 53° N having a temperate maritime climate, modified by the north Atlantic current with mild winters and summers; Vienna, Austria at latitude 48° N having a temperate continental climate with cold winters and warm summers; and Athens, Greece at latitude 38° N, having a subtropical Mediterranean climate with mild winters and hot, dry summers. Ventilation was assumed to be achieved by the combination of a mechanical extract system with natural supply via elements integrated into the façade. Possible renewable energy production via building-integrated photovoltaic modules on the roof and the south-, east- and west-facing façades was also estimated for the various typologies. The results show that for some climate zones, the specific thermal energy demand based on the usable floor area is similar for all three typologies, while in other climate zones, the energy demand for the single-family dwellings is significantly greater than for the apartment

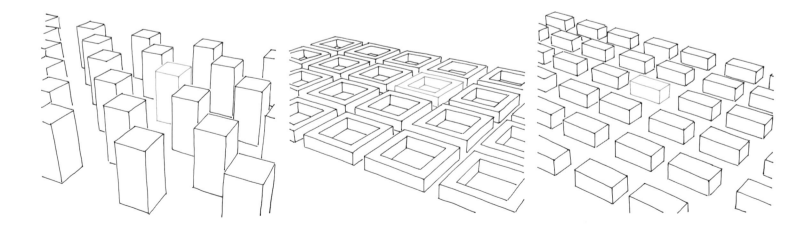

Fig. 5.13

buildings (Fig. 5.14). At the four locations studied, the choice of typology matters most in Helsinki, where the energy demand of the single-family home typology is nearly 40 % higher than in the best apartment building typology and least in Vienna, where it is less than 20 % higher.

Calculations also show that if the single-family typology is constructed with timber, the embodied energy is nearly 30 % lower than for the multistory apartment buildings. In a doctoral dissertation currently being completed at my institute, different city models employing these typologies are developed and the total energy demand for the city calculated, in order to test the optimal density hypothesis outlined above.

When the potential for building-integrated renewable energy production is taken into account, the single-family dwelling typology outperforms the apartment building typologies in terms of operating energy at all four locations studied (Fig. 5.15). Implications of the choice of typology for the goal of achieving Zero Energy Buildings also emerge, as even with very high standards of insulation and mechanical ventilation with heat recovery, the apartment building typologies in the sort of urban context outlined above, would have difficulty achieving this goal in many European climate zones, as long as energy consumption for household appliances is not drastically reduced. One important aspect related to the single-family home typology studied is that the spaces in the residential units receive more sunlight in winter than the majority of the apartments in the apartment building typologies do, with all the associated comfort and health benefits this implies.

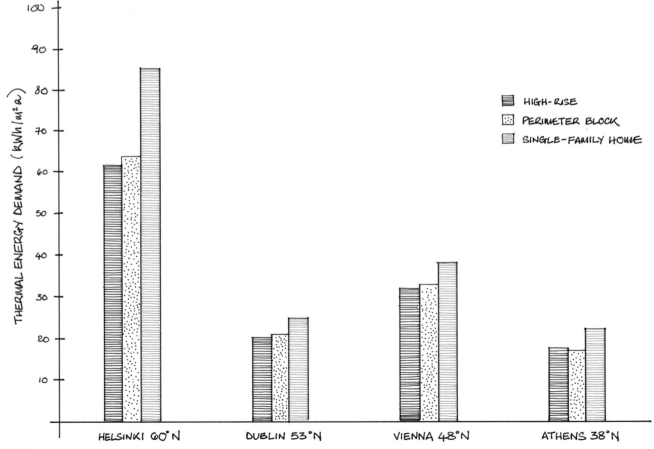

Fig. 5.14

Preliminary findings show that the differences in urban density achievable by the use of the different typologies, measured as described above, is less significant than expected. The work suggests that increasing urban density beyond a certain point has no appreciable effect on land use, as the decrease in land required for urban development is compensated for by an increase in land required for energy production. In fact, at some point it may even become counterproductive to increase the density further, as the creation of high-density urban areas by the stacking of energy demand into super-tall structures will require large tracts of land to accommodate the energy production areas to meet this demand (Fig. 5.16). What is interesting about this approach, and also about recent research carried out on vertical farming (see next section), is that it becomes apparent that ultimately, the currency of comparison for various options may well be land and not energy or economics as land is – leaving aside water – perhaps the ultimate resource. With sufficient land, it is possible to generate all the energy a city requires with renewable sources. Total land use is probably also a good indicator for economic performance.

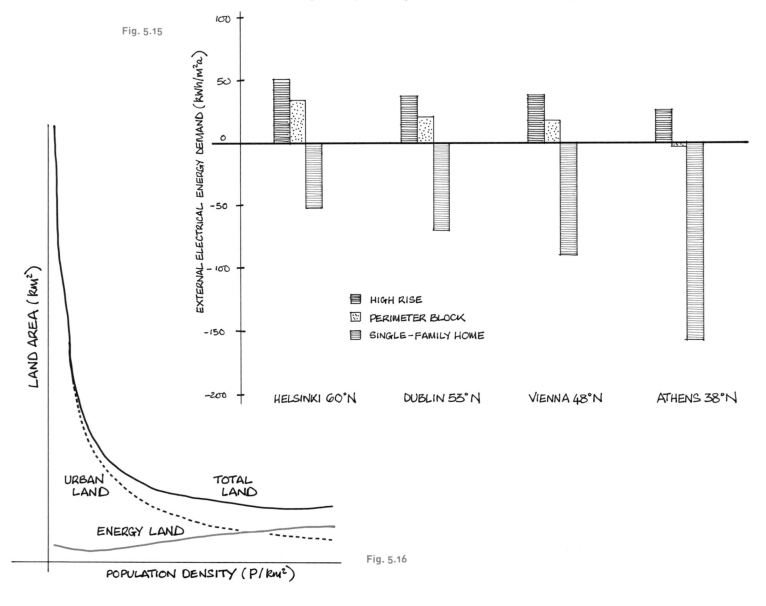

Fig. 5.15

Fig. 5.16

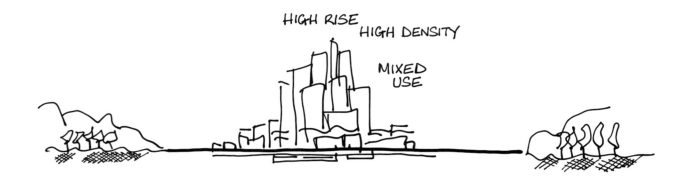

Fig. 5.17

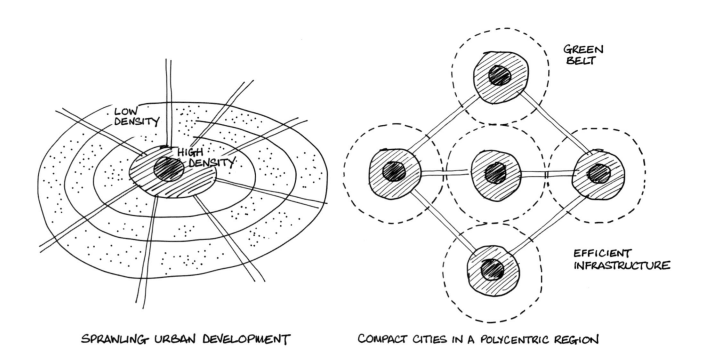

SPRAWLING URBAN DEVELOPMENT   COMPACT CITIES IN A POLYCENTRIC REGION

Fig. 5.18

These findings should not be interpreted as advocating that the path to a sustainable future is the single-family home typology. Firstly, the use of land is more effective with apartment block typologies, even if the difference is less significant than expected. Secondly, there are other issues to be considered; for example, the potential of typologies to create attractive urban conditions, mixed-use development and pleasant street spaces. Here, the potential of the perimeter block development in particular has definite advantages, as can be seen in the older parts of many cities around the world. Also, although a typological approach may be used predominantly in a particular urban area, hybrid mixtures of different typologies are more likely to be successful. However, it is interesting to see how the incorporation of energy production surfaces into buildings, and the solar geometry necessary to ensure solar access to these surfaces, challenges the dogma of compactness in both building and city design.

In any case, cities should be concentrated urban places with a clear boundary to a surrounding green belt (Fig. 5.17). Good quality of life in a large city depends on the integrity of natural environments in the surrounding areas. An interesting question is also the optimal maximum size of a city. Structures employing compact cities in a polycentric region instead of sprawling urban conurbations would seem to offer advantages (Fig. 5.18).

Another research project at my institute is concerned with the energy aspects and potential of **vertical farming**. Concepts for buildings comprising vertically stacked levels of food production areas – primarily vegetables and fruit – have been much discussed in recent years. Our research is focused on the potential to increase the energy efficiency of the food production system when compared to the conventional agricultural system used at present. Aside from the possible reduction in land required, other advantages of the vertical farm concept are that fertilizers and pesticides are not required, less crops are lost due to extreme weather incidents, water is more efficiently used, crops can be grown all year-round in the temperate climate zone and transportation energy demand can be reduced as the food is grown nearer the point of consumption. Potential disadvantages are the energy demand for artificial lighting and conditioning of the spaces and the associated high costs. Sometimes reservations are expressed regarding the artificiality of such a food production system. On the other hand, a critical look at how natural our current system really is may put this into perspective.

Figure 5.19 shows the vertical farming concept and the present conventional food production system in schematic form. In the present system, food is grown on agricultural land outside the city. Fossil fuels are used to manufacture the necessary fertilizers and pesticides in order to achieve the required crop yields and power the agricultural machinery for ploughing, sowing, reaping, harvesting etc. After harvesting, the foodstuffs are transported to facilities at other locations where processing and packaging takes place, and are then distributed – usually via a chain of various stages – to retail outlets in the city. For all of these processes, further energy use is required; today largely derived from fossil fuels. In the vertical farming concept, food production takes place in buildings with stacked levels on compact urban plots, significantly reducing land use for farming compared to the conventional system. However, if the energy is supplied by renewable sources, the land use for this could become very significant owing to the high energy demand, particularly for lighting. Therefore, the concept becomes viable if the total land area required, including the land required for the energy supply systems, is less than that required for conventional farming. The potential of vertical farming thus depends strongly on the following main factors:

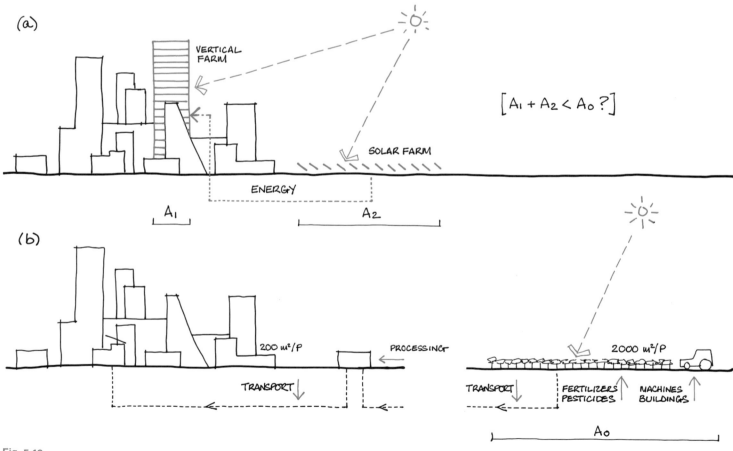

$$[A_1 + A_2 < A_0 \, ?]$$

Fig. 5.19

Fig. 5.19
(a) Vertical farming
(b) Conventional farming

- the possible increase in crop yield
- lighting level requirements of the plants to be grown
- lighting concepts (potential for daylighting, efficiency of artificial lighting)
- energy yield of renewable energy supply plant

As an example, assuming a yield increase factor of 5 (vertical farming compared to conventional), a usable-to-total floor area ratio of 0.66 and a stacking factor of 20 (i.e. 20 food production levels stacked vertically), the vertical farm area required might be 400 m² and the land use taken by the vertical farm building roughly 30 m² per person, compared to roughly 2000 m² for the conventional system. If we assume that an installed electric lighting load of 55 W/m² is necessary to meet the photosynthetic light requirements of the plants and that this operates roughly 3500 full-load hours per year (51 weeks per year, 14 hours per day and assuming daylighting provides 30 % of the annual light required), the electrical energy demand for lighting will be 190 kWh/m²a. Assuming a further 50 kWh/m²a for HVAC, elevators etc. we arrive at a total electrical energy demand of 240 kWh/m²a to operate the vertical farm. If this energy is to be supplied by a PV farm, the area required will be 1940 m², assuming a solar electricity yield of 100 kWh/m²a and an area factor of 2 as discussed above. Therefore, the total land area required will be 1970 m² per person, more or less the same as for conventional farming. Note that the figures chosen are purely given as an example. Other assumptions obviously alter this result significantly and future research work will need to concentrate on the study of the four main parameters listed above.

Other factors to be considered include the energy demand for operating agricultural machinery and for the manufacture of fertilizers and pesticides in conventional soil-based farming, the operating energy demand for heating, cooling, ventilation, moisture control, elevators etc. in vertical farms, the embodied energy of both systems, energy demand for transportation, processing, distribution, storage and water consumption as well as social and economic factors.

Interesting questions for architecture, urban design and city life pose themselves should this new typology be introduced on a large scale. This building type is essentially an industrial production facility with sparse human occupation, and while these types of buildings have been traditionally located in the peripheral regions of cities, the whole premise of vertical farming is to locate the buildings in central urban areas close to the human population in order to reduce transportation energy demand. This aspect has obvious implications for the city. Aside from the spatial implications, in terms of the physical manifestation of the structures in the cityscape, and the social and economic factors for both city and countryside, the ecological implications in terms of use of land, energy, water, materials etc. will need to be investigated in detail.

In 2008, in collaboration with Ortner & Ortner architects in Vienna, we developed an energy masterplan for a carbon-neutral development on a peninsula with an area of approximately 100 hectares, which closes Bigova Bay in Montenegro off from the Adriatic sea. Most of the land on the site is hilly and the highest peak is approximately 110 m above sea level.

On the northeastern side there are some existing buildings. The rest of the peninsula is covered with dense vegetation. The site is to be developed as a tourist destination with vacation homes, resort hotels, leisure and sport facilities, retail and gastronomy and a total gross floor area of over 400 000 m² and for an expected total number of approx. 5000 people. The approach was to concentrate most of the development on three locations in a village-like typology with high urban density, thus reflecting local urbanistic and architectural traditions. A large portion of the land could thus be retained in its present form.

In a conventional solution, if you were to draw a system boundary around the island, food, fuels for heating and vehicles, and electricity for building cooling, lighting and small power would pass through the boundary from outside. Waste water, refuse and combustion products would exit from inside. In the proposed solution, on the other hand, only food needs to be brought across the system boundary (Fig. 5.20). The energy demand of the entire development including all buildings and vehicles is supplied by on-site renewable energy sources. The use of solar and wind energy,

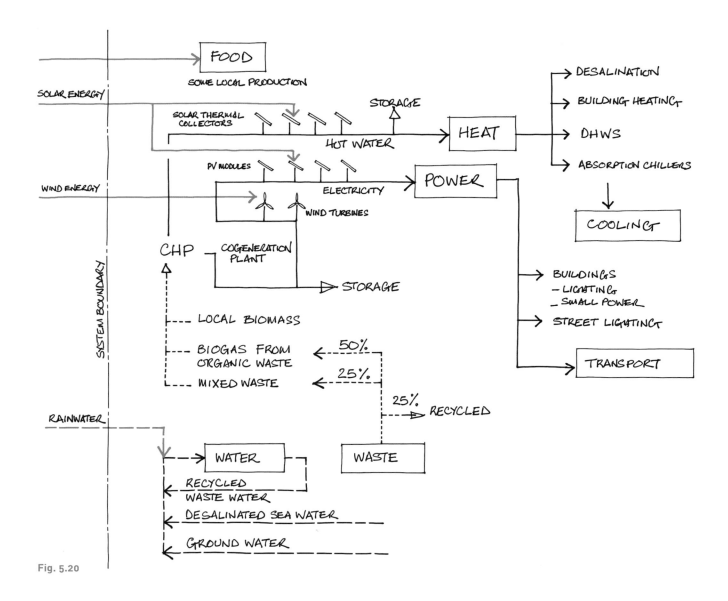

Fig. 5.20

Fig. 5.20
Bigova Bay, Montenegro,
whole energy system

Fig. 5.21
Bigova Bay, Montenegro,
energy grid

rain water, even waste water and garbage are integrated into the system. An integrated building and vehicle network called the Energy Grid is proposed, which is supplied with renewable energy via a combination of centralized plant and decentralized building-integrated energy supply systems (Fig. 5.21). An interchange building provides the transformation from the primary conventional transportation system outside the site to a secondary transportation system on the peninsula, comprising electrical taxis in which the batteries are recharged by renewable energy. Buildings and vehicles are connected together via the energy grid and both buildings and cars can extract and supply energy from and to the grid.

As explained above, energy storage is a vital component of any energy system employing renewable energy sources in order to match supply and demand, and the electrical mobility system partly fulfils this important function by providing storage capacity. The topography of the site is also used to store energy. Surplus electrical energy produced by solar and wind sources is utilized to pump water to the highest point of the peninsula and store it in a large reservoir. This potential energy in the form of water mass is used, when required, to drive turbines and generate electrical power (Fig. 5.22). The system is also combined with a system for collecting and using rainwater. Solar cooling systems employ solar energy to drive absorption chillers, and sea water is used as a cooling source. Concentrating the urban development in densely built villages means that a large part of the peninsula can be left in its natural condition, the biodiversity can be preserved to a large extent and the transportation demand can be minimized. Solar geometry and wind analysis were used to generate urban morphologies which provide pleasant microclimatic conditions in the external urban spaces.

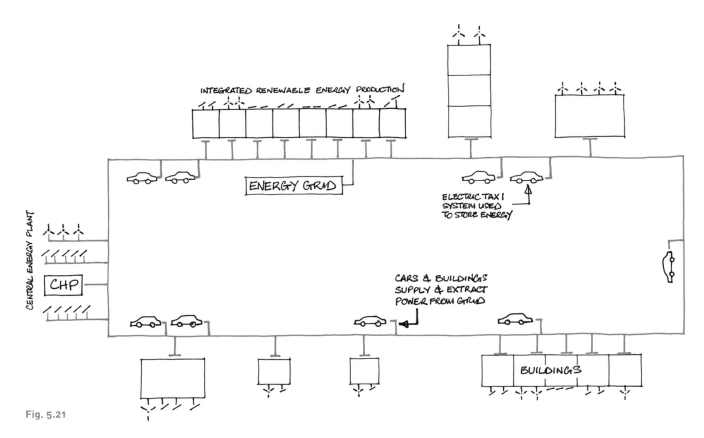

Fig. 5.21

Figure 5.23 shows a schematic representation of a simple model built to study the energetic structure of a typical developed country, in this case Austria. Fuels flow across the borders and are combusted in thermal power plants to supply electricity and some heating energy via district heating systems to energy consumers in the building, industry and transport sectors. Imported fuels are also combusted in boiler systems within buildings to provide heating energy, and used to provide power for mobility systems such as the internal combustion engines of cars, motorcycles and trucks. In Austria, the geographical situation allows a large share of the electrical energy demand to be met by the use of hydroelectricity. A relatively small share of the total energy demand is met by biomass, wind and solar energy. Electrical energy is imported and exported on a daily basis with some net electrical energy import over the course of a typical year. Imported and exported goods also flow through the system boundary with associated embodied energy. Note also the use of fossil fuels for non-energy use and the energy demand of the energy sector itself (so-called energy for energy). The model used data from the country's official statistics,

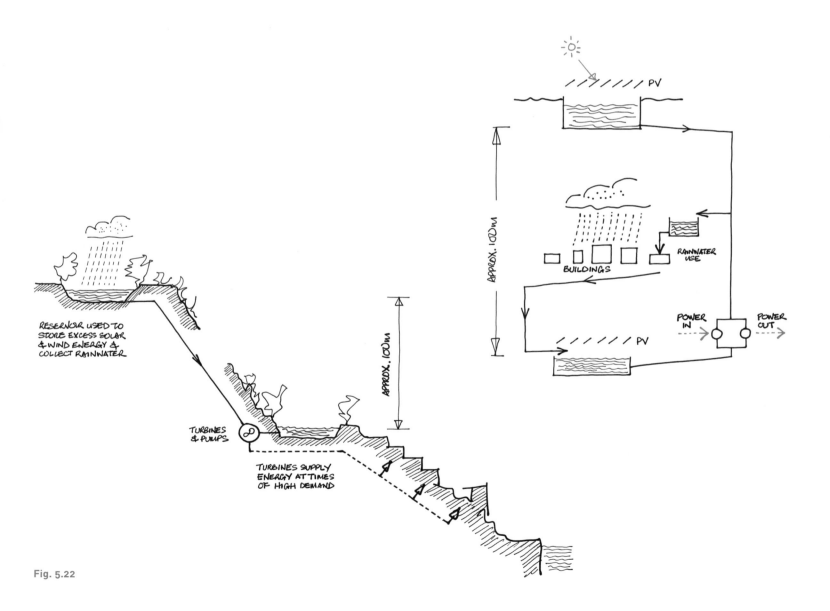

Fig. 5.22

which were converted to primary energy values for energy demand to better reflect energy use on a global scale; using factors of 2.6 for electricity and 1.0 for fossil fuels[6]. Due to the fact that a large proportion of electrical energy generation in Austria is derived from hydroelectricity, the actual primary energy consumption is lower, as can be seen in the supply-side part of the model. Using this simple model, various future scenarios can be explored, e.g. renovating all buildings to a very high thermal standard, converting all transportation to electrically powered vehicles, installing solar panels on all suitable roof areas or radically expanding the use of wind power and biomass.

The results of these studies show that while all of these strategies are effective in their own way, achieving real progress in sustainable development and reducing the present energy consumption rate of over 5000 W/P to the global average of roughly half this figure would probably entail the radical restructuring of society's physical infrastructure. Alongside spatial densification as discussed above, strategies for temporal densification need to be considered. A step in this direction was provided by an interdisciplinary research project which was led by my institute and included experts in transportation, sociology and IT. This research was concerned with the nature of the relationship between different forms of **teleworking and energy efficiency** in society. In recent years, the use of new forms of working involving information and telecommunication systems has unquestionably increased energy consumption. However, there is the poten-

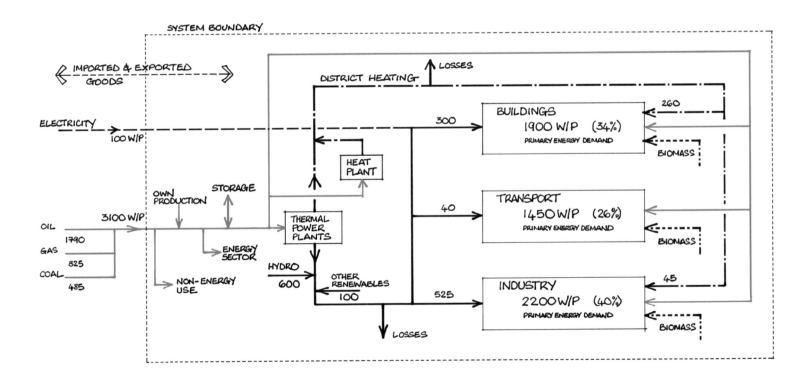

Fig. 5.23

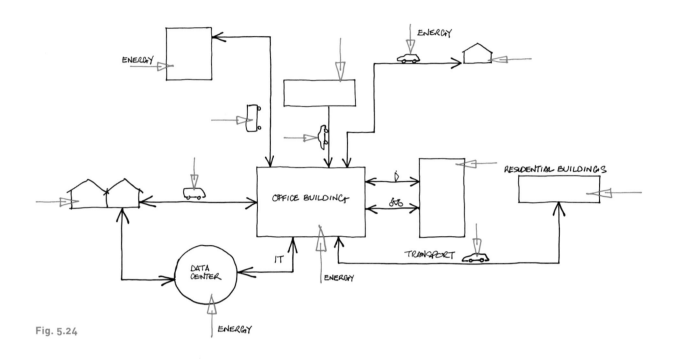

Fig. 5.24

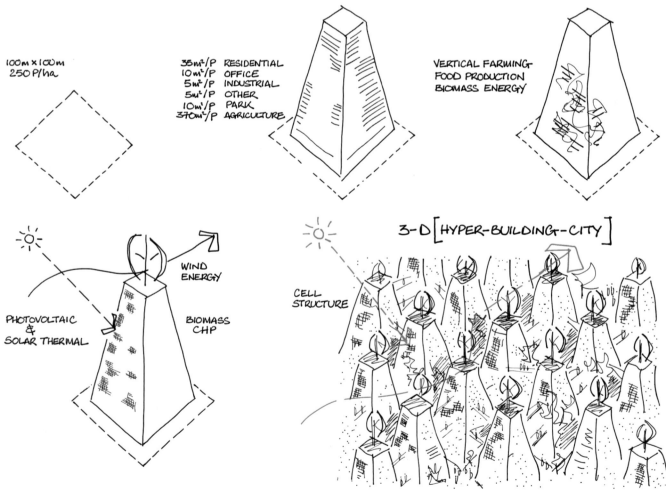

Fig. 5.25

Fig. 5.24
Rethinking the city

Fig. 5.25
Hyper-Building-City

tial to use these new technologies to allow the generation of radically new forms of building and transport systems with the aim of increasing total energy efficiency. To study this, we modeled the energetic structures of typical corporate organizations (Fig. 5.24).

A key research question in the field of architecture and urban design is the consequences of the increasingly flexible structuring of work for the design of future office and residential buildings in both spatial and temporal terms. The use of information and telecommunication systems, and an associated spatial flexibility in terms of where the work is carried out, is the starting point for all concepts involving teleworking. Against the background of the necessary improvement of energy efficiency in society, this topic assumes a new relevance.

In the context of this research, various scenarios relating to teleworking were studied to determine how these could be expected to influence total energy demand. All of the scenarios studied in the project assumed that office buildings retain their social function of providing a place for communication amongst the employees. The time spent in office buildings to allow face-to-face communication, meetings etc. is however so structured that the majority of office workers are expected to spend no more than approximately 20 % of their time in the office. A central issue is the effective use of space and time, and in the course of the project we derived a new unit to measure the degree of utilization of the building stock; m^3h, the product of space and time. The research results show that the implementation of various teleworking models can reduce the total energy consumption of a typical company structure by about 25 %. Moreover, extrapolating these results in a process of rethinking the city could lead to an urban model with much smaller commercial office buildings than those we know today. These would become centers of face-to-face communication, while residential buildings would be configured to allow effective office work at home. The reduction in energy demand achievable by this reconfiguration of the whole system was shown to be potentially greater than that achieved by strategies to increase the energy efficiency of present-day building and transportation systems.

Building on these results, in further research work we studied more generally the consequences of more effective use of building space and the use of synergies between physical and virtual infrastructure, living and working spaces, teleworking etc. In the search for strategies toward spatial, temporal and digital densification, new typologies for vertical structures incorporating all the necessary infrastructural elements of society – even including industrial and agricultural uses, food production, energy generation etc. – were developed (Fig. 5.25). In the cell-like structure of the **Hyper-Building-City** model, each Hyper Building-cell has the ability to work independently and function in a self-sufficient manner. However, when linked together, they mutually assist each other so that the whole is more than the sum of the parts. The Hyper Building itself is a structure which allows a population density roughly equal to that of Manhattan, needs no external energy supply, no external water supply, produces no waste, emits no CO_2 and needs little or no external food supply. Space for residential, office and industrial use is provided alongside parks and areas for agriculture, biomass and energy production. Linked together,

Fig. 5.26
City of the future?

they form a three-dimensional urban structure combining urbanity and nature, density and diversity. A central feature of the conceptual approach is the synergetic integration of the different systems and the exploitation of symbiotic relationships between nature, man and technology; e.g. plants supplying oxygen for humans, humans supplying CO_2 for plants, biological waste as fertilizer, waste heat use, water recycling, biological waste water treatment etc.

I believe that the urban design of cities needs to be conceived of in more spatial terms than has been the case until now. Circulation, mobility systems and public spaces need not remain trapped on the ground plane. Various layers at different vertical levels are conceivable in a truly three-dimensional spatial arrangement of public and private life. A radical rethinking of our urban structures could provide solutions for the energy question and at the same time lead to a higher quality of urban life. Often when people see this work, they immediately think of applications for new cities which are currently being built in countries like China and India, but they discount any relevance for cities in places such as Western Europe or the US. This is based on the misconception that cities there are more or less "completed" and that our future efforts will be concerned only with their upkeep and ongoing renovation. That this is not true can be easily understood if you project the future, say 50 years, of a typical European city (Fig. 5.26). Based on the assumptions that the annual rate of demolition is 1% of total building stock and the annual rate of new build is 1.5% of total building stock (i.e. there is a total annual growth in city size of 0.5%), it can be seen that 50 years from now, more than 50% of the buildings standing by this time will be buildings that are yet to be built. Therefore, the considerations outlined above are not limited to the design of new cities. With the knowledge that in the course of the next 50 years existing city structures will drastically change, it is imperative now to develop a masterplan and a vision for every city in 50 years' time. Why? Because every intervention we make between now and then – every new building, every renovated old building – is a fragment of the "City of the Future".

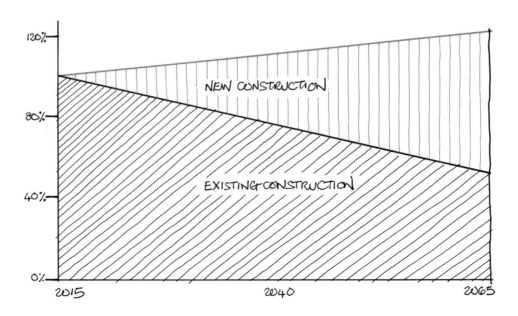

Fig. 5.26

Fig. 6.1
Discipline of Energy Design

Energy design is a fundamentally new way of collaborating on the design of buildings. It is essentially a new discipline which sets itself apart from the traditional building design disciplines of architecture, structural engineering, MEP engineering, building physics, façade engineering etc. While all of these disciplines are concerned with aspects affecting the energy performance of the building, an integrated overarching energy concept seldom results due to the traditional boundaries between the disciplines and missing areas of expertise (Fig. 6.1).

In the energy design of a building, concepts are developed which minimize building energy demand while optimizing internal environmental conditions in the spaces. This is achieved by using transient energy flows in the building's external environment as well as those generated in the building as a result of its use. At the same time, renewable energy is produced for use in the building and/or for export to the surrounding urban infrastructure. Instead of deploying standard solutions, the scientific principles of thermodynamics, heat transfer and fluid mechanics are applied in order to develop solutions which use multifunctional building elements and systems to maximize building performance.

A building is designed to operate within a natural environment of continuingly changing conditions, and to provide internal conditions which diverge significantly from these most of the time. Two approaches can be followed to achieve this goal. The conventional approach is to exclude the external environment as much as possible and employ mechanical systems to provide the desired internal conditions. An alternative approach is to design the building's form, construction and skin to capture and utilize energy flows in the environment, in order to create the desired internal conditions. This second approach, in which the energy of the dominant natural forces which seem to pose the problem (wind in a skyscraper, solar radiation in a hot climate, daylight in a museum building) are captured and used in a controlled way to achieve the desired result, is for obvious reasons the more challenging. It also offers however much more potential with regard to the efficient use of resources.

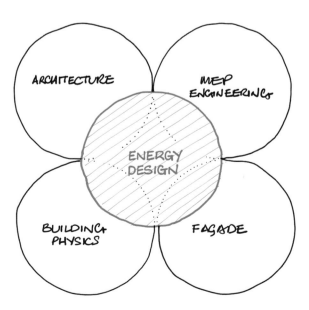

Fig. 6.1

$$e = mc^2$$

Fig. 6.2

1. $du = dq_v - dw$

2. $dS = \dfrac{\delta Q_{rev}}{T}$

$$\dfrac{dS}{dt} \geq 0$$

$$\eta = (Q_H - Q_c)/Q_H$$

$$= 1 - T_c/T_H$$

Fig. 6.3

As described in chapter four, the energy design approach uses building form, skin and construction to modify the sea of ever-changing conditions the external climate of a particular location has to offer and bring it as close as possible to the desired internal environmental condition, thus minimizing the energy demand of the climate control systems. In energy design, the focus and aim of the design is a building with optimal internal climate, minimized energy demand and a high spatial quality. The materials, technical systems etc. used to achieve these goals are merely elements of the solution and not aims in themselves. As explained in the next chapter, energy performance is the relationship between the quality of the internal environment achieved and the quantity of energy required to maintain this environment.

In the approach to energy design taken both in real projects carried out by my engineering design firm and in research and teaching activities at my institute, achieving energy-efficient solutions is not seen – as is often the case – as a process in which energy demand is added up on one side and energy production on the other until they match, much like the approach used in financial accounting or bookkeeping. Rather, it is recognized that everything is essentially energy (Fig. 6.2). The bookkeeping approach corresponds to the use of the first law of thermodynamics. In the work described in this book, systems are also analyzed according to the second law of thermodynamics, which allows energy quality to be properly considered (Fig. 6.3). By considering the interactions and dependencies of all the elements that comprise a given system, the whole system is always within view, even when the focus is on the optimization of a smaller subsystem (Fig. 6.4). The key to sustainable future development lies in **whole systems thinking**. If, in our approach to problem solving, we draw a system boundary around the problem and ignore the effect potential solutions will have on other parts of the whole system, we run the very real risk of potentially contributing unwittingly to an unsustainable development of the whole system. Currently prevailing misguided developments concerning energy efficiency in the building sector stem largely from a lack of systems thinking and the lack of a holistic approach to the analysis and design of buildings. Instead of considering whole systems, the focus is placed on the development of subsystems without consideration of the interactions and dependencies with and on the other subsystems making up the whole.

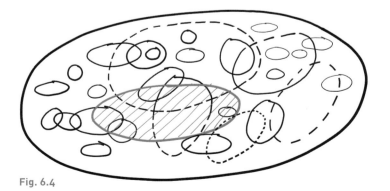

Fig. 6.4

As explained in chapter two, energy has quality as well as quantity. As an example of how insufficient consideration of the quality of energy forms involved in building construction and operation can lead to undesired results, a study carried out at my institute showed that in many cases the installation of mechanical ventilation systems with heat recovery in office buildings led to lower energy performance than natural ventilation via operable windows (Fig. 6.5), when the qualities of the various forms of energy involved were considered (electrical energy for the fans, thermal energy for heating). This type of situation, whereby measures intended to reduce energy demand inadvertently lead to greater energy use, is unfortunately a typical one. Conclusions are arrived at by the analysis of energy flows, sometimes in great depth, but without due consideration of the accompanying effects on entropy.

One important reason for the better performance of natural ventilation in office buildings is that in a typical office, heat gains due to solar radiation via windows and internal heat sources from people, lighting and machines are often greater in magnitude than losses due to transmission and infiltration through the building envelope. Therefore, in a naturally ventilated office, the heat energy required to raise the temperature of incoming air from the external temperature to room temperature can often be supplied by excess heat gains in the space. In a mechanically ventilated space with isothermal supply air, the supply air is heated to room air temperature before supply to the space and thus the system cannot take full advantage of the heat gains in the space. The natural ventilation system is in effect employing 100 % heat recovery in these situations.

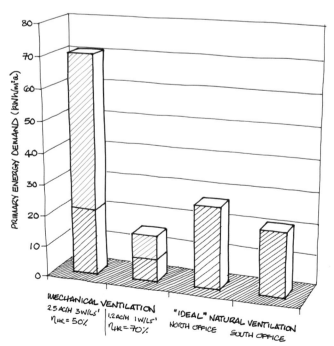

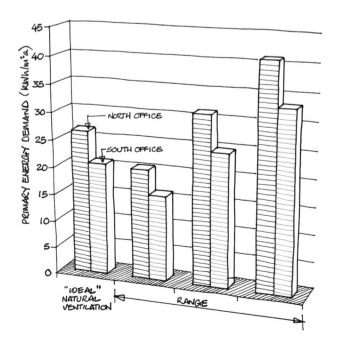

Fig. 6.5

The example above gives a first insight into the importance of considering not just the magnitude of energy flows in a system but also their quality, in a way which allows their true impact in ecological, economic and social terms to be assessed. The purpose for which energy is used in various buildings depends heavily, of course, on the nature of the building's use and its location. Nevertheless, there is one universal issue which appears to be important, and that is our preoccupation with the thermal energy needs of buildings. For example, in Northern and Central Europe, the overemphasis on heating energy is problematic, as more important issues are often ignored or the strategies employed to improve this one factor lead, in the worst cases, to a reduction in the total energy efficiency of the building. Figure 6.6 shows, for example, the breakdown of the energy consumption of a building, originally built in the 1960s, on which my institute was asked for advice by the building owner in 2006 regarding various strategies for improving energy efficiency prior to the selection of the winner of an architectural competition for its refurbishment. Contrary to the client's expectations, the contribution of thick thermal insulation layers to reduce heat loss from the external walls is relatively insignificant in the context of the building's total energy consumption as can be seen from the diagram. Of course, insulation would improve this part of the building's energy performance; it is just that this part is not a significant portion of the whole. Given the fact that there is usually a limited budget, it is vital to invest in the right measures.

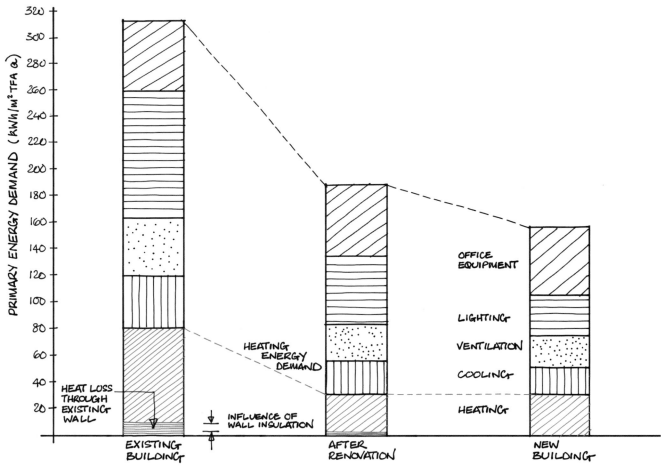

Fig. 6.6

Heating energy demand in a modern office building accounts for only a fraction of the total energy demand of the building. Figure 6.7 shows a rough breakdown of the energy demand of a typical modern office building in Central Europe. The relatively modest portion attributable to heating is evident. So where does the preoccupation with heating energy demand in our codes, our practice and in our heads derive from? Humans are essentially a subtropical species, and for those who arrived in regions like Central and Northern Europe, where the climate is relatively cold for a substantial part of the year, the climatic challenge in the past was to achieve reasonably warm indoor temperatures in the winter. This cultural background and line of thought still tend to dominate our thinking today, although the reality of the modern buildings we need and use clearly requires much more sophisticated thinking. Modern buildings not only need to be heated but also artificially lit, ventilated and – increasingly – cooled. This has only partially to do with the architectural concepts employed and largely results from the changed requirements due to modern usage of spaces.

A further example of the lack of a holistic approach in the construction sector is the emphasis on energy demand in operation without consideration of the embodied energy necessary to manufacture the measures employed to save energy during operation. When various alternative solutions in the building context are compared with each other, too often only the energy efficiency in operation is considered. We need to think more holistically. The total energy efficiency including manufacturing, construction and disposal in most cases needs to be considered. As an example, our research showed that in many buildings employing double façades to improve energy efficiency, the time taken to recover the embodied energy of the second skin via energy savings in operation can be in the order of a quarter of a century (Fig. 6.8). This amortization period was calculated purely in terms of primary energy; the economical payback period is substantially longer. Double skin façades can improve building performance in operation but they also increase capital costs and embodied energy significantly. Their viability therefore, in economic terms but also in terms of energy efficiency, depends not only on their potential to reduce energy demand in operation but also on their potential to eliminate the need for other systems, usually HVAC, in the building. In the majority of the buildings built to date employing double skin façades, all that was achieved was a mere reduction in the size of some of the HVAC systems. All the usual systems for heating, cooling and ventilation were however still provided in some form. The results of our study showed that in these cases, approx. 25 years are needed to recover the embodied energy of the second skin via energy savings in operation. On the other hand, if whole systems such as mechanical ventilation or conventional heating systems can be omitted due to the presence of a double façade, these savings can be offset against the increased costs and grey energy of the extra skin and the energy payback period reduces to a couple of years. The research shows that the success of the implementation of an architectural device such as a double façade, designed to increase energy efficiency, depends on developing strategies which improve the performance of the skin to such a degree that the complete omission of other building systems becomes possible.

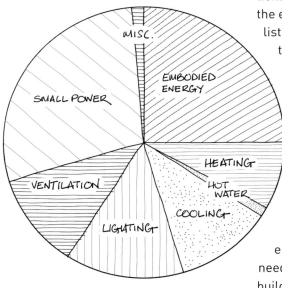

Fig. 6.7

The Braun headquarters building near Frankfurt in Germany, completed in 2000 and briefly introduced in chapter three, is one example of this approach. On account of the relatively high external noise level due to traffic on the nearby road, in the architectural competition held in 1996 we proposed a double skin façade on this side of the building to enable natural ventilation. During the development of the design, it was decided to extend the double façade around the whole building (Fig. 6.9). The reasons were twofold. On the one hand, the double skin envelope gave the optical appearance of a smooth glass façade while still retaining the benefits of a quasi-external shading device. The second reason was more important to me. We set out to improve the thermal performance of the skin to a level which would enable us to drastically simplify the mechanical systems required in the building.

The thermal effectiveness of the high-performance double-skin façade developed with schneider + schumacher architects in Frankfurt allowed a conventional heating system to be dispensed with. A network of capillary tubing integrated into a thin plaster layer on the underside of the concrete slab, fed with warm water in cold weather and cool water in warm weather, is the only system needed to provide comfortable internal conditions in the offices (Fig. 6.10). The system is zoned in accordance with

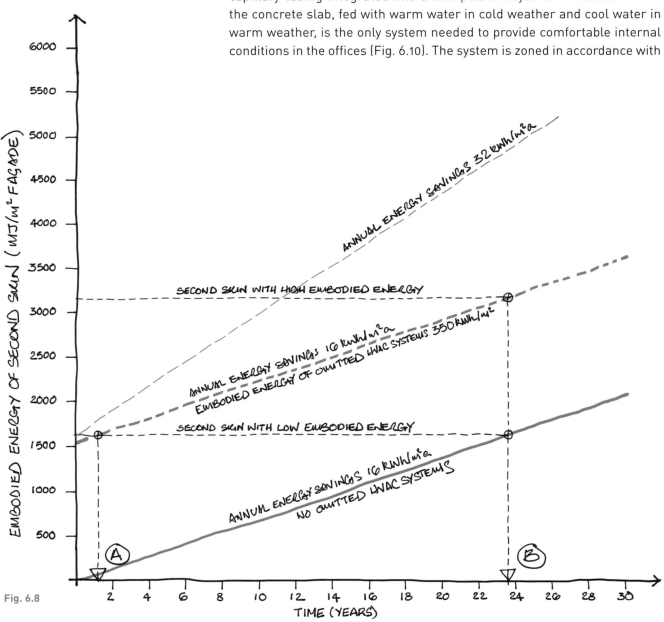

Fig. 6.8

Fig. 6.8
Embodied energy,
double façades

Fig. 6.9
Braun HQ Germany,
double skin concept

Fig. 6.10
Braun HQ, office section

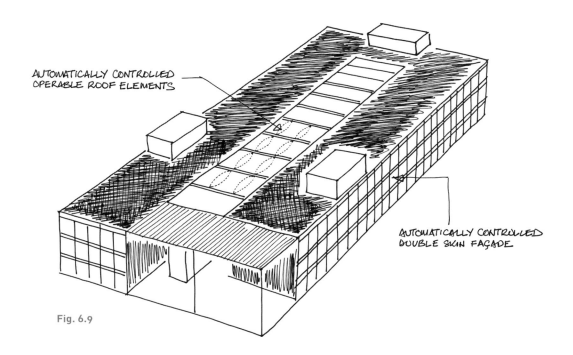

AUTOMATICALLY CONTROLLED
OPERABLE ROOF ELEMENTS

AUTOMATICALLY CONTROLLED
DOUBLE SKIN FAÇADE

Fig. 6.9

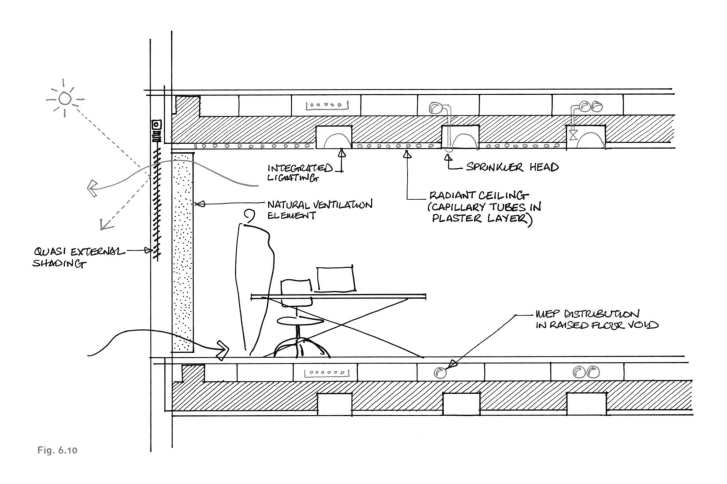

INTEGRATED
LIGHTING

SPRINKLER HEAD

RADIANT CEILING
(CAPILLARY TUBES IN
PLASTER LAYER)

NATURAL VENTILATION
ELEMENT

QUASI EXTERNAL
SHADING

MEP DISTRIBUTION
IN RAISED FLOOR VOID

Fig. 6.10

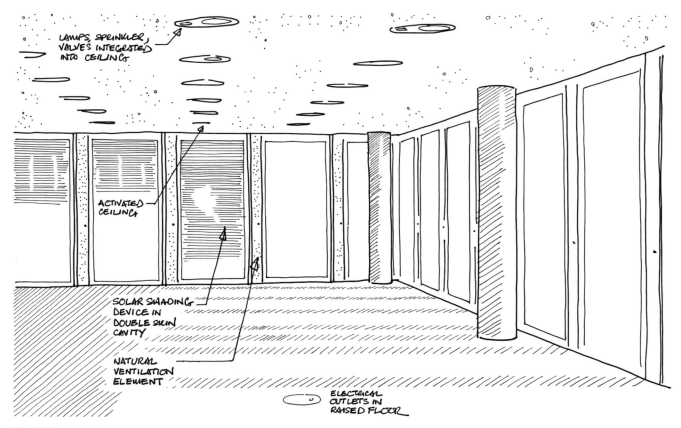

LAMPS, SPRINKLER, VALVES INTEGRATED INTO CEILING

ACTIVATED CEILING

SOLAR SHADING DEVICE IN DOUBLE SKIN CAVITY

NATURAL VENTILATION ELEMENT

ELECTRICAL OUTLETS IN RAISED FLOOR

Fig. 6.11

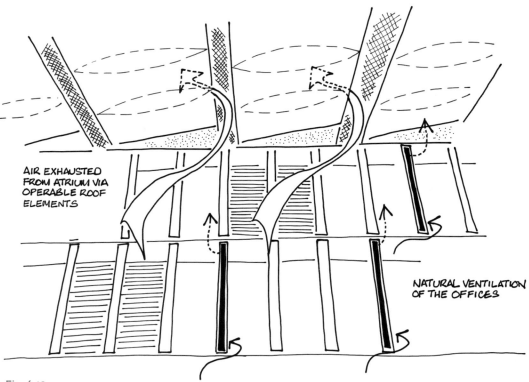

AIR EXHAUSTED FROM ATRIUM VIA OPERABLE ROOF ELEMENTS

NATURAL VENTILATION OF THE OFFICES

Fig. 6.12

orientation but otherwise there are no individual room controls. The external zone up to approximately 5 m from the façade is naturally ventilated. The internal zone is ventilated via a displacement ventilation system. The thermal inertia of the exposed slabs, the high performance of the building skin and the possibility of natural ventilation via operable windows make more complicated controls superfluous. The fact that a fully glazed office building can be conditioned with such minimal climate control systems is attributable to the high thermal performance of the building skin (Fig. 6.11).

The additional external skin is wrapped around the entire building. On the external façades, horizontal separations are provided in the cavity at each floor level and vertical separations for each 1.35 m wide façade planning module. Each module has an external window which is automatically controlled and a narrow, vertically aligned opaque element in the inside skin which is manually operated for ventilation (see chapter three). The shading device is located in the cavity. In the middle of the U-formed building plan, a central atrium is formed with a PTFE foil cushion roof construction, which provides the second skin for the office façades facing into the atrium (Fig. 6.12). The atrium is an unheated buffer zone. In summer, its roof can be completely opened to allow unwanted heat to escape. Underground concrete ducts integrated into the building foundations supply tempered fresh air to the atrium and from there via operable windows to the offices (Fig. 6.13). The outer skin of the building is automatically controlled via the building management system. The outer layer is opened according to external conditions and the solar control blinds in the façade cavity are automatically adjusted depending on the degree of incident solar radiation. Artificial lighting is controlled to match external light intensity. All settings can be overridden at any time by the users. The high performance of the building envelope means that the ceiling temperature does not have to be higher than approx. 27 °C or lower than approx. 20 °C. The

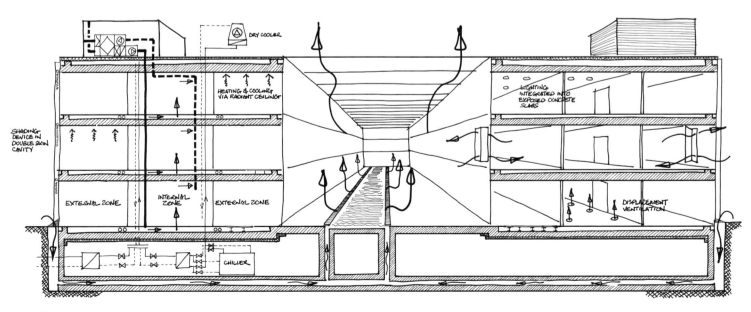

Fig. 6.13

concept proved that the economic feasibility of double skin façades could be much improved in comparison to completed buildings having used these concepts to date. The effectiveness of the high-performance double skin façade allowed whole building systems – the conventional heating system and the mechanical ventilation of the external office zone – to be completely dispensed with, and thus led to considerable capital cost savings on the building's mechanical services.

Building on this experience, these concepts were further developed and refined and – in collaboration with the same architects ten years later – the Fronius office and laboratory building in Wels, Austria was also designed with a double skin concept and hybrid ventilation system and completed in 2013. Again, a highly effective façade design makes a conventional heating system at the perimeter superfluous. In a similar zoning of the floor plan, the external zone with a depth of approximately 5 m from the façade is naturally ventilated, while the internal 5 m deep middle strip is mechanically ventilated. In this building, an element in the building envelope is rotated to allow various ventilation scenarios. Figure 6.14 shows the proposed concept at the competition stage. This was subsequently refined but the essential principle remains. In cold weather, the air is preheated in the cavity of the double skin before entering the room at high level. The path through the façade cavity, together with the entry position at high level, ensures that the air is tempered and sufficiently mixed with the room air so that the fresh air supplied to the room is at a comfortable temperature, thus avoiding cold drafts and solving one of the main problems with conventional ventilation via windows (Fig. 6.15). In warm weather, the element is rotated to allow air to flow directly from the outside to the inside without the heating effect in the skin cavity, while air flow through the cavity from low to high level removes excess heat from the shading device, which is protected by the outer skin of the façade from strong winds but is in a thermal sense equivalent to an external shading device. The upper portion of the horizontal blind system is controlled separately to distribute daylight into the deeper parts of the floor plan, this being assisted by glass partition walls between the external and internal zones. A multifunctional element suspended from the ceiling fulfils acoustical and light reflection functions as well as providing heating and cooling (Fig. 6.16). Nighttime

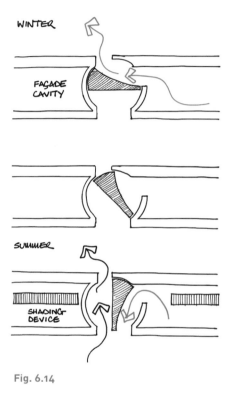

Fig. 6.14

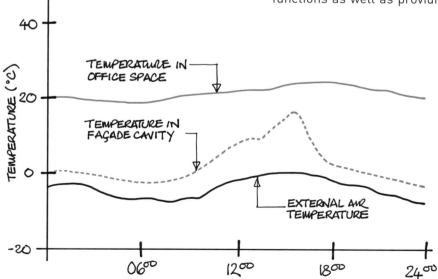

Fig. 6.15

ventilation of the spaces allows the exposed thermal mass of the concrete ceilings to be cooled by cool, summer night air. Building integrated photo-voltaic modules and geothermal ground heat exchangers in combination with heat pumps and the use of the nearby river for cooling allows a high proportion of the building's energy demand to be met via renewable energy (see chapter four). These projects show that double façades can, under certain circumstances, present very efficient solutions.

The forerunner for both of these projects was an office building de-signed in collaboration with schneider + schumacher architects in 1995 in Schwedlerstrasse, Frankfurt, which was configured in three distinct zones; naturally ventilated offices with exposed concrete slabs and balconies to the south, an internal zone with displacement ventilation and a fully glazed winter garden as circulation and communication space which provides an unheated thermal buffer zone on the north side (Fig. 6.17).

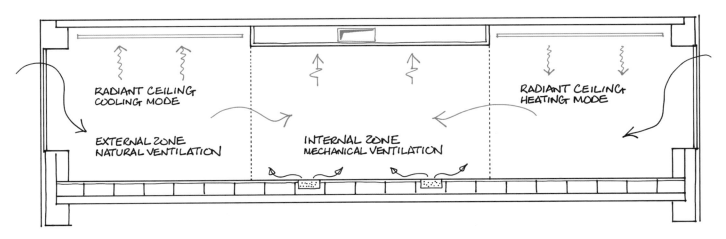

Fig. 6.16

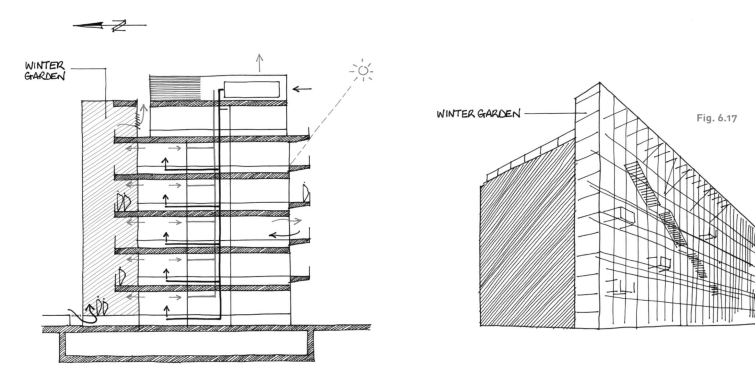

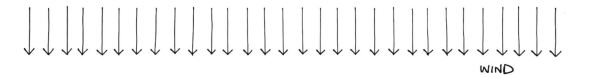

WIND

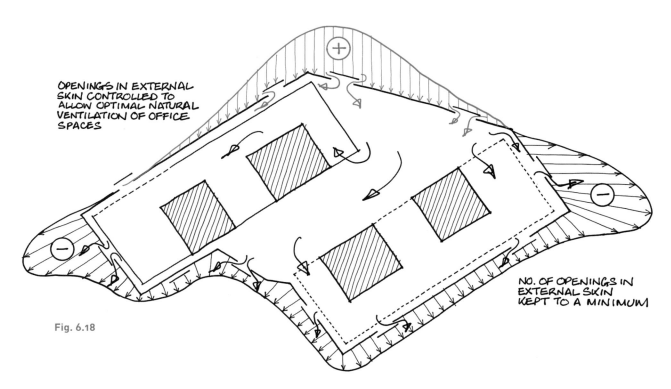

OPENINGS IN EXTERNAL
SKIN CONTROLLED TO
ALLOW OPTIMAL NATURAL
VENTILATION OF OFFICE
SPACES

NO. OF OPENINGS IN
EXTERNAL SKIN
KEPT TO A MINIMUM

Fig. 6.18

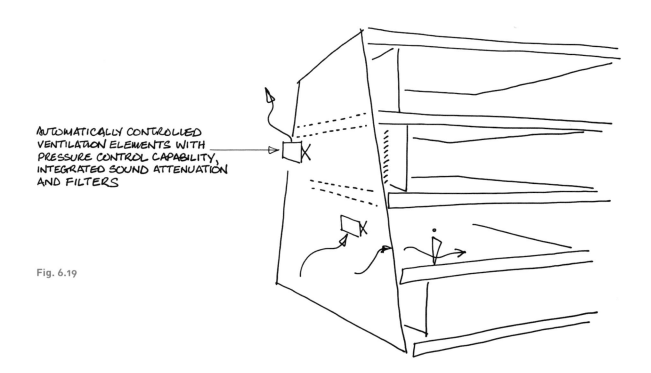

AUTOMATICALLY CONTROLLED
VENTILATION ELEMENTS WITH
PRESSURE CONTROL CAPABILITY,
INTEGRATED SOUND ATTENUATION
AND FILTERS

Fig. 6.19

Fig. 6.18
Office tower, Baku,
Azerbaijan, ventilation
concept

Fig. 6.19
Office tower, Baku,
façade concept

If I were asked to reduce energy design to a simple formula, it is probably this: the **use of natural forces**, such as wind, sun and thermal buoyancy to achieve the goals outlined above and maximize building performance. In the design of tall buildings, for example, wind is normally seen as a problem. Figures 6.18 and 6.19 show a conceptual approach for a system of natural ventilation which was developed in collaboration with Coop Himmelb(l)au for a skyscraper in the windy city of Baku, Azerbaijan, in which the use of wind is integrated into the concept to provide the motive force to drive the building ventilation system. The "enemy" becomes a friend.

Detailed analysis of many building types shows that often the areas with the highest potential for increasing energy efficiency are the mechanical ventilation and artificial lighting systems, primarily because the quality of energy used to power these systems is conventionally high exergy, low entropy electricity. In the case of mechanical ventilation a further reason is the potential reduction in embodied energy due to the fact that the building space taken up by these systems is very substantial.

All buildings of course require a ventilation system in order to achieve adequate air quality and, regardless of whether this is a mechanical, hybrid or natural ventilation system, it needs to be conceived and designed as a system. Tall buildings have traditionally been sealed and mechanically ventilated. The skyscraper or tall building type originated in the US and has been without exception equipped with a mechanical ventilation system and cooling from the postwar era onwards. Wind speed increases exponentially with height and high wind pressures at the upper levels lead to difficulties associated with operable windows, one of the major ones being the resulting large force necessary to open internal doors (other problems being windows and doors blowing closed, uncomfortable drafts and papers flying from desks).

As we have seen, in recent years advances have been made which allow the natural ventilation of tall buildings. The motivation has been both energy savings and occupant comfort. The projects realized thus far, such as the GSW building described in chapter two, use double skin façades and operate on the mixed mode principle. Natural ventilation is employed for a portion of the annual period. Under certain wind and external temperature conditions, mechanical systems take over. On top of the energy efficiency potential of natural ventilation, there are also the well-known psychological benefits. Mixed mode systems can function well and allow energy

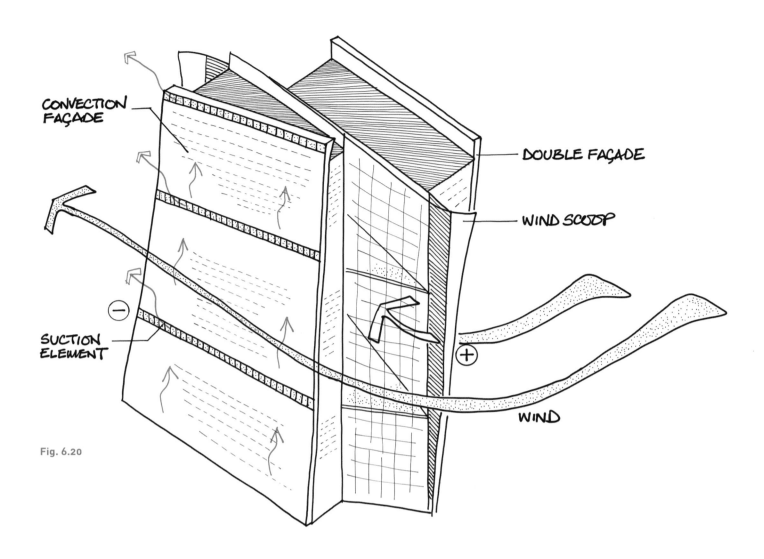

CONVECTION FAÇADE

DOUBLE FAÇADE

WIND SCOOP

SUCTION ELEMENT

WIND

Fig. 6.20

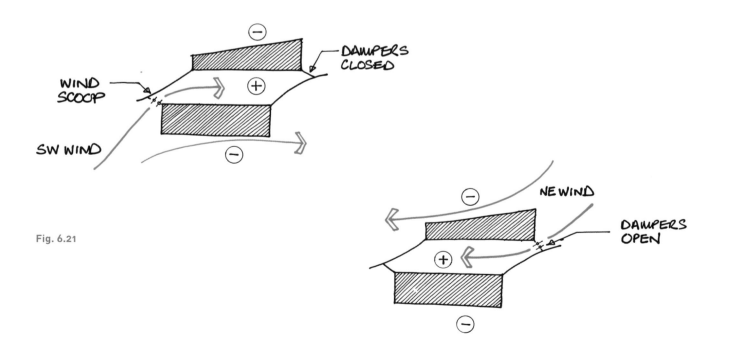

WIND SCOOP

SW WIND

DAMPERS CLOSED

NE WIND

DAMPERS OPEN

Fig. 6.21

Fig. 6.20
ECB HQ, Frankfurt,
natural ventilation concept

Fig. 6.21
ECB HQ, wind

savings in operation as well as improved occupant comfort. However, our research has shown that the economic viability of these concepts is poor due to the fact that in such concepts, two systems are provided which essentially perform the same task; a situation which rarely makes economic or ecological sense. As described above, the energy efficiency of double façade concepts depends strongly on the potential to eliminate mechanical systems from the design.

As discussed in chapter five, tall buildings can be employed to increase urban density and contribute to the sustainable development of our cities. However, as mentioned above, high rise buildings have an inherently low operational energy efficiency. This is mainly due to wind-related issues. On account of the increased wind pressures due to height, external solar shading and natural ventilation with operable windows become difficult and thus tall buildings employ mechanical ventilation and air conditioning. Strategies allowing the natural ventilation of tall buildings therefore offer significant potential to improve energy efficiency. If a system of natural ventilation could be refined so as to perform in an acceptable way all year round and mechanical ventilation systems were thus dispensed with, a paradigm shift in the ecological and economic viability of naturally ventilated tall buildings could be the result.

In the 2003 competition for the new headquarters building for the European Central Bank in Frankfurt with Coop Himmelb(l)au architects, a concept was developed which enabled the natural ventilation of an approx. 180 m tall building in an urban location and allowed us to dispense with mechanical systems completely, thus marking a radical departure from conventional skyscraper building design (Fig. 6.20). The building form was strongly influenced by considerations for the maximization of energy performance and the employment of wind and thermal buoyancy to provide all-year-round controlled natural ventilation of the offices. Two – in terms of building energy performance – optimally orientated towers with their main façades facing north/south were placed on the site, positioned so that an effective shading of the first tower is provided by the second. Then, an additional skin was wrapped around the two towers to create a central atrium and double-skin façades on the external sides of the towers.

The atrium façades were designed to act as wind scoops to channel wind from the predominant wind directions into the atrium (Fig. 6.21). Air flows from outside into the atrium and from there across the office floors before leaving the office spaces on the external sides of the towers, thus ensuring effective cross ventilation of the office floors. The double façade on the external sides of the towers also acts as a solar thermal flue. The less dense, warmer air rises up through the flue and is replaced by cooler, heavier air flowing through the office floors (Fig. 6.22). On account of the height of the building, the façade was horizontally divided up into three sections with a height of approximately 60 m each, in order to keep the pressure differences between floors manageable. Dampers in the external skin of the atrium and office façades were provided to control the pressure difference acting across the office floors and so regulate the natural ventilation of the offices. Due to the special design of the "suction elements" in the external façades of the office towers, the pressure coefficient at the air exhaust points is always lower that the pressure coefficient at the air inlet points on the atrium façade, independent of the prevailing wind direction (Fig. 6.23). Functional areas (meeting rooms, recreation zones, communication bridges, lifts etc.) were moved out of the office towers and into the atrium, improving the relationship between gross and net floor area in the towers. The dynamically formed atrium connects the two towers and improves communication within the building complex, creating a vibrant vertical city.

The elimination of mechanical ventilation in the office spaces offers enormous advantages in capital costs and grey energy (mechanical systems, plant rooms, shafts) as well as operating energy savings and main-

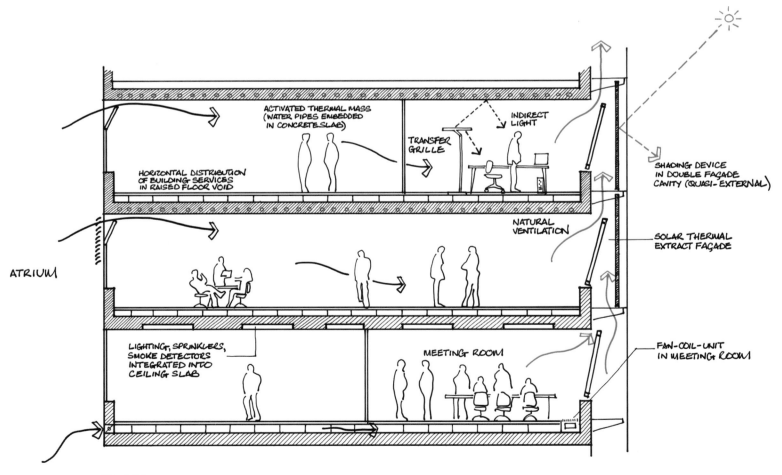

ACTIVATED THERMAL MASS
(WATER PIPES EMBEDDED
IN CONCRETE SLAB)

INDIRECT LIGHT

TRANSFER GRILLE

HORIZONTAL DISTRIBUTION
OF BUILDING SERVICES
IN RAISED FLOOR VOID

SHADING DEVICE
IN DOUBLE FAÇADE
CAVITY (QUASI-EXTERNAL)

NATURAL VENTILATION

SOLAR THERMAL
EXTRACT FAÇADE

ATRIUM

LIGHTING, SPRINKLERS,
SMOKE DETECTORS
INTEGRATED INTO
CEILING SLAB

MEETING ROOM

FAN-COIL-UNIT
IN MEETING ROOM

Fig. 6.22

Fig. 6.22
ECB HQ, climate
control concept

Fig. 6.23
ECB HQ, suction
element, façade

tenance costs. As explained above, all contemporary naturally ventilated high-rise buildings of this height are in fact also provided with mechanical ventilation systems, which are used in extreme weather conditions. This is however wasteful, as the systems thus provided need to be dimensioned for the worst case scenario and are effectively the same systems that would be provided in a sealed, mechanically ventilated building with all the attendant disadvantages of increased capital costs and space required for shafts and plant rooms. The savings potential in maintenance and electrical energy costs is significant, particularly as the systems also tend to be used by the occupants at times when they were not designed to be.

During design development, mechanical ventilation systems were however added, primarily due to building owner concerns regarding reliability and the innovative nature of the proposal. Nevertheless, the ECB building, completed in 2014, is a very good example of an energy-efficient tall building design. The façade incorporates selective glazing, quasi-external automatically controlled movable solar shading and specially designed ventilation elements, which allow natural ventilation during a large part of the year. Waste heat from the buildings data center makes a substantial contribution to meeting the building's heating energy demand. The naturally ventilated atrium is a buffer zone with minimal thermal conditioning, offering spatial and communication potential in the form of a vertical city. Office workers coming and going via the atrium are offered mag-

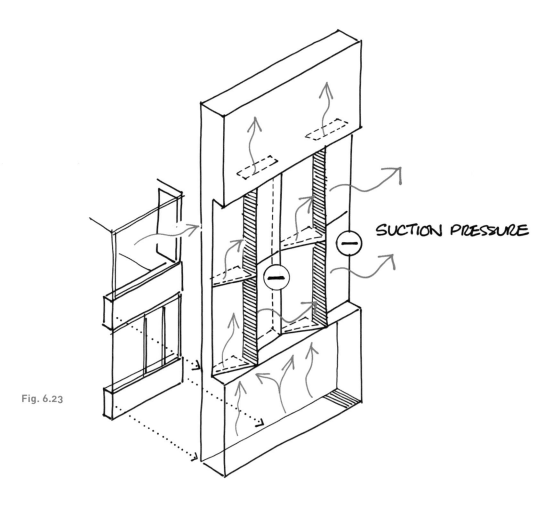

SUCTION PRESSURE

Fig. 6.23

nificent views of the city and a sense of connection with the whole spatial volume enclosing the institution. The location of the lift cores in the atrium also allows more efficient spatial organization of the office towers.

In a research project which expanded on the work done on the concepts for the ECB headquarters and other buildings, a high-rise building typology was developed which allows all-year-round controlled natural ventilation at almost any desired building height. Figure 6.24 shows one compartment of such a structure, which would be composed of many such compartments stacked vertically. The central principle is the controlled use of wind and thermal buoyancy via a central atrium space which can be

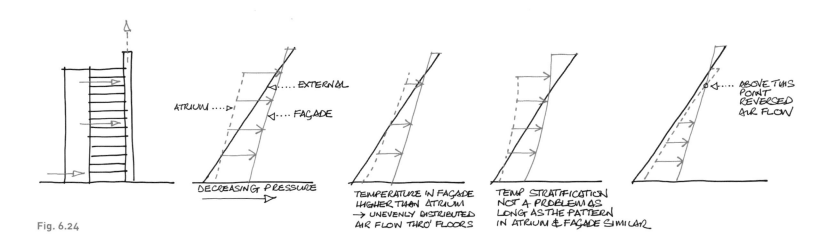

Fig. 6.24

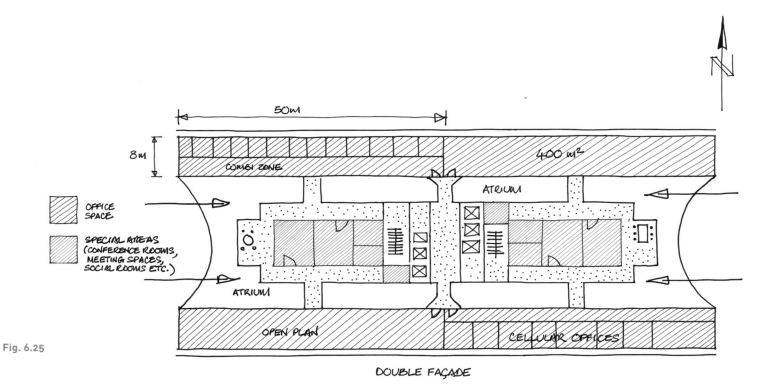

Fig. 6.25

DOUBLE FAÇADE

opened on all building sides and which is combined with a double skin façade system on the external building faces. This research work led on the
one hand to a building structure which would enable year-round optimized
natural ventilation and on the other hand to a specific typological solution,
expressed in the unique configuration of floor plan and section which opens
up an exciting potential of spatial possibilities; an example of new building
form generated by energy performance considerations (Figure 6.25).

Figure 6.26 shows a concept for the ventilation of the lecture theaters and seminar rooms in the new school of management building at the
Fudan University in Shanghai, in collaboration with the architects Miralles
Tagliabue EMBT in Barcelona, which won first prize in the architectural
competition in 2011. In this concept, the driving force for natural ventilation
is the thermal buoyancy generated by the heat gains from the people using
the spaces. Based on analysis of the climatic data for Shanghai, the energy
performance of various system options was compared and a system employing vertical shafts combined with underground ducts to provide thermally induced natural ventilation was subsequently chosen. The thermal
mass of the concrete shafts alongside that of the ground is employed to
assist in temperature regulation. Cooling coils are used in hot weather to
cool and dehumidify the incoming air and are positioned so as to support
the thermal buoyancy driving forces. The system offers savings in capital,
maintenance and energy costs when compared with conventional air conditioning systems.

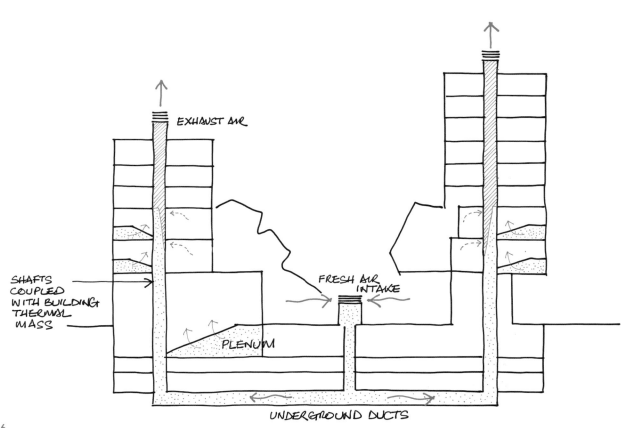

Fig. 6.26

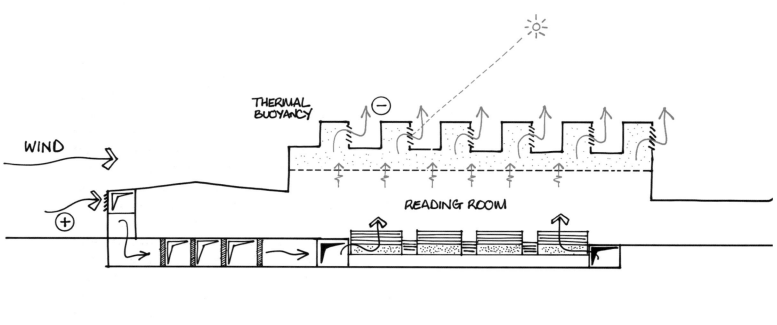

THERMAL
BUOYANCY

WIND

READING ROOM

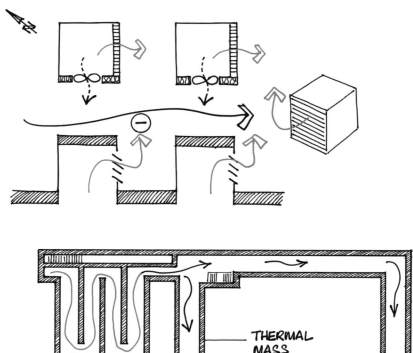

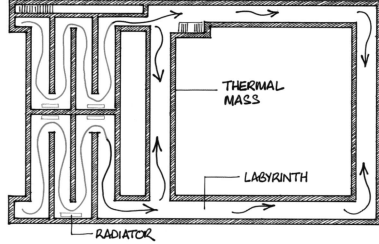

THERMAL
MASS

LABYRINTH

RADIATOR

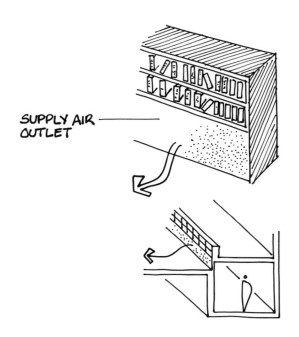

SUPPLY AIR
OUTLET

Fig. 6.27

Fig. 6.27
Adlershof library, Berlin,
energy concept

Fig. 6.28
Adlershof library,
roof elements

The form of the new University Library Building in Adlershof, Berlin with Daniel Goessler architects was developed with the goal of creating a deep-plan reading room which could be naturally lit and naturally ventilated. During the competition in 1998, which we subsequently won, I argued for a central reading space surrounded by bookshelves instead of a configuration with mixed areas of bookshelves and reading spaces. This space could then be naturally ventilated and provided with daylight using a combination of specially developed roof elements and a concrete labyrinth system (Fig. 6.27). In summer, the thermal mass of the labyrinth is cooled at night by the colder night air and acts as a cooling source for the supply air during the warm day, which enters the space via large displacement ventilation outlets. In winter, radiators in the labyrinth preheat the supply air. Both wind and thermal buoyancy forces are used to drive air flow through the space. The system was designed as a hybrid-system, incorporating small fans which support air flow at times when the natural forces are too weak. As it turned out, on this project not all the original environmental concepts were followed through. The daylighting design was retained while the natural ventilation concept was changed to mechanical ventilation. The architectural features which resulted from the concept remained (Fig. 6.28).

The energy efficiency of many building types, currently designed as "windowless boxes" which depend entirely on the use of artificial lighting systems to achieve their purpose such as museums, galleries, exhibition halls, lecture theaters, retail units and many more, could be vastly improved by the incorporation of well-designed daylighting systems. A daylighting system is, of course, more than the provision of transparent areas in the building skin, and in fact the difficulties in designing such systems have led to the proliferation of buildings which deliberately shut out the natural environment and rely on energy-intensive artificial lighting systems. On account of the fact that too much light can damage the exhibition contents, all fenestration is omitted in order to keep daylight out of

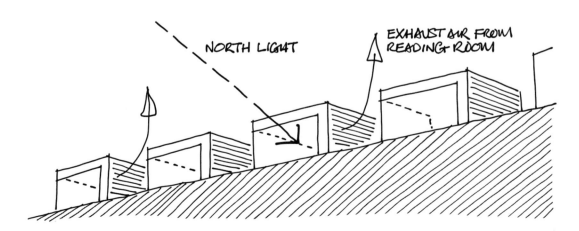

Fig. 6.28

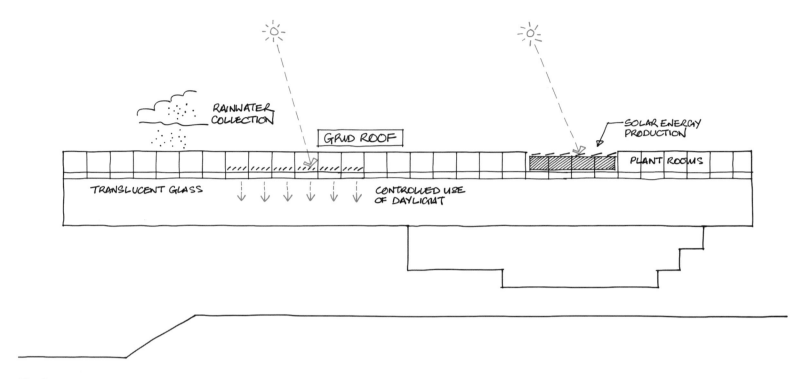

Fig. 6.29

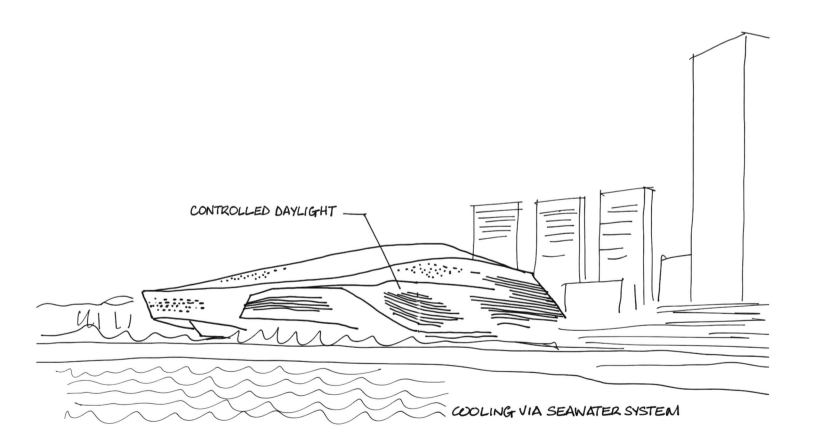

Fig. 6.30

museum and exhibition buildings and the necessary lighting levels are provided by energy-intensive artificial lighting systems. In the competition phase of the MOCAPE exhibition building in Shenzen, China in 2007 with the architect Coop Himmelb(l)au, we developed a "Grid Roof" which incorporates many elements, including energy production and roof gardens (Fig. 6.29). The main function, however, was the controlled use of diffuse daylight in an appropriate manner for exhibition spaces via a multi-layered skin construction incorporating two glass layers and an automatically controlled louver system. In collaboration with the same architects, a similar approach was followed in the design of the International Conference Center in Dalian, China, which was designed after MOCAPE but completed earlier in 2012 (Fig. 6.30). It goes without saying that the design of buildings such as these is complex and requires more effort than the design of conventional buildings. Allowing external forces to infiltrate the building in a controlled manner requires a more sophisticated approach. Nevertheless, the approach of working with, instead of against, natural forces is without doubt the future of building design.

In 2013 we worked with Coop Himmelb(l)au architects to design a residential tower structure in Murray street, Manhattan, NYC, which incorporated an innovative natural ventilation system. At the competition stage, I proposed the use of a double skin façade which would provide a new type of winter garden space (Fig. 6.31). In the outer layer, vertical clear glass louvres could be modulated to react to different conditions relating to wind, noise, security etc. Sliding doors in the inner façade layer,

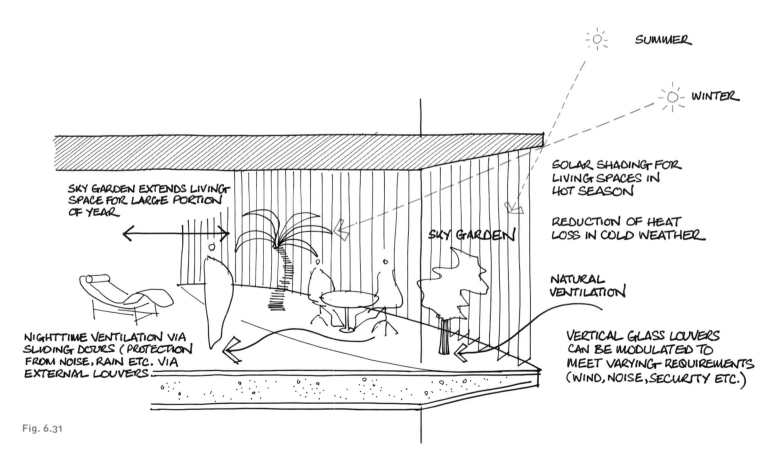

Fig. 6.31

positioned roughly 2 m back from the outer layer, allow the living space to be extended for a large portion of the year. The so-called sky garden acts a buffer zone in cold weather, reducing heat loss and providing solar shading for the living spaces in the hot season. Natural ventilation can be controlled by the modulated opening of the two façade layers. In summer, nighttime cooling can be achieved by opening the sliding doors with protection against noise, rain etc. provided by the external glass louvres, which would be partially opened. The proposed typology offers a new type of living experience in Manhattan; better than a roof garden, much better than a balcony. The streamlined building form developed also gives optimized aerodynamic performance and improved pedestrian comfort. Figure 6.32 shows the site plan with data relating to sun, wind and noise emissions. Figure 6.33 shows the wind flow patterns and pressure distribution around the building for wind from the north-west.

After winning the competition, the design was developed. The idea of the winter garden as an inhabitable space was given up, as the real estate developer preferred to maximize the conventional living space and instead we developed a system with controlled air inlets to the building via elements in the façade which we called "The Lungs" and air distribution to the spaces in the residential units via a horizontal bulkhead element which we called "The Belt" (Fig. 6.34). The external skin of "The Lungs" comprises fixed glass louvers and air inlet elements (Fig. 6.35). A finned convector heating element incorporated in the bulkhead heats the air in cold weather

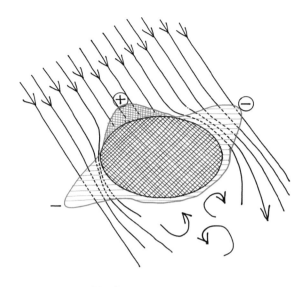

Fig. 6.33

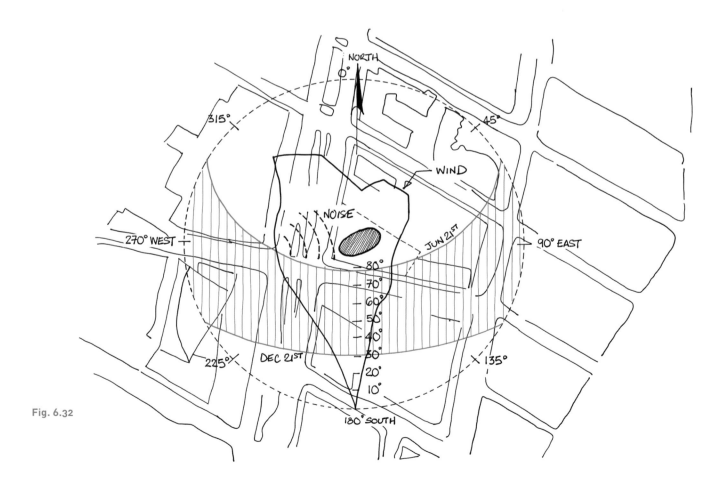

Fig. 6.32

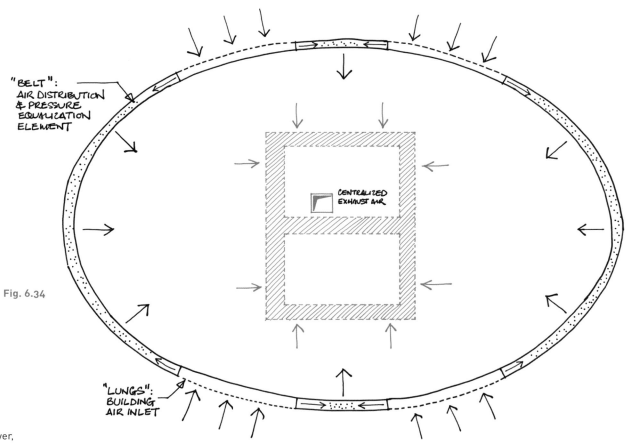

"BELT": AIR DISTRIBUTION & PRESSURE EQUALIZATION ELEMENT

CENTRALIZED EXHAUST AIR

Fig. 6.34

"LUNGS": BUILDING AIR INLET

Fig. 6.32
Residential tower,
NYC, site plan

Fig. 6.33
Residential tower, NYC,
wind flow around building

Fig. 6.34
Residential tower, NYC, air
flow diagram, floor plan

Fig. 6.35
Residential tower,
NYC, "Lungs"

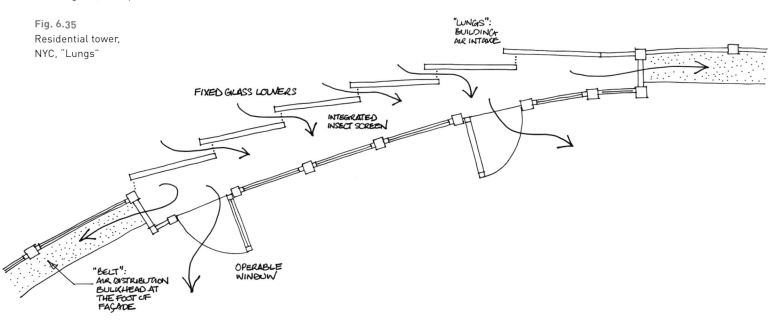

"LUNGS": BUILDING AIR INTAKE

FIXED GLASS LOUVERS

INTEGRATED INSECT SCREEN

"BELT": AIR DISTRIBUTION BULKHEAD AT THE FOOT OF FAÇADE

OPERABLE WINDOW

Fig. 6.35

before entry into the space (Fig. 6.36). Operable windows in the internal layer of the lungs element also allow increased natural ventilation, manually operated by the occupants. Pressure equalization is achieved by "The Belt", so that the pressure differences are kept to a manageable level. Air leaves the building via a centralized stack effect-assisted mechanical extract system with heat recovery.

Fig. 6.37 shows one of the challenges that every tall building with a system of natural ventilation must meet. The greater pressure differences caused by increasing wind speed at height have to be dissipated within the air flow path through the building when elements for natural ventilation are opened on two sides of the building with different pressure coefficients. In a normal building, the entire pressure differential can act across a single door and be of such magnitude that some occupants may not be able to open the door – with obvious negative implications for safety in an emergency situation. In this design, "The Lungs" reduce the pressure difference and "The Belt" serves to equalize pressure within the façade cavity. The natural ventilation elements in the outer layer of the façade are clearly articulated in the architectural design (Fig. 6.38). Similar to fish gills, these are the elements which allow the building to breathe in a controlled way.

An older example, and in fact the first project on which I collaborated on with Coop Himmelb(l)au architects, perhaps illustrates the principle of using natural forces most graphically. In the 2002 competition for the Grand Egyptian Museum in Giza, Egypt, near the pyramids, my idea from the outset was to use the large roof area to generate the required energy to cool the building. The first approach was a high-tech photovoltaic roof. However, after my first meeting with Coop Himmelb(l)au, we decided to follow a more low-tech approach, using a black stone roof (Fig. 6.39) de-

Fig. 6.36

SUPPLY AIR

FINNED CONVECTOR

AIR DISTRIBUTION PLENUM

RADIANT FLOOR

Fig. 6.37

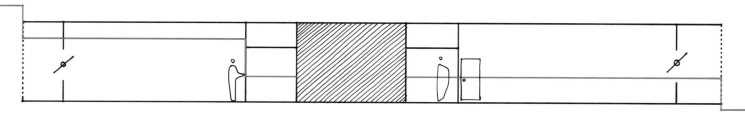

PRESSURE DISTRIBUTION AT HIGH WIND SPEED WITH OPEN WINDOWS & DOORS

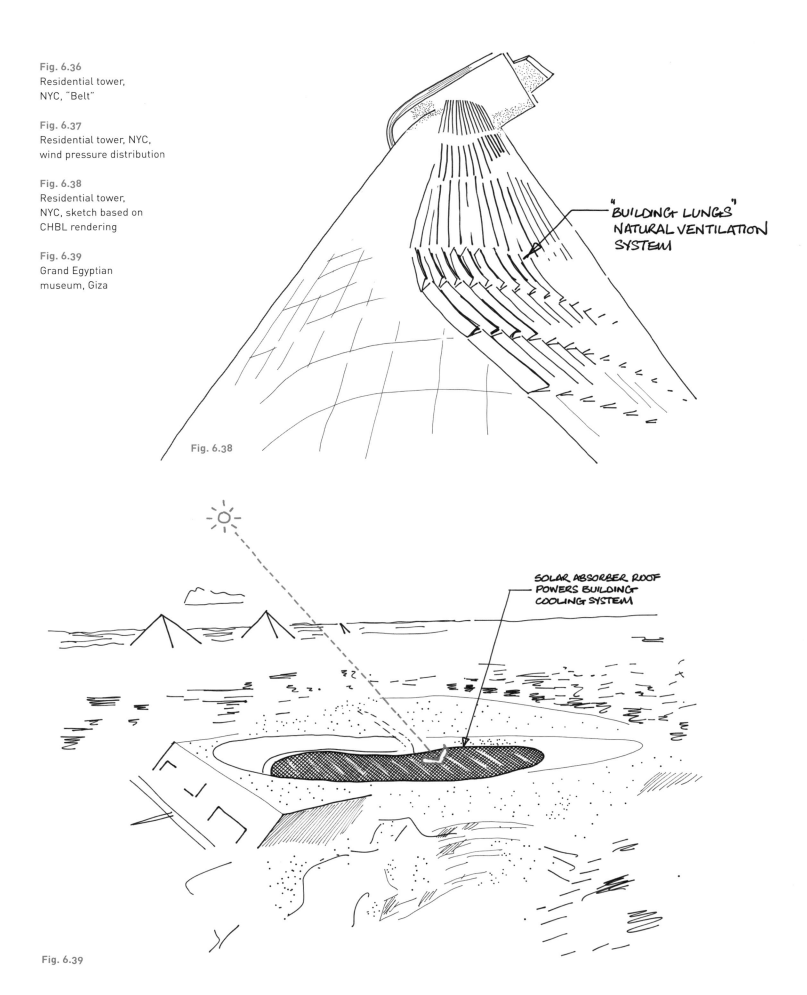

Fig. 6.36
Residential tower,
NYC, "Belt"

Fig. 6.37
Residential tower, NYC,
wind pressure distribution

Fig. 6.38
Residential tower,
NYC, sketch based on
CHBL rendering

Fig. 6.39
Grand Egyptian
museum, Giza

"BUILDING LUNGS"
NATURAL VENTILATION
SYSTEM

Fig. 6.38

SOLAR ABSORBER ROOF
POWERS BUILDING
COOLING SYSTEM

Fig. 6.39

signed to absorb solar radiation. Return air from the conditioned spaces is fed through a cavity in the double skin roof construction, heating the air to a temperature sufficient for it to power a heat-driven cooling system. The thermodynamic principles employed are shown in Fig. 6.40. The incoming air is dehumidified by a desiccant wheel rotating between the extract and supply air streams. Indirect evaporative cooling is achieved by spraying water into the return air and by means of a rotating heat transfer wheel using the return air to cool the incoming outdoor air. Further cooling of the supply air is achieved by direct evaporative cooling in the supply air stream. The heat energy needed to regenerate the desiccant wheel is supplied by the hot air from the roof. The more intensive the solar radiation on the hot black roof in the desert is, the higher the cooling capacity of the system. This type of approach is unconventional, and at first sight counterintuitive. If conventional design can be thought of as trying to overcome nature using brute force, this approach is similar to the one used in some Asian martial arts – capture the force of your opponent and re-direct it to achieve your aims. As briefly mentioned in the opening paragraphs, the forces which seem to constitute the problem, e.g. wind in a skyscraper, light in a museum, solar radiation in a hot climate, can be put to work as

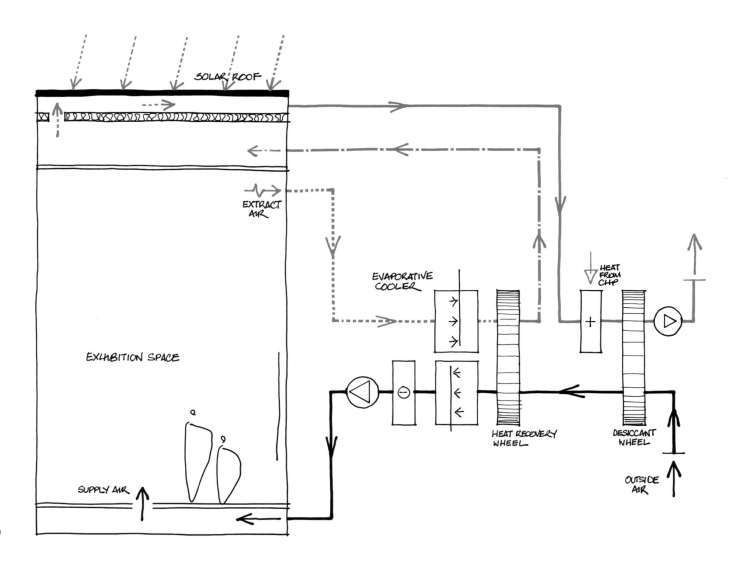

Fig. 6.40

Fig. 6.40
Grand Egyptian
museum, energy
concept

Fig. 6.41
Patna Museum,
India

the forces which help us achieve the desired result. Unfortunately we did not win this competition, which turned out to be one of the largest architectural competitions ever held with more than 1500 entries; but we did receive second prize.

On the competition entry for the Patna Museum in India with Coop Himmelb(l)au architects in 2011, we again turned to the sun as a source of cooling. The external layer of a double skin concrete roof including a selective coating is utilized to capture solar heat energy which is transported away by integrated air ducts and used to power the building's cooling system. In a secondary system, the treated air flows through the inner layer of the concrete construction to activate the exposed thermal mass before entering the space (Fig. 6.41). The activation of the thermal mass of the floor and ceiling slabs via the supply air system allows radiant cooling of the spaces.

A similar approach was used in a proposal for a healthcare facility in Doha with Delugan Meissl Associated Architects (DMAA) in Vienna in 2013 (Fig. 6.42). The exterior surface of the double-skinned concrete construction is specially treated with very thin, spectrally selective coatings – so that the solar absorptivity is very high (approx. 90 %) and the emissivity for long wave radiation is low (< 25 %) – and covered with an outer glass layer.

A further example of a solar-powered cooling system is provided by the proposal for the Dubai Design District in 2014, with Coop Himmelb(l)au. On this project, we decided to reinterpret traditional typologies with a composition of individual buildings which house retail, showroom and workshop units, creating a dense network of urban streets. The energy roof is again a glass-covered black concrete solar absorber construction,

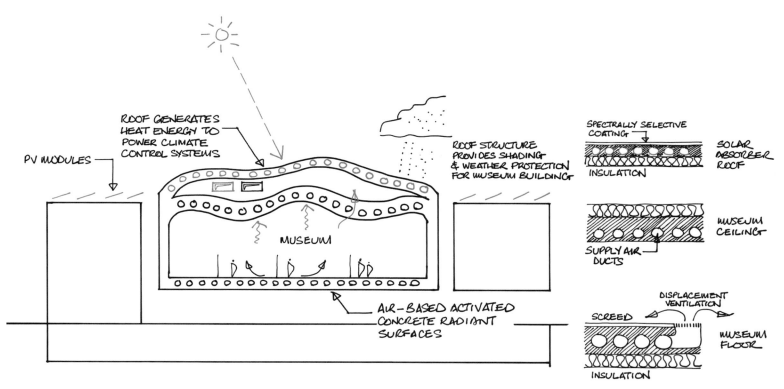

Fig. 6.41

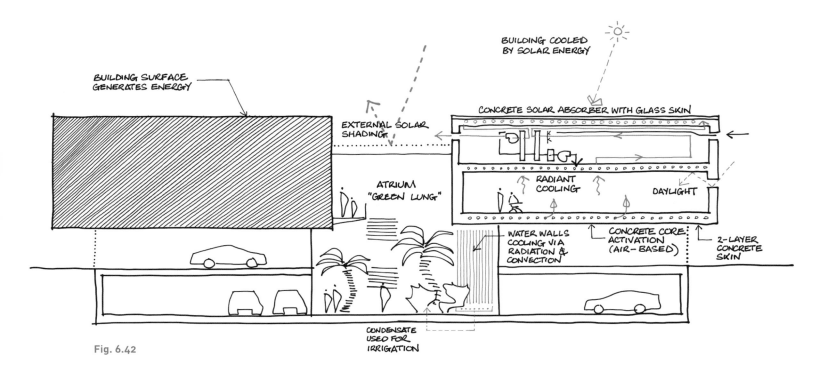

BUILDING SURFACE
GENERATES ENERGY

BUILDING COOLED
BY SOLAR ENERGY

CONCRETE SOLAR ABSORBER WITH GLASS SKIN

EXTERNAL SOLAR
SHADING

ATRIUM
"GREEN LUNG"

RADIANT
COOLING

DAYLIGHT

WATER WALLS
COOLING VIA
RADIATION &
CONVECTION

CONCRETE CORE
ACTIVATION
(AIR-BASED)

2-LAYER
CONCRETE
SKIN

CONDENSATE
USED FOR
IRRIGATION

Fig. 6.42

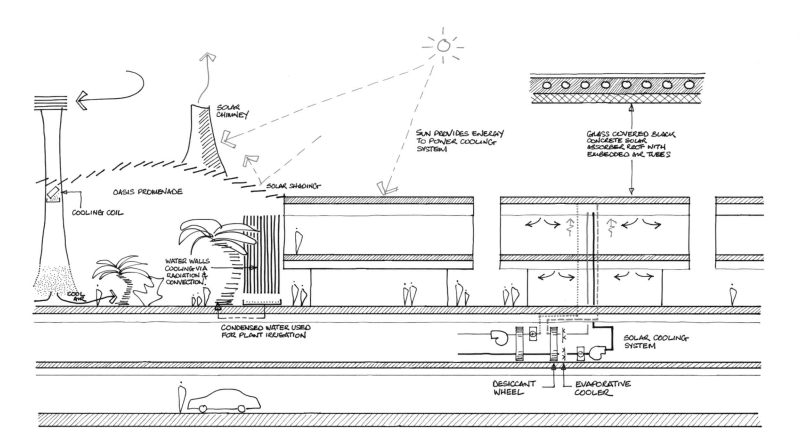

SOLAR
CHIMNEY

SUN PROVIDES ENERGY
TO POWER COOLING
SYSTEM

GLASS COVERED BLACK
CONCRETE SOLAR
ABSORBER ROOF WITH
EMBEDDED AIR TUBES

OASIS PROMENADE

SOLAR SHADING

COOLING COIL

WATER WALLS
COOLING VIA
RADIATION &
CONVECTION

COOL
AIR

CONDENSED WATER USED
FOR PLANT IRRIGATION

SOLAR COOLING
SYSTEM

DESICCANT
WHEEL

EVAPORATIVE
COOLER

Fig. 6.43

activated with an embedded network of air tubes. At nighttime, the structural composition of the creative community complex reveals itself from an aerial view in the form of light emanating from the street network through the expansive black roof, almost like cracks of light in a sea of black polished marble (Fig. 6.43). Running through the whole development is the "Oasis Promenade", essentially a shaded outdoor space with a pleasant microclimate created by a variety of measures including wind towers (designed to capture the prevalent winds and, after cooling, channel the air down into the occupied zone via textile ducts), solar chimneys (providing effective extraction of hot exhaust air) and "Water Walls" (providing cooling via convection and radiation, with the condensed water used for the irrigation of plants in the promenade).

Figure 6.44 shows the schematic arrangement of the technical approach used on these projects. Incoming air is dried by a silica gel-coated desiccant wheel. The temperature of the extract air is lowered by evaporative cooling and an energy recovery wheel is used to transfer sensible heat from the supply to the extract air stream, thus cooling the incoming air. The exhaust air is heated by the solar roof and/or waste heat from another source, e.g. on the Dubai design district project by an on-site CHP system, and used to regenerate the desiccant wheel before being discharged to the atmosphere.

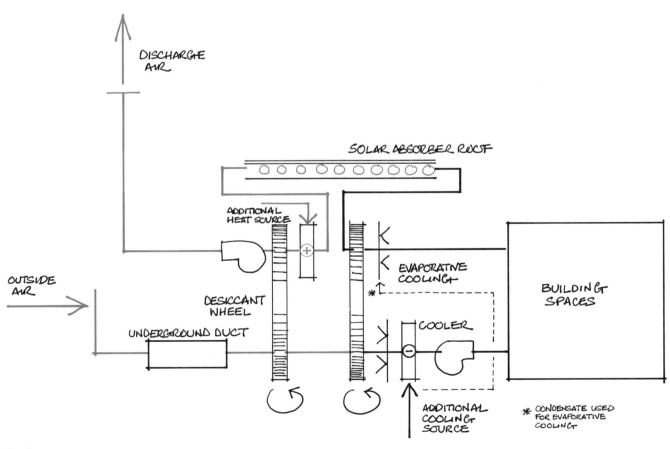

Fig. 6.44

Figure 6.45 shows the site plan of a large house in Doha, developed in collaboration with OMA architects in 2012. The house was conceived as a composition of different microclimates under a large roof. Figure 6.46 shows the concept of superimposed vertical and horizontal thermal zoning strategies. The multifunctional roof incorporates a concrete solar absorber, thermal solar collectors, photovoltaic modules and daylighting elements. To provide a pleasant microclimate in the "in-between spaces", a concept employing "Water Walls" for cooling and dehumidification in combination with natural ventilation was developed (Fig. 6.47). The energy source for cooling is provided by the solar absorber roof in a similar way

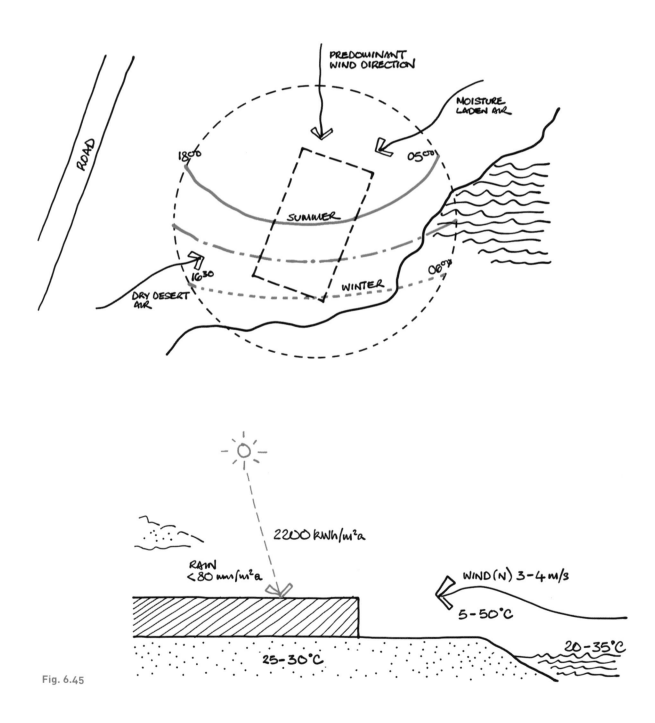

Fig. 6.45

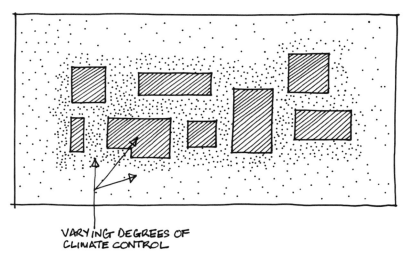

VARYING DEGREES OF
CLIMATE CONTROL

SUPERIMPOSED VERTICAL
AND HORIZONTAL
ZONING STRATEGIES

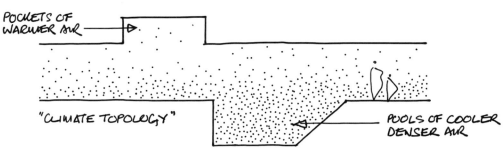

POCKETS OF
WARMER AIR

"CLIMATE TOPOLOGY"

POOLS OF COOLER
DENSER AIR

Fig. 6.46

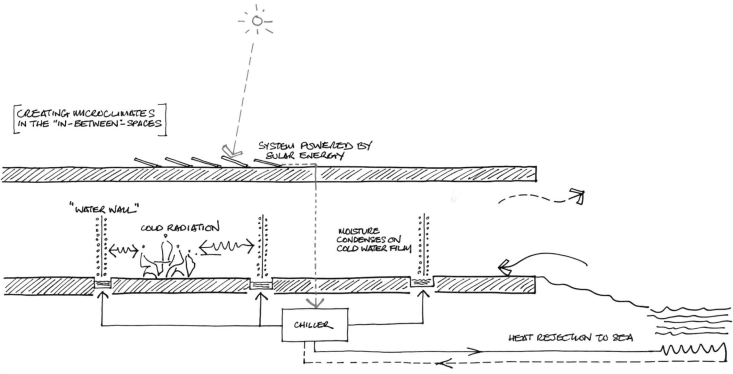

CREATING MICROCLIMATES
IN THE "IN-BETWEEN"-SPACES

SYSTEM POWERED BY
SOLAR ENERGY

"WATER WALL"

COLD RADIATION

MOISTURE
CONDENSES ON
COLD WATER FILM

CHILLER

HEAT REJECTION TO SEA

Fig. 6.47

to the projects just described. Figure 6.48 shows an alternative concept in which decentral heat pumps are used to cool the spaces, providing cool dry air directly to the rooms without the use of ducted air systems, and rejecting the heat at the roof level of well-shaded glass enclosed gardens which punctuate the space at regular intervals. A network of underground tubes supplies outdoor air to these garden elements, and from there into the living spaces. The rejected heat from the cooling process is used to drive the air circulation in the spaces by thermal buoyancy. The energy is supplied from photovoltaic modules integrated into the roof design.

Solar energy also powers the climate control concept for the New Parliamentary Building in Tirana, Albania with Coop Himmelb(l)au architects, which won first prize in the architectural competition in 2011. The air conditioning system for the main hall employs desiccant dehumidification and indirect evaporative cooling to condition the supply air using solar energy supplied via hot water from the south-facing energy generating surface of the building's façade structure. Outside air is taken in at high level, treated, dropped to the floor level of the hall in a massive heavyweight shaft and supplied into a plenum located underneath the seating in the hall. Thermal buoyancy effects are used to support the circulation of air in the space (Fig. 6.49). The height of the volume is used to allow temperature stratification to take place. In the unoccupied part of the volume at high level, higher temperatures can be tolerated. This reduces the size of the conditioned volume and allows thermal buoyancy to drive the ventilation, both effects contributing significantly to energy efficiency. A second skin is wrapped around the office building and specially configured to improve building performance with regard to optimum daylight use, views, solar control, glare protection, thermal insulation, natural ventilation and noise protection. The exact configuration of the envelope form and the degree of skin perforation varies according to the orientation of the various façades.

In the conceptual approach for a new convention center building in Baku with Coop Himmelb(l)au, the special form and structure of the external envelope was also designed to capture solar heat energy which is used

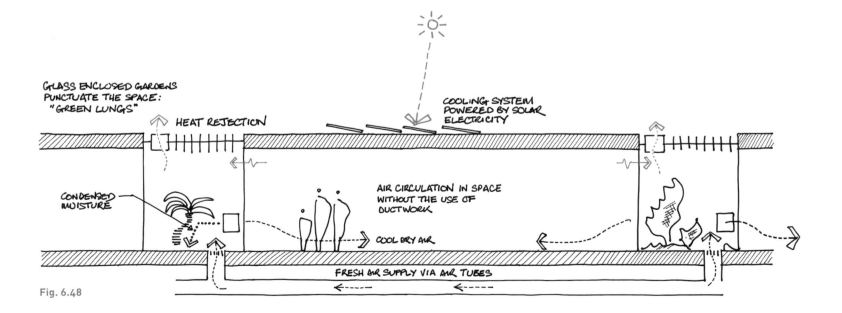

Fig. 6.48

to power the building's cooling system, while at the same time optimizing solar protection, the use of natural daylight and natural ventilation in the spaces (Fig. 6.50). On the north side (the predominant wind direction) the skin "scales" are configured to form an air inlet area, to allow air to enter the building in a controlled manner using the natural pressure differences caused by wind and thermal buoyancy. After flowing through a heating/cooling coil and filter system, where the air is conditioned and cleaned, the air enters a system of underground ducts, from where it is distributed throughout the lobby spaces. In milder weather, the air can be tempered by the thermal mass of the concrete ducts and the earth alone. Exhaust air leaves the space at high level though outlets in the roof structure.

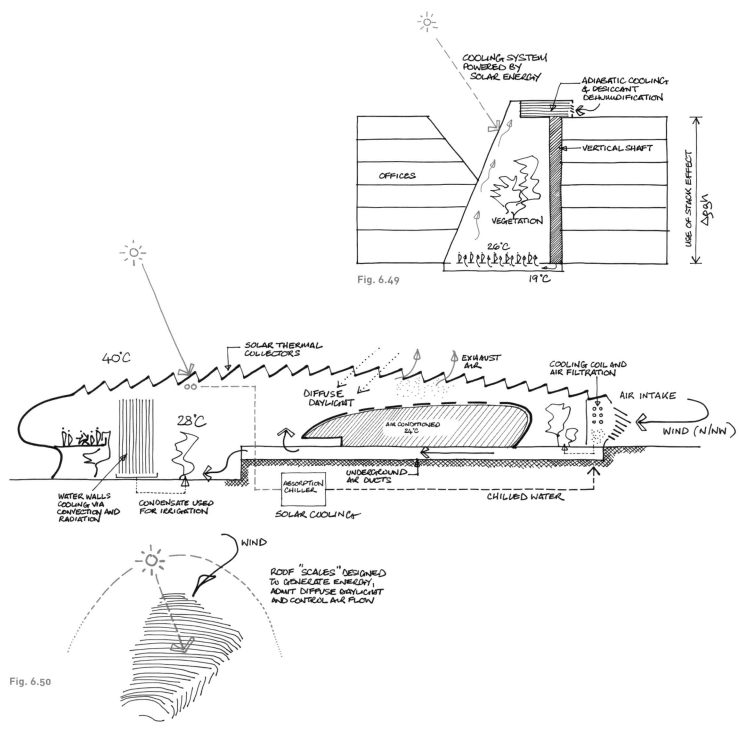

Fig. 6.49

Fig. 6.50

199

The next example shows an entirely different way of cooling a building based on biological principles found in nature. For the EXPO 2000 in Hanover, the Duales System company, a provider of take-back packaging systems, wanted a pavilion which avoids overheating without resort to conventional air conditioning, in line with their corporate philosophy of a closed ecological loop. The anticipated large number of visitors in the summer months and the high internal loads due to the exhibition lighting and equipment, together with the wish that the pavilion could be dismantled after the EXPO and rebuilt somewhere else, provided quite a challenge. Conventional thermal mass in the form of a heavyweight building structure was obviously not an option. The design, developed with Atelier Brueckner in Stuttgart, responds to this challenge with the provision of thermal mass which can be easily transported (Fig. 6.51). Water tanks, which can be emptied and re-filled after moving to a new location, were integrated into the spiraling exhibition ramp (Fig. 6.52). Spray nozzles incorporated into the façade allowed water to be sprayed from the façade at night and thus cooled by evaporation (Fig. 6.53). This water was circulated in a secondary circuit coupled to the water tanks by means of heat-exchanging tubing. The thermal mass could thus be activated and cooling energy regenerated. Similar to the way humans and some animals perspire to lose heat in warm conditions, the building "sweats". In the case of the pavilion, this does not occur as a direct response to overheating as is the case in the natural world, but at nighttime when it is cooler, in order to regenerate itself for the anticipated hot day ahead. The concept of an ecological closed loop embodied in the concept matched the corporate philosophy of the company so well that they decided to include it in the exhibition. The climate control and energy concepts became part of the exhibition, including monitors with touch screens which allowed visitors to interact with the

Fig. 6.51

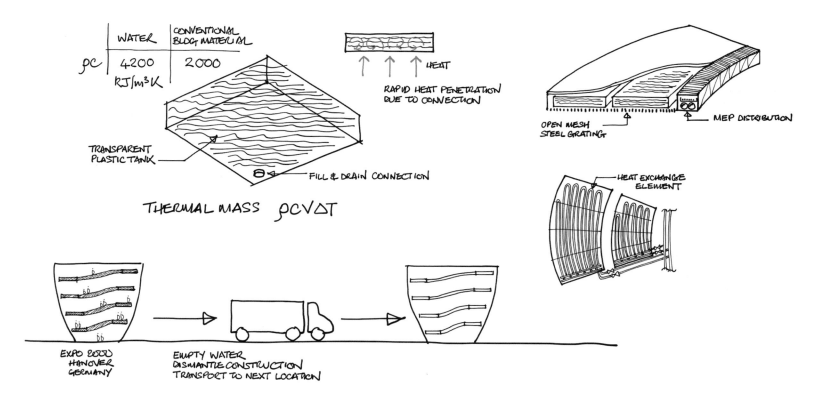

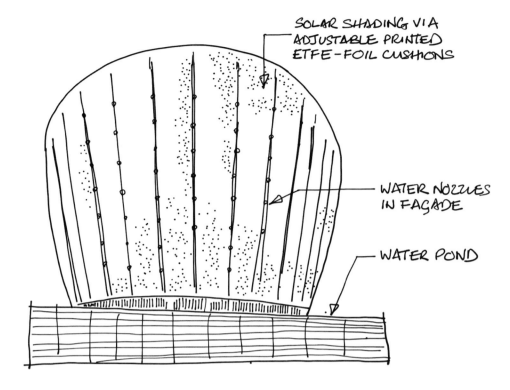

SOLAR SHADING VIA
ADJUSTABLE PRINTED
ETFE-FOIL CUSHIONS

WATER NOZZLES
IN FAÇADE

WATER POND

Fig. 6.53

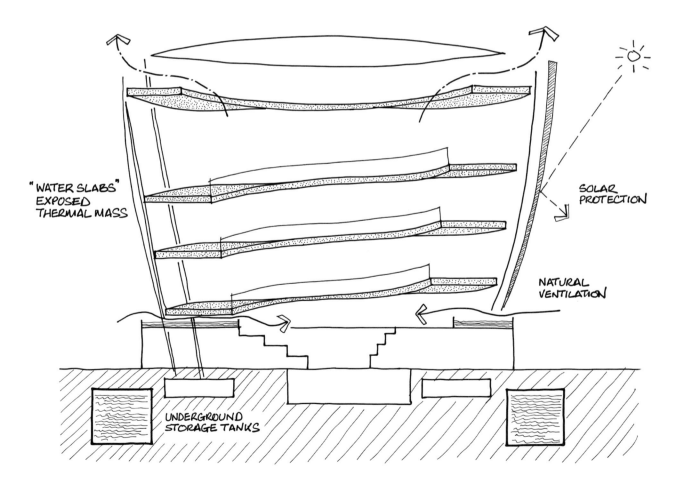

"WATER SLABS"
EXPOSED
THERMAL MASS

SOLAR
PROTECTION

NATURAL
VENTILATION

UNDERGROUND
STORAGE TANKS

Fig. 6.52

building and its systems and take part in a virtual simulation of the buildings energy systems, whereby the effect of changing parameters such as the nighttime evaporative cooling system operation could be experienced, or data on the real-time operation of the systems viewed. Here, the influence of the energy design did not stop at the architecture of the building containing the exhibition, but became a part of the exhibition itself.

In recent decades, many efforts have been undertaken in an attempt to reduce the negative impact of our buildings on the environment. However, design professionals and industry seem to be preoccupied with protective functions. This becomes apparent if we pause to reflect on the terms used to describe the functions and elements of the building skin – solar protection, wind protection, insulation, vapor barrier etc. Perhaps there are psychological aspects involved. Is the need to insulate, isolate and protect ourselves from the external environment driven by other concerns rather than purely energy issues? In any case, it is time for a paradigm change. We need to use the natural forces, not just protect ourselves against them. We need to develop buildings which not only minimize their negative impact but maximize positive impact. **Buildings which give,** not just take; buildings which clean the air in the atmosphere and provide clean water and energy to the surrounding urban area – buildings as power plants.

For the competition proposal for the new opera house in Guangzhou with Coop Himmelb(l)au in 2003, the interaction of incident solar radiation with the building envelope was analyzed in order to determine the optimal degree of transparency for the various modules in the building skin, depending on their position within the skin; i.e. their orientation and tilt angle (Fig. 6.54). The glass skin incorporates photovoltaic cells which help to shade the internal public areas and at the same time generate electricity for use within the building. The degree of transparency of the individual modules depends on the annual solar intensity for the particular position of the module concerned, thus giving a texture to the appearance of the building skin.

Fig. 6.54

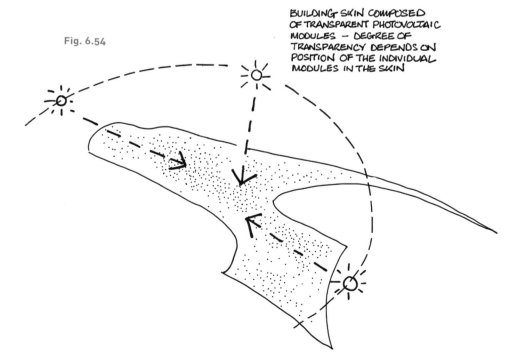

BUILDING SKIN COMPOSED OF TRANSPARENT PHOTOVOLTAIC MODULES – DEGREE OF TRANSPARENCY DEPENDS ON POSITION OF THE INDIVIDUAL MODULES IN THE SKIN

A similar approach was used in the design of the Beethoven Halle concert hall in Bonn in a 2008 competition proposal with Zaha Hadid architects in London. By superimposing the values calculated for the varying effectiveness of photovoltaic cells for different tilt angles and orientations onto a pattern of opaque and transparent panels in the building skin, an interesting appearance was arrived at, while at the same time optimizing energy performance (Fig. 6.55). At this location, groundwater can be used effectively for cooling and heating the building (Fig. 6.56).

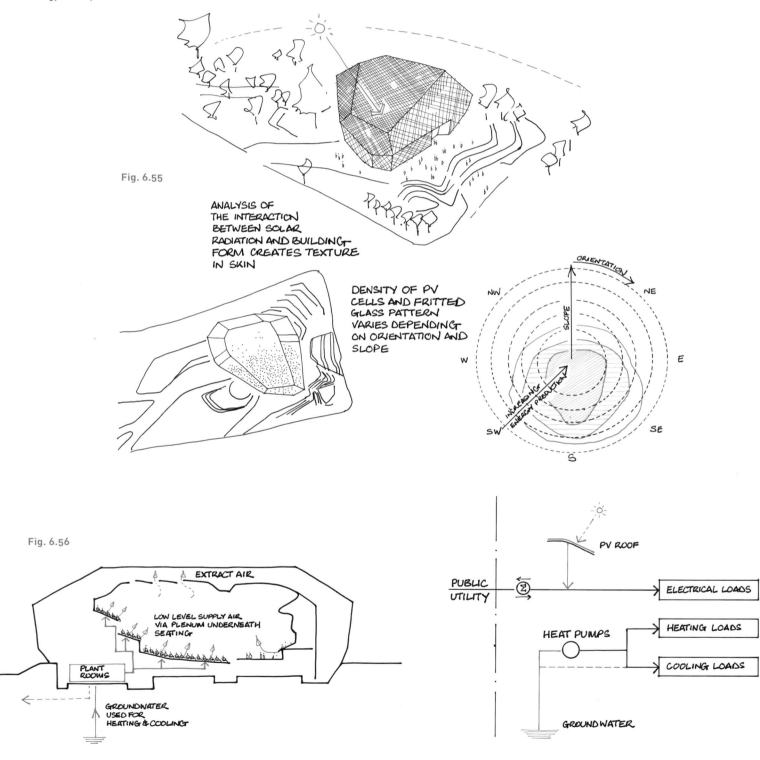

Fig. 6.55

ANALYSIS OF THE INTERACTION BETWEEN SOLAR RADIATION AND BUILDING FORM CREATES TEXTURE IN SKIN

DENSITY OF PV CELLS AND FRITTED GLASS PATTERN VARIES DEPENDING ON ORIENTATION AND SLOPE

Fig. 6.56

EXTRACT AIR

LOW LEVEL SUPPLY AIR VIA PLENUM UNDERNEATH SEATING

PLANT ROOMS

GROUNDWATER USED FOR HEATING & COOLING

PV ROOF

PUBLIC UTILITY

ELECTRICAL LOADS

HEAT PUMPS

HEATING LOADS

COOLING LOADS

GROUNDWATER

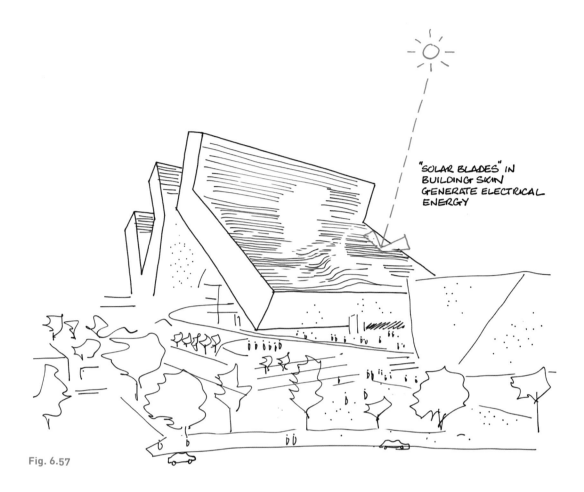

"SOLAR BLADES" IN BUILDING SKIN GENERATE ELECTRICAL ENERGY

Fig. 6.57

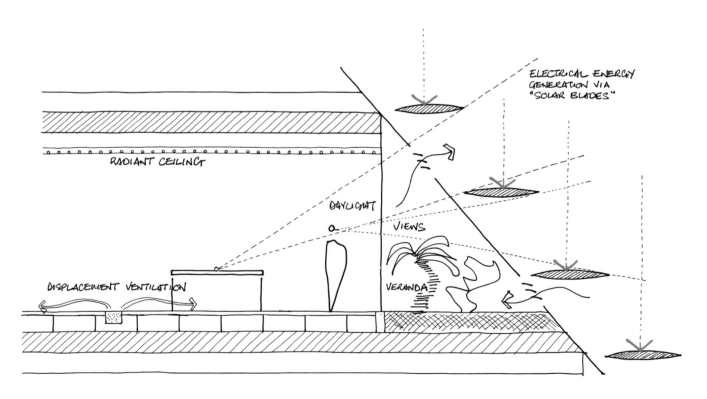

ELECTRICAL ENERGY GENERATION VIA "SOLAR BLADES"

RADIANT CEILING

DAYLIGHT

VIEWS

VERANDA

DISPLACEMENT VENTILATION

Fig. 6.58

Fig. 6.57
Office tower for Singapore,
based on CHBL rendering

Fig. 6.58
Office tower for
Singapore, concept

Figures 6.57 and 6.58 show a concept for a tall building in Singapore with Coop Himmelb(l)au architects, also designed in 2008, in which the geometry of the proposed building form enables year-round energy production at this equatorial location via specially designed "solar blades" with integrated photovoltaic modules, while at the same time avoiding mutual shading and allowing simultaneous daylight usage and views. The main façades are orientated north and south, which is the optimal orientation of a building in Singapore in terms of energy performance. The well insulated technical cores are located on the east and west sides, in order to eliminate low angle solar gain to the office areas and further improve performance. The multi-layered skin construction enables the users to remain in contact with the external environment and creates a thermal buffer zone, providing protection against rain and noise and reducing infiltration. Planting in the buffer zones provides shading and improves air quality.

The concepts for the Bank Austria Campus in Vienna, in collaboration with Boris Podrecca Architects, which won the first prize in the architectural competition in 2011, were developed with the goal of designing a zero-energy building with regard to thermal energy needs on a dense site in the city of Vienna. An energy-generating roof landscape, comprising sloped roof surfaces clad in photovoltaic modules and green roof areas which help to cool the photovoltaic modules and thus improve their performance, is combined with a large geothermal energy system to supply the necessary energy for the heating and cooling systems (Fig. 6.59). At the same time, energy demand is minimized by an optimized configuration of the building form and an optimized façade and HVAC system design (Fig. 6.60).

In 2013 in collaboration with Coop Himmelb(l)au architects, we developed an energy concept for the former Intercontinental hotel site with a popular outdoor ice skating area in Vienna. A large part of the building is lifted up to hover over and thus maximize the outdoor ice skating area. Energy production via photovoltaic modules is integrated into both the roof and the underside of the building volume. Adjustable mirrors are used together with the ice surface to reflect sunlight onto the building's underside and thus maximize the surface area available for energy production (Fig. 6.61).

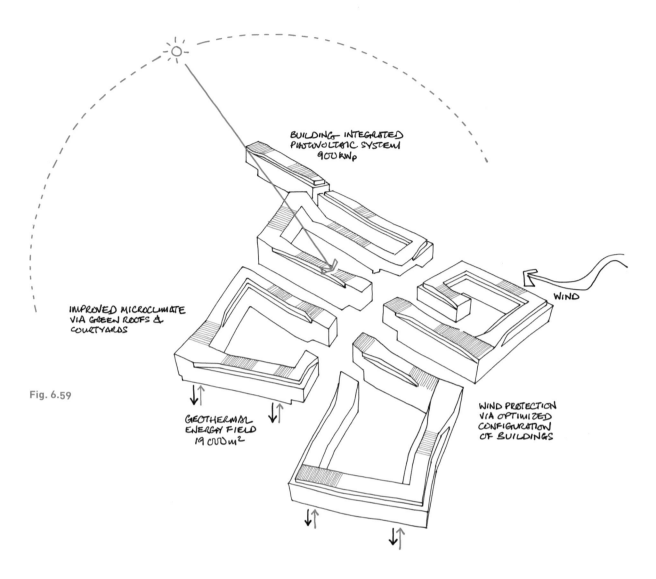

BUILDING INTEGRATED PHOTOVOLTAIC SYSTEM 900 kWp

IMPROVED MICROCLIMATE VIA GREEN ROOFS & COURTYARDS

WIND

Fig. 6.59

GEOTHERMAL ENERGY FIELD 19 000 m²

WIND PROTECTION VIA OPTIMIZED CONFIGURATION OF BUILDINGS

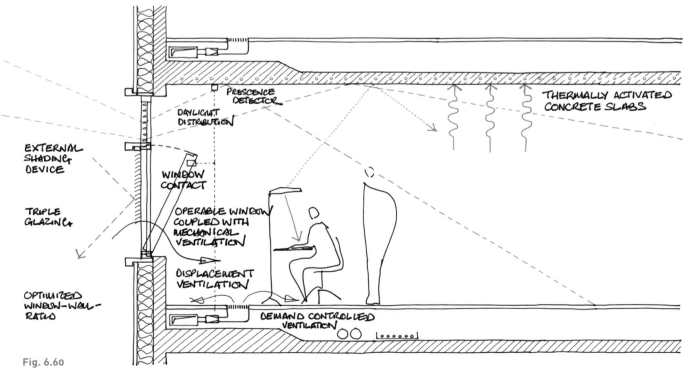

THERMALLY ACTIVATED CONCRETE SLABS

PRESCENCE DETECTOR

DAYLIGHT DISTRIBUTION

EXTERNAL SHADING DEVICE

WINDOW CONTACT

TRIPLE GLAZING

OPERABLE WINDOW COUPLED WITH MECHANICAL VENTILATION

DISPLACEMENT VENTILATION

OPTIMIZED WINDOW-WALL-RATIO

DEMAND CONTROLLED VENTILATION

Fig. 6.60

Alongside minimizing energy demand and maximizing building-integrated renewable energy production, another major challenge is the need to develop innovative energy storage systems. The proposed design for Central Park Taopu in Shanghai, China, developed in collaboration with DMAA in 2014, is a hybrid composition of nature, water systems, public space for city residents, buildings, renewable energy technology and innovative energy storage systems, providing a recreation and leisure area with pleasant microclimatic conditions and clean air for people living and working in the area. The vast majority of the energy required for the operation of the park, including the buildings which are located underneath the park, is generated by renewable sources on-site. A large-scale solar electrical system comprising photovoltaic modules is integrated into the park landscape with optimized orientation and tilt angle to maximize energy production at this location. The efficiency of the modules is increased in hot weather by a water cooling system forming an integrated part of the park's water systems design. As discussed in chapter four, national grid systems are increasingly coming under pressure to cope with wide variations of supply and demand, and thus future-orientated solutions look to integrated energy storage on-site. Conventional methods of storing elec-

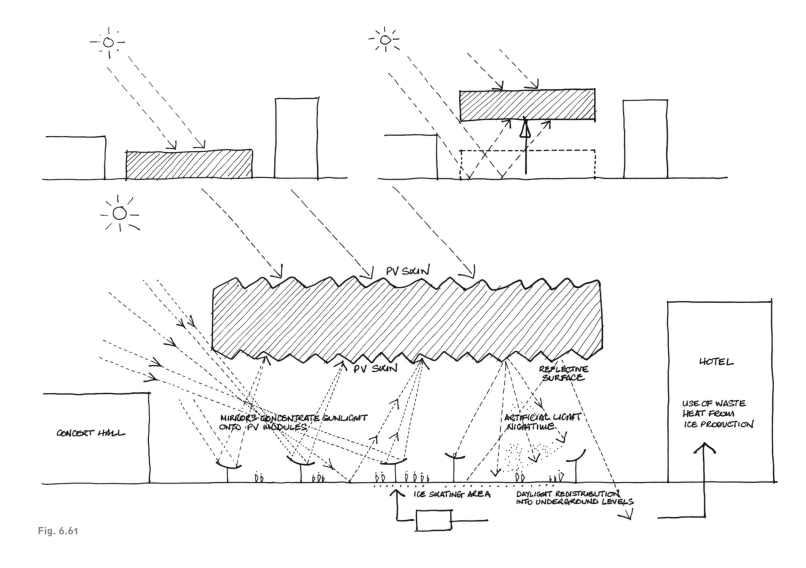

Fig. 6.61

OPTIMALLY ORIENTATED
PV MODULES & LED
LIGHTING INTEGRATED
INTO TOWER STRUCTURE

Fig. 6.62

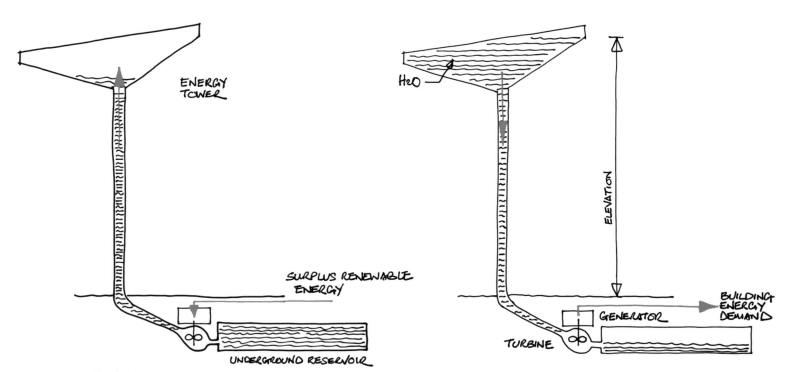

ENERGY TOWER

SURPLUS RENEWABLE ENERGY

UNDERGROUND RESERVOIR

H₂O

ELEVATION

BUILDING ENERGY DEMAND

GENERATOR

TURBINE

Fig. 6.63

tricity such as batteries are possible, but introduce problems related to embodied energy, durability and cost as well as disposal issues. For Central Park Taopu, we developed a unique solution which utilizes the potential energy of elevated water mass in the form of water towers, which are integrated into the park landscape as a form of iconic eye-catching element that also gives the park a visible and easily recognizable identity within the whole region (Fig. 6.62). At times when production exceeds demand, excess electrical energy is utilized to pump water into the towers, where the water is then stored at a substantial elevated height (approx. 100 m) in relation to the counterpart storage reservoir located in the vicinity underground. At times of low or no solar radiation, energy can then be supplied by releasing water from the towers to drive a turbine generator set and supply the building's energy demand (Fig. 6.63).

A similar energy storage system was designed for the new Botanical Garden in Taiyuan, also in collaboration with DMAA, briefly introduced in chapter four (Fig. 6.64). The system helps to smooth load variations on the site power grid, which is supplied with energy from a large solar electric system and a biomass CHP plant, permitting the base-load CHP plant to operate continuously at peak efficiency. The diagram shows electrical energy generated by the on-site renewable energy sources together with the anticipated building electrical energy demand during a period of four days in summer (Fig. 6.65). At times when supply is greater than demand, the excess energy is used to pump water into the storage towers. This stored energy is then used to match demand at times when the demand is greater than the supply.

These projects are intended to act as demonstration projects to illustrate the possibilities and opportunities in dealing with the challenges facing our society in general and cities in particular. In both projects, integrated LED lighting is proposed on the tower's external surface to visualize the energy storage system, indicating the energy level situation at any particular time and thus communicating the concept to visitors and the public at large. The strategies employed not only considerably reduce primary energy demand and CO_2 emissions but also dependency on the local supply grids for electricity and gas.

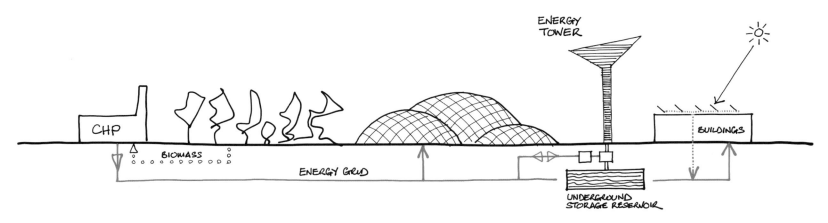

Fig. 6.64

During a collaboration with DMAA in 2016 on a competition proposal for a new spa complex in the city of Seoul, my first thought on seeing the amount of outdoor pool area in the program was concerning the associated energy demand. Then I realized these large volumes also offer the potential for energy storage. In the proposed concept, a gas-fired CHP plant provides the building with both heat and electrical power. This solution has both ecological and economic advantages compared to more conventional alternatives (less CO_2 emissions) and also provides advantages regarding the security of energy supply. The heat generated is used to meet the substantial hot water supply demand associated with this building type and the building heating loads. Thermal solar collectors located on the roof areas provide further heat energy. In summer, the heat is used to power absorption chillers, which in combination with reversible heat pumps supply chilled water to meet cooling loads. An important element in the total concept is an array of energy storage technologies in combination with the reversible heat pump system which are employed to match the energy supply and demand profiles and allow the cogeneration plant and solar thermal collectors to operate at maximum efficiency. These include conventional water storage tanks for hot water as well as underground ice

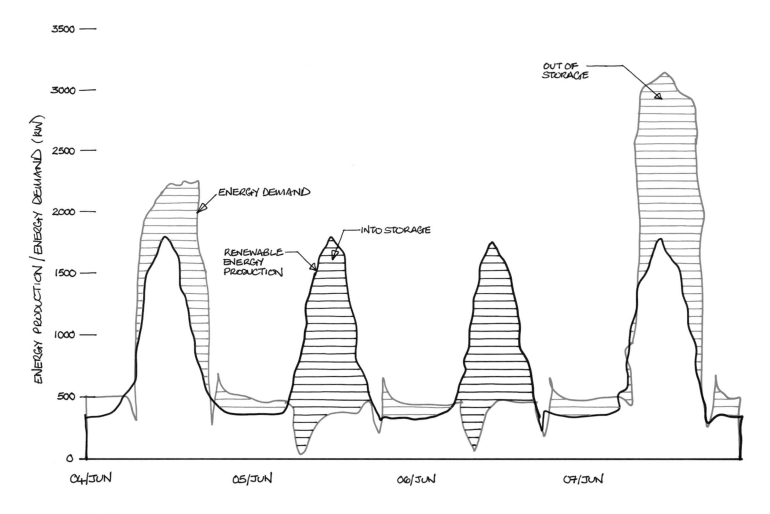

Fig. 6.65

Fig. 6.65
Botanical Garden Taiyuan,
China, energy production
and storage

Fig. 6.66
Atrium climate control
in office tower for Baku,
Azerbaijan

storage tanks, but also the use of the outdoor swimming pools in winter for energy storage in the form of ice. At external temperatures above 3 °C, the ambient air is used as the heat source for the heat pump system via external units which are also used as dry coolers for heat rejection in summer. At external temperatures below 3 °C, the outdoor swimming pools and the underground ice storage tank serve as the heat source. A special system comprising flexible tubing and a water–glycol mixture is used to activate the swimming pool for ice storage, while the upper surface of the pools is maintained for use as an ice skating area.

The creation of comfortable microclimates in transitional spaces, and even in outdoor areas, is an increasingly interesting area of work. Figure 6.66 shows a concept developed for the large vertical atria in the skyscraper project in Baku, which was introduced briefly above. The conceptual approach shown uses a "hanging garden" tube element, combined with "Water Walls" to provide cooling and dehumidification. The water wall element provides a wetted surface at a temperature which causes moisture from the space to condense on the surface. Condensate is collected at low level and used for irrigation of planting and vegetation in the atrium. The large surface area also removes heat by convection and provides radiant cooling to the occupants in the space. The hanging garden tube element contains a convective cooling element at high level to cool the inflowing air and cause it to flow via thermally induced pressure difference down the tube and enter the space in the occupied zone, providing cooling to the occupants. An underfloor piping system removes absorbed solar radiation at higher chilled water temperatures. The use of cooling breezes (air movement) and cold radiation to achieve comfort at higher air temperatures, the elimination of the need for fans and the higher chilled water temperatures employed (higher COP) lead to a higher energy performance than that associated with conventional systems.

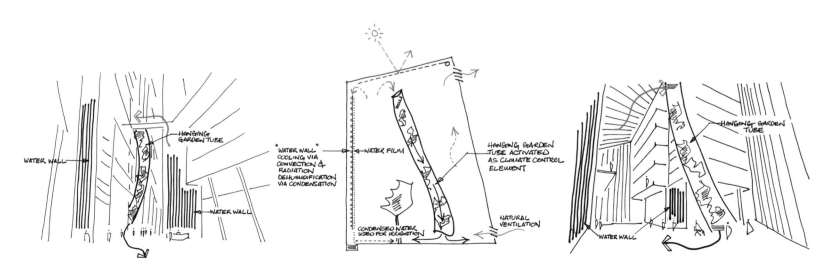

Fig. 6.66

Figure 6.67 shows the conceptual approach for the Busan Cinema Center in Busan, South Korea, with Coop Himmelb(l)au architects which won first prize in the architectural competition in 2005 and was completed in 2012. Pleasant microclimatic conditions for an open-air cinema space during the Busan International Film Festival can be achieved by the use of a large roof structure which spans the entire complex and a radiant floor system in combination with a geothermal heat exchange system. The roof above the open-air cinema has a significant impact on the usability of the open-air area and the comfort of the audience, alongside its more obvious function to protect from rain and direct sun. It reflects long-wave radiation back to the audience, working especially well in combination with a radiant floor system, and helps to increase the number of comfortable days for an open-air cinema audience. The topography of the complex is also used to reduce wind and external noise entering the area.

In a proposal for the new Central Park in Baku, Azerbaijan with Coop Himmelb(l)au architects, we developed pavilion structures which use the energy of the Sun to provide active cooling of shaded outdoor spaces, while at the same time harvesting water from the humid air and using this – in combination with stored rainwater from the roof and pumped ground water – to provide irrigation for adjoining lawn areas. The pavilion roof is designed to generate energy via integrated photovoltaic modules and to collect rainwater (Fig. 6.68). The provision of comfortable outdoor

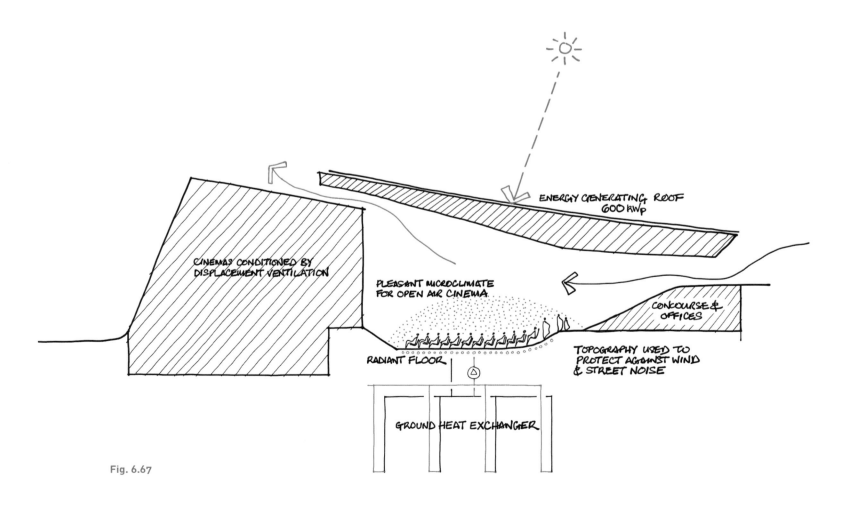

Fig. 6.67

Fig. 6.67
Busan Cinema Center,
South Korea, open air
cinema concept

Fig. 6.68
Central Park Baku, Azer-
baijan, energy concepts

spaces for the city's population, especially in the hot summers, is an important goal of this new park. The most pressing energy issue associated with the provision of a large park in Baku is related to the water demand for irrigation of the grass, plants and vegetation. To address both of these issues, we developed a very specific concept for the subtropical semi-arid climate with its warm dry summers and cool wet winters. The electrical energy generated by the pavilion roof is used to power an integrated cooling unit which cools incoming air from the surroundings. The cooled air is supplied to the shaded area underneath the pavilion roof at low level via a vertically aligned shaft, thus providing a pleasant microclimate for the people. The air flow is driven by buoyancy. Water condensing out of the humid outdoor air as a natural part of the cooling process is captured and piped to an underground storage tank underneath the pavilion floor, where it is stored together with the collected rainwater and with water pumped from the ground via pumps that are also powered by the energy roof. The collected water is subsequently used for controlled irrigation of the surrounding lawn areas. Surplus electrical energy is stored in a battery system and used to power outdoor lighting of the spaces at night.

The energy design of urban areas is similar in approach to the energy design of buildings. On an urban scale, it is important to recognize that the spaces between buildings are equally as important as the spaces within. Making a successful urban place necessitates the creation of a pleas-

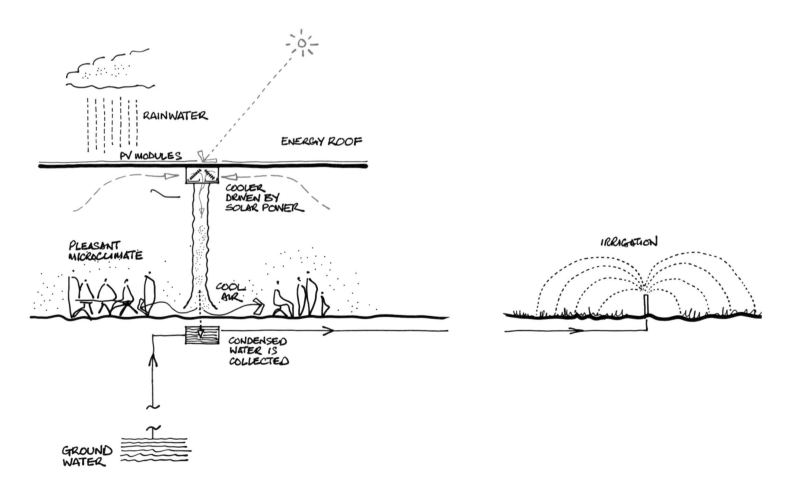

Fig. 6.68

ant microclimate, e.g. ensuring solar access to and reducing wind turbulence in outdoor places where people might congregate in cold weather, or providing shade and breezes in hot weather. In the work we are doing on master planning, for several university campuses in particular, these are central aspects. Fig. 6.69 shows conceptual strategies for a university campus in Baku, in collaboration with Coop Himmelb(l)au architects.

An interesting area of research at my institute in recent years has been the development of what we call **Smart Skins** – façades which maximize energy performance by varying their properties to adapt to changing external and internal conditions. Building skins can act as an adaptable filter between the external and internal environments. The physical prop-

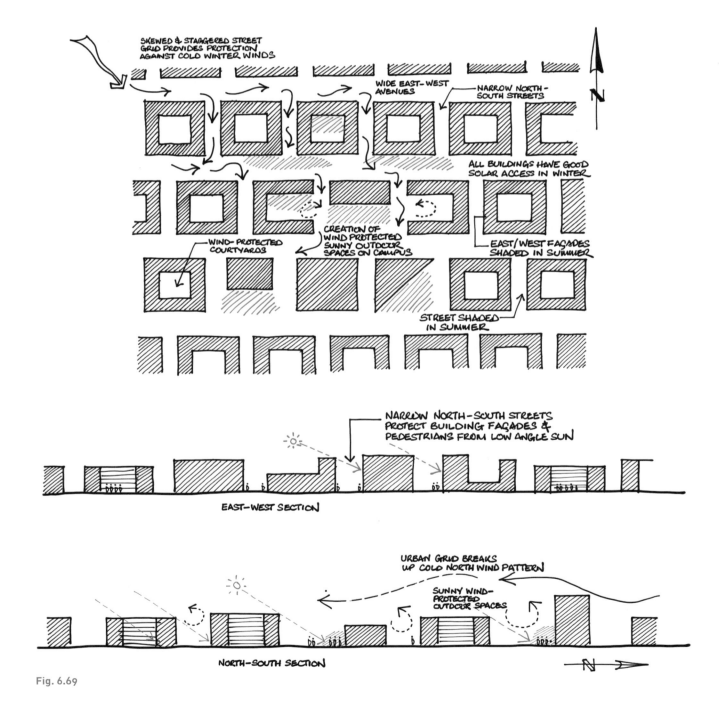

Fig. 6.69

Fig. 6.69
University Campus Baku,
Azerbaijan, strategies

Fig. 6.70
Building skin as interface

erties of today's building façades are however unable to adapt to changing conditions in a significant manner. This applies to both the ever-changing external conditions such as climate, noise, air quality and light, and the fluctuating demands and needs of building occupants on the internal side of the façade interface. Their specific properties in terms of thermal conductivity, solar heat gain transmission, light transmittance, porosity etc. are static and remain essentially constant with time, although the requirements for an energy efficient building skin differ significantly under the widely varying climatic conditions and patterns of use at different times of the day and year. Existing responsive façades are limited to one-dimensional approaches such as automated shading systems. If you refer back to the diagrams showing the external climatic conditions for the four chosen locations in chapter three and the diagrams of the energy design process introduced in chapter four, it is clear that if we are to achieve desirable internal conditions within the sea of ever-changing conditions the external climate exhibits, the building skin must play a very important role. Fig. 6.70 shows the skin as the interface between inside and outside

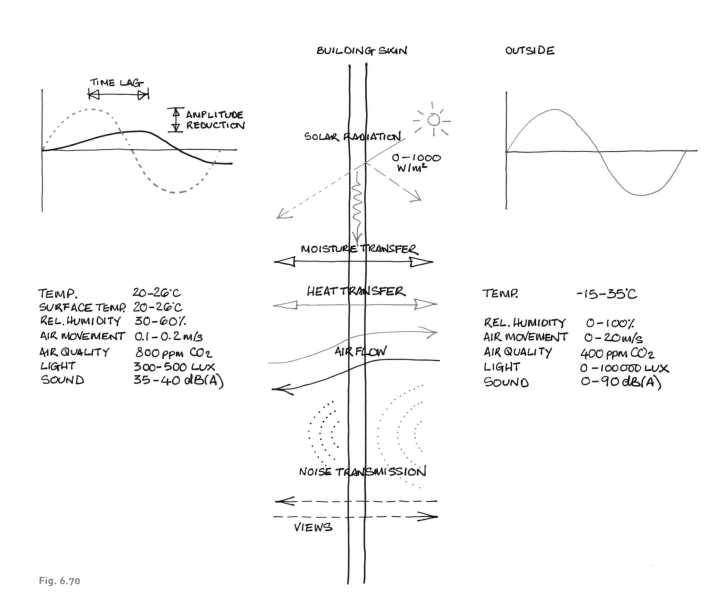

Fig. 6.70

with typical internal conditions and external design conditions for a location such as Seoul or New York City. The external conditions vary during the course of the day and more so over the course of a year. The internal conditions considered comfortable for human occupation are, as we have seen, more or less constant. However, due to the fact that we occupy and use buildings in a dynamic way, coming and going, changing our activity etc., the internal side of the interface also includes a highly dynamic component. We would expect, therefore, that for a building skin to be effective in energy design terms, the skin as interface should reflect the dynamic worlds on both sides of the interface. If we look around us, however, whether in Manhattan, Moscow, Berlin or Hong Kong we see static surfaces of stone, concrete and glass: building envelopes which remain unresponsive and unchanging, totally oblivious to whether it is -20 °C and dark or 35 °C and sunny outside. This passive behavior of conventional building envelopes leads inevitably to increased activity of the building HVAC systems in order to achieve thermal comfort.

    Building skins should be active and dynamic. They should act as a filter, selecting, mediating and modulating between inside and outside and not only providing protection against the elements. The fact that they for the most part do not has of course to do with cost and complexity, but also perhaps with certain architectural dreams we are still chasing. The famous unbuilt glass skyscrapers Mies van der Rohe designed in the 1920s come to mind. Sometimes, the buildings which were not built are more important than those which were. If we look around at contemporary architecture, the static unchanging envelopes make this apparent. On the other hand, if we look back to buildings from past centuries, we see building envelopes which evolved to include many elements which react to sun, light, privacy, temperature – "adaptable skins" (Fig. 6.71). In a research project, we studied the possibility of reinterpreting this type of adaptability using the technology available today. This research forms the scientific basis for

Fig. 6.71

Fig. 6.71
Building façade in Venice

Fig. 6.72
European Central Bank
HQ, Frankfurt

the development of a completely new approach to façade design. An adaptable and variable building skin could react and adapt to both internal and external conditions, effectively creating "Space on Demand". One simple example would be movable, highly insulated elements which in a closed position form an air-tight connection with the primary building façade, and thus allow the transparent portion of the building skin to vary, for example, down to 0 % if the spaces behind the façade are not in use or if the use of the spaces at a given time does not require daylight.

Some of the completed projects already described in this book include façades which incorporate elements of this conceptual idea of a "smart skin". The designs of the Braun and Fronius buildings described above include façades with a large degree of adaptability. Architecturally, Braun undergoes an architectural metamorphism when conditions outside become warm and sunny, changing from a "Miesien" glass box to a much more expressive architecture. The façade developed for the ECB also incorporates an array of devices which offer a high degree of selectivity and adaptability, including selective glass coatings, automatically controlled movable solar shading and elements specially developed to provide the natural ventilation of a high-rise building in a windy environment. Yet, the building façade presents a monolithic homogenous exterior appearance, showing once again that similar energy design approaches can lead to different architectural expressions (Fig. 6.72). This is not to say that the energy design concept does not affect the architecture, which it most certainly does, but that it does not lead to a monotonous architectural language in a deterministic way.

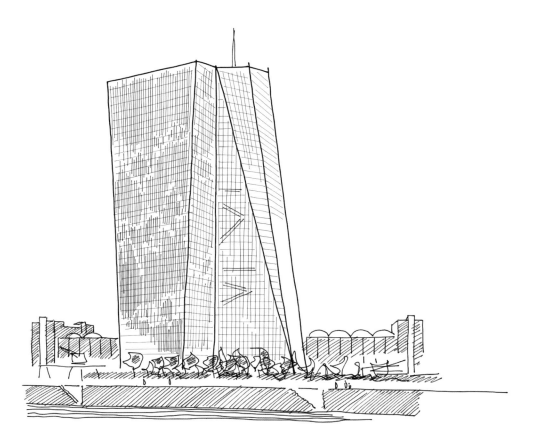

Fig. 6.72

The original concept for the skyscraper in Manhattan described above, with a double skin façade containing a void which offers inhabitable space and at the same time incorporating strategies to provide energy-efficient ventilation and maximize energy performance, is also a form of smart skin. It fulfills the functions usually provided by the typical present-day complex multilayered external wall constructions with all their associated problems relating to embodied energy, disposal etc. and mechanical ventilation systems with heat recovery systems. In a sense, the concept replaces the traditional wall construction with an inhabitable space.

Working on a residential apartment building for a site in Vaduz, Liechtenstein, with Falkeis architects in 2010, we were faced with the challenge of designing a plus-energy building on a site which in effect only allows the construction of a building form with the worst orientation, namely long façades facing east and west. Fig. 6.73 shows the conceptual approach adopted in the early design stages. By incorporating dynamic elements into the building skin which can be rotated into the direction of the incident solar radiation in winter, and supplemented with solar panels integrated into the roof and south façade, the east-west orientated building

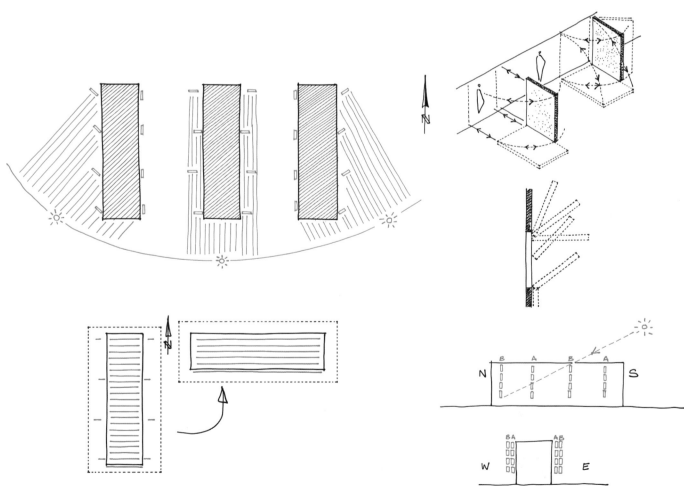

Fig. 6.73

Fig. 6.73
Active energy building,
Vaduz, Liechtenstein,
concepts

Fig. 6.74
Smart façade concept

can – in a sense – be transformed into an optimally orientated building. To achieve effective thermal storage of the absorbed thermal energy, a concept using an optimized absorber panel, phase change materials (PCM) with a suitable melting point and vacuum insulation panels to minimize heat loss was developed. A means of transferring the stored heat to the spaces could be found by coupling the element to the ventilation system to supply the necessary outdoor air. Other functions were also proposed for the elements, including night-time cooling in summer, sound protection, solar control, wind pressure control to support natural ventilation, daylighting reflection and variable thermal insulation.

The proposed smart skin concept we are developing in the research project, however, goes far beyond the strategies we have been able to implement in practice and incorporates and uses forecast data relating to future weather and likely user behavior (based on past experience and using an embedded artificial intelligence approach) as well as present time data to decide the optimal configuration of physical properties and thus optimize performance (Fig. 6.74). A novel dynamic simulation model which was specially developed for the project provided meaningful insight into the

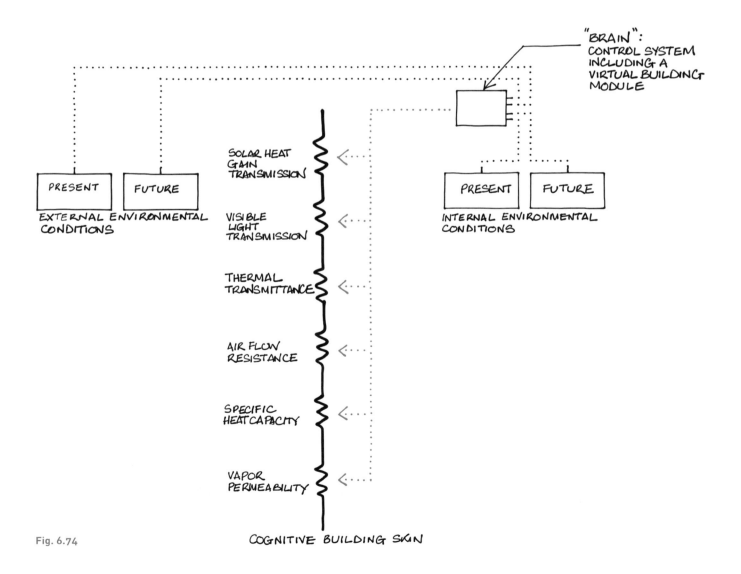

Fig. 6.74

potential and possibilities. This type of model could also serve as a virtual model to be incorporated into the completed buildings automatic control system and so provide part of the intelligence necessary for optimal performance of the smart skin. Further research will look at how the necessary degree of adaptability can be physically accomplished. Many possibilities are conceivable; mechanical devices, fluid-filled cavities or smart materials which can change their physical and/or chemical characteristics in order to accomplish the desired adaption to changing conditions. The final goal is the development of adaptive façades which automatically change their thermal and optical properties, constantly adapting to changing requirements by the manipulation of variable parameters for thermal insulation, solar energy transmittance, light transmission, thermal energy storage, air tightness and moisture diffusion to achieve the desired internal conditions with the least amount of energy expenditure. The results of the intensive investigations carried out in the first stage of this project show that the potential is enormous, with possible energy savings of up to 90 % compared with conventional energy efficient façade systems today.

The energy design of buildings is a **design process** not unlike the architectural design process in which invisible energy flows, inside and outside the proposed building, are manipulated to achieve the design goal of an optimal internal environment. Instead of standard engineering solutions, the laws of physics, especially thermodynamics, heat transfer and fluid mechanics are invoked to develop solutions from first principles. The discipline of energy design requires a synthesis of creative design talent and precise analytical skills. Dynamic simulations are used to assess and verify the feasibility of the proposed concepts and to optimize and validate the design solutions. The implementation of technology in design can often

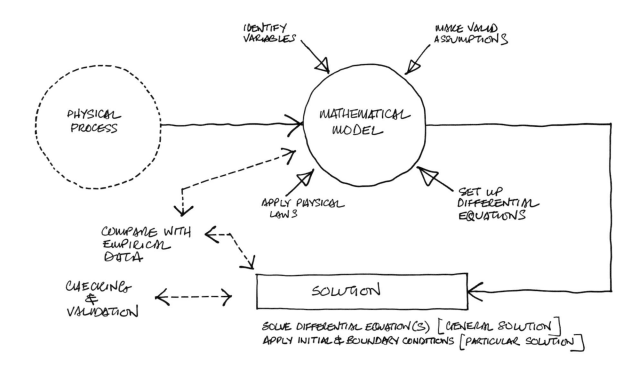

Fig. 6.75

lead to a lower requirement for technical systems in the completed building. Important words in my work are **system**, **analysis** and **design**. Design means creating something new, pushing the boundaries and designing from first principles. An important part of the work is the preparation of mathematical models, sometimes very simple, other times very complex; and the use of computer simulation to develop, test and optimize the concepts. An engineering model should be as simple as possible to achieve the required accuracy (Fig. 6.75). An equally important part of the work is the development of ideas, often by sketching and drawing diagrams. These are made during design team meetings with the architects and other team members, as well as back in the office. During the critical parts of the early design phase, ideas go back and forth in rapid succession between the principal designers involved. Figure 6.76 shows ideas developed in the competition for a glass pavilion in the botanical gardens of Montreal, in collaboration with Cecil Balmond in London and the VS-A group in Lille, France. Communicating ideas and concepts, whether as rough sketches during design meetings or in formal presentations to the client or building owner, is also a very important – and often underestimated – element in the success of a design. A good idea, poorly communicated, will often remain just that; an idea.

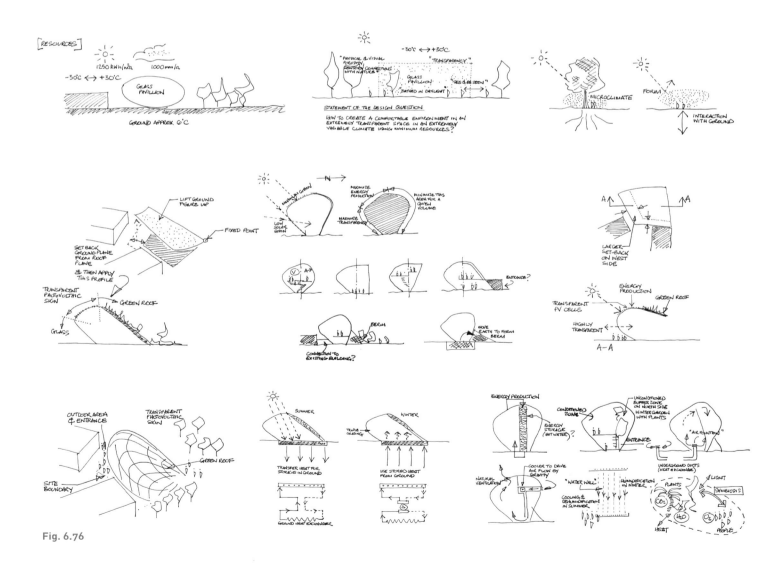

Fig. 6.76

The method of design varies, depending on the situation and the project. Sometimes, I will approach the problem in a very analytical, almost scientific way; carrying out rigorous analysis, coming at the problem from different angles, until the solution almost "magically" and often suddenly appears. Other times, the approach is more about playful experimentation, sketching and diagramming ideas and the analysis is performed afterwards to verify the assumptions. Sometimes it is a mixture of both. Other times, the ideas are born while sitting together with the architects at a table, maybe around the site model, possibly with a copy of the competition brief strewn around the table, where ideas and proposals are exchanged almost like the moves in an intense chess game.

In engineering design, it is often easier to make the argument that a difficult or complex concept will not work or will pose too much risk, and it is often much more difficult to support a daring and radical idea which may harbor great potential. Due to the traditional understanding of the roles in the design process and to a flawed understanding of the commercial aspects of the design profession, many engineering consultants in the building industry today also tend to try and delay their real input on a project for as long as possible, letting the architect firm up and hopefully freeze his design before investing time and fees. While there would seem to be obvious commercial advantages to this way of working, all my experience has shown that in fact the opposite is true. A more effective approach, not only in terms of benefit for the project, but also in commercial terms with regard to the profitability of a consultant's business is to start early, provide input, ideas and concepts early and influence the design. The likelihood of costly design changes being introduced at a later stage is much lower and if these are necessary, the likelihood of being paid for extra work much higher.

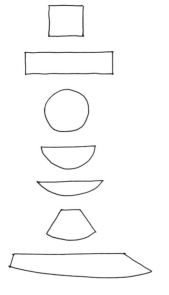

Fig. 6.77

Fig. 6.78

A question which has pervaded my work in practice, research and teaching is the relationship between form and energy in architecture and urban design. Energy strategies in the form-finding process of building design can be used to generate new architectural forms. Energy design can lead to new aesthetical qualities in architecture. The form of a building can be optimized to reduce the energy consumed by the building but also to maximize the energy generated by the building's surface. For over 25 years now, I have been collaborating with architectural offices on the design of buildings which set out to achieve these aims.

I first used the phrase "**Form follows Energy**" when writing about the design of the Low Energy Apartment Building in Marzahn, Berlin which was completed in 1996. In the early 1990s I went to an interview with the client, a residential building developer, who was interested in building a pioneering low-energy building in former East Berlin in an area called Marzahn. Apparently, they had been told by all the consultants which they had interviewed to date that after receiving the architects' completed preliminary drawings, they would review these and suggest ways to optimize the design in terms of energy efficiency. The client asked whether there was another approach. I suggested to carry out a study to find the optimal form in terms of energy performance, and that the results of these investigations could be used to help generate the architectural form.

Various generic forms to incorporate the required building program were studied initially and then subsequently further developed with the architects Assmann Salomon & Scheidt. The form was driven by the desire to minimize the heating energy demand in winter (Fig. 6.77). The building has a large, curved south-facing façade with a high proportion of glass while the area and the glass proportion of the north façade are minimized (Figures 6.78 and 6.79). The building is structured in three thermal zones, the

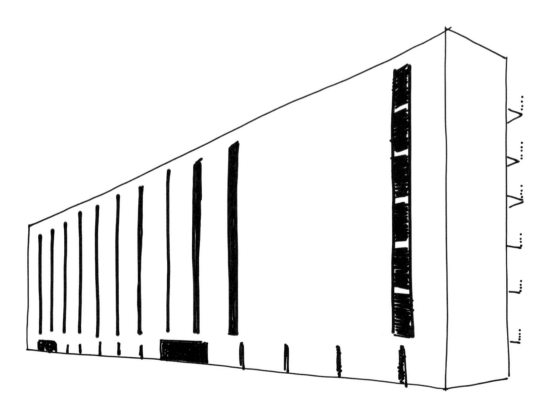

Fig. 6.79

living rooms on the south side, an unheated buffer zone on the north side in which the staircases and lifts are located, and the rooms requiring the highest internal temperatures – the mechanically ventilated bathrooms – in the middle (Fig. 6.80). The projecting balconies on the south side provide effective shading in summer but allow the lower winter solar radiation to penetrate into the apartments. Sliding doors in the walls separating the rooms on the south side enable the sun to reach deeper into the spaces and also allow a more flexible use of the rooms (Fig. 6.81).

Many projects on which I explored this theme with various architects followed. Strategies which maximize the energy performance of a building can influence the architectural form language in a variety of different ways; we have already seen many examples. Now, we will look at some more projects where the form of the building structure was derived explicitly from such considerations.

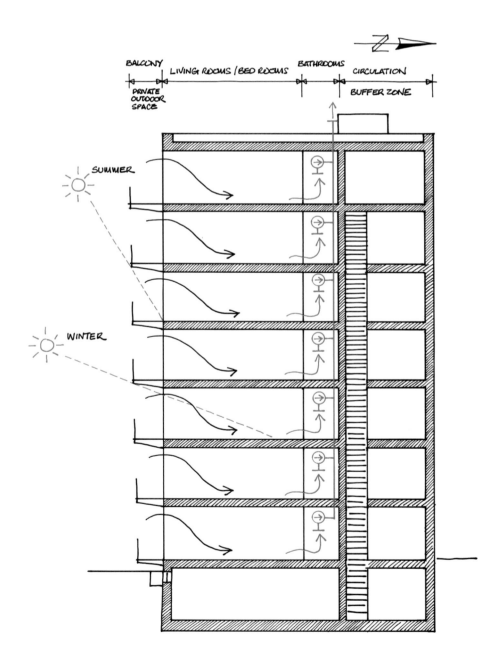

Fig. 6.80

In the design of the Sunbelt Management office building in San Diego, California with schneider + schumacher architects in 2001, the form of the building was derived directly from a consideration of the interaction of incident solar radiation with the building envelope. By connecting an oval-shaped floor plan with a circular roof, the slope of the building façade was optimized in relation to the orientation so that the cooling load is considerably lower than for a building with conventional vertical façades in the same location (Fig. 6.82).

Fig. 6.81

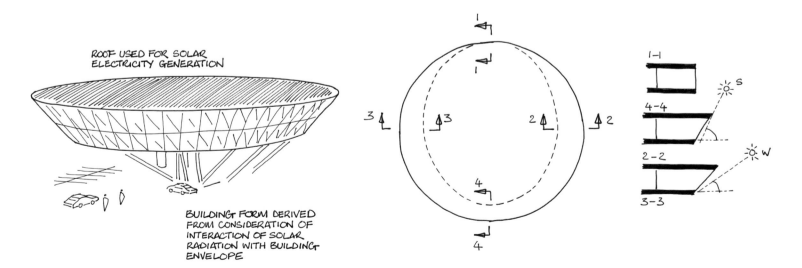

ROOF USED FOR SOLAR ELECTRICITY GENERATION

BUILDING FORM DERIVED FROM CONSIDERATION OF INTERACTION OF SOLAR RADIATION WITH BUILDING ENVELOPE

Fig. 6.82

A similar approach was used for the membrane atrium roof of the Infineon Asia Pacific Headquarters Building in Singapore with the Los Angeles-based architectural firm tec pmc (Fig. 6.83). Due to its location near the equator, a horizontal surface would be very unfavorable in terms of solar heat gains. To reduce the solar load, the horizontal area of the atrium roof was broken up into vertical surfaces which face north and south. In addition, the design creates spaces underneath the roof surface in which a warm air layer can form without it negatively impinging on the environmental conditions of the adjacent offices on the top floor.

In the summer of 2007, we received a commission at the institute to develop an energy concept for a sports hall building for a small community called Puconci in Slovenia. The idea was to look at the design problem of the required new sports building from the point of view of maximizing energy efficiency and to develop concepts which were to serve as the basis for an architectural competition, scheduled to take place after completion of the research. In many ways, the challenge was similar to the low-energy apartment project in Berlin more than 10 years earlier. Concepts for building form derived from energy considerations were to be developed prior to the normal architectural design process and then used to support the generation of the architectural design. In this case, however, this was a full-blown research project and the considerations were to extend beyond the

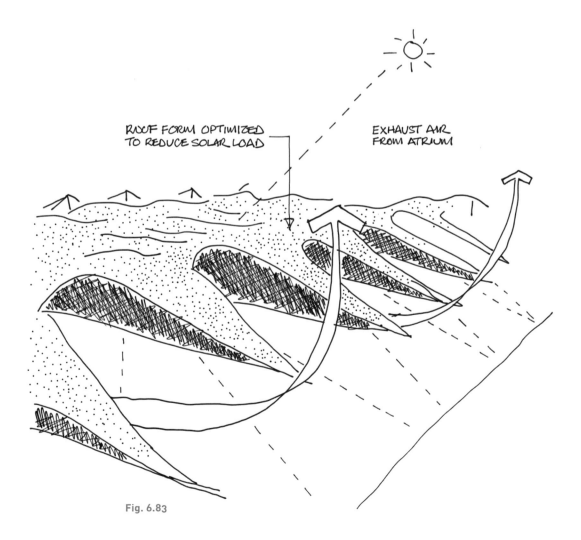

Fig. 6.83

Fig. 6.83
Infineon Asia HQ,
Singapore, atrium roof

Fig. 6.84
Sport hall of the future,
Slovenia, ventilation
concept

building form to include the type of construction and MEP systems etc. to be employed. We approached the problem by building a virtual model of the proposed building and then optimizing this model in an analytical process.

We started off by studying the external climate conditions, the requirements of the program and suitable choices of internal conditions and then started to look at different ways of arranging the building program on the site. The building was to include a three-court sports hall and the usual ancillary spaces. After choosing the most promising arrangement, we built a computer model with standard assumptions pertaining to building envelope, construction materials, climate control systems and energy supply. This model was then simulated in a dynamic thermal simulation environment and the results analyzed to suggest which areas held the greatest potential for optimization. Many alternatives were then studied, including orientation, positioning the building partly underground, various options relating to the envelope and construction systems and different approaches to climate control and ventilation.

As a result of these studies, a prototypical building design was developed in which the long axis was orientated east-west, so that the main façades of the building face south and north. The concept that was developed includes a system of automatically controlled natural ventilation which uses sensors for temperature, humidity and air quality to operate motor-controlled ventilation elements in the façades and roof (Fig. 6.84). In winter, outdoor air is taken in via the south façade, which comprises a heavyweight solar absorbing concrete wall with a layer of insulating glass on the outer side. Solar energy is absorbed by the concrete wall and used to preheat the incoming outdoor air. In warm weather, the required outdoor air is taken in at the north façade which is similarly constructed. Here, the thermal mass is cooled by nighttime ventilation so that the incoming air during the day can be precooled. A cooling coil at high level supplied with ground water is used to cool the air further before it drops by gravity into the sport halls. In both summer and winter, the extracted air is exhausted at high level though automatically controlled opening elements in the roof. The roof construction includes double skin transparent areas

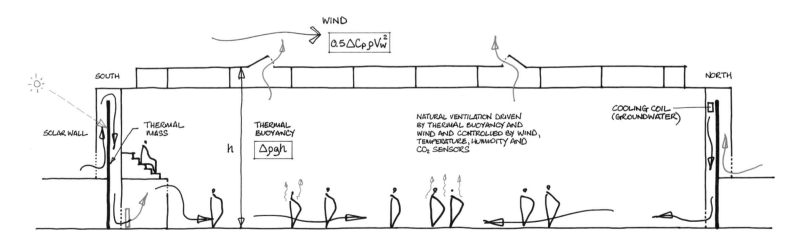

Fig. 6.84

with louvers in the interstitial cavity which are automatically controlled. The ratio of transparent to opaque areas is optimized to achieve minimum energy demand for lighting, heating and cooling (Fig. 6.85). As there is no need for a mechanical ventilation system, the ceiling remains uncluttered from the usual technical systems – with obvious advantages for the sports activities – and daylight is introduced into the spaces predominantly from the ceiling. Once or twice a year, larger events are held at the facility with more than 400 visitors. The conventional solution would be to size the mechanical ventilation system for the normal case and hire temporary mobile ventilation units to deal with the competition event situation. A further advantage of the natural ventilation concept that was developed is that the self-regulating characteristics of the system mean that it can cope with both the normal and the special situation without any need for further equipment (Fig. 6.86).

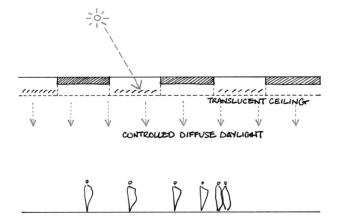

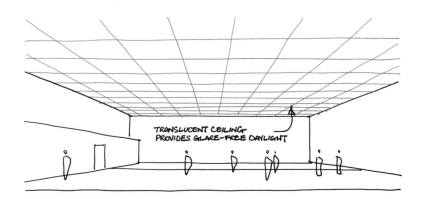

Fig. 6.85

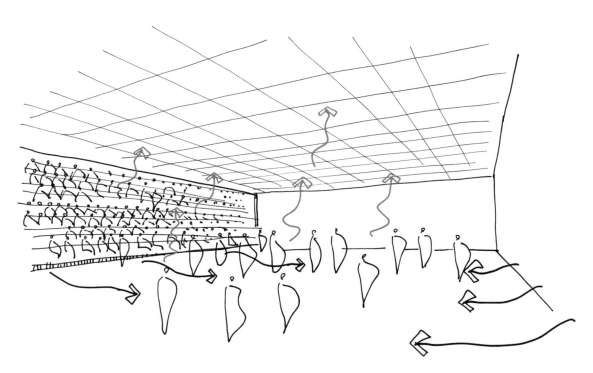

Fig. 6.86

Fig. 6.85
Sport hall of the future,
daylighting concept

Fig. 6.86
Sport hall of the future,
natural ventilation
during event

Fig. 6.87
Adidas office building,
Herzogenaurach, Germany,
site plan

In research work, we are developing "parametric energy design" software which can generate possible building volume envelopes for specific sites under the constraints that the building envelope should generate the maximum amount of renewable solar energy while minimizing the shading effect on neighboring sites. The volumes thus derived are not intended to directly represent a building form, but offer an envelope within which the building form can be developed.

In the first prize-winning design in the 2014 competition for a new office building for Adidas in Herzogenaurach, Germany, I encouraged the architects DMAA to develop a very deep-plan building form in defiance of the prevailing conventional wisdom that an energy-efficient office building should have a shallow floor plan for natural light and ventilation (Fig. 6.87). Instead, the design comprises office platforms within a large volumetric

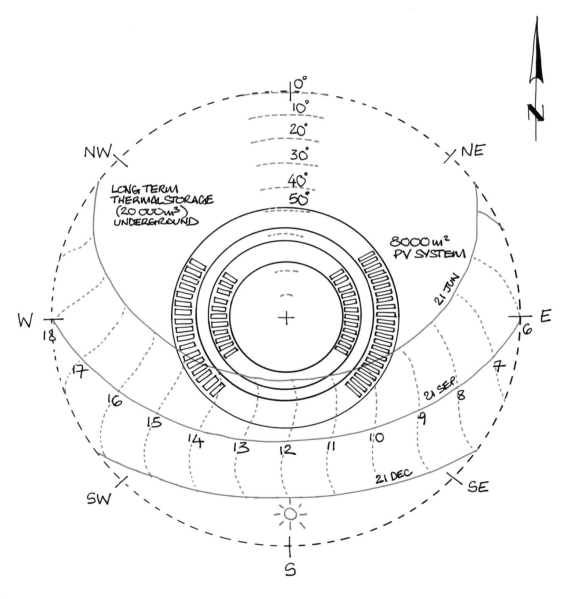

Fig. 6.87

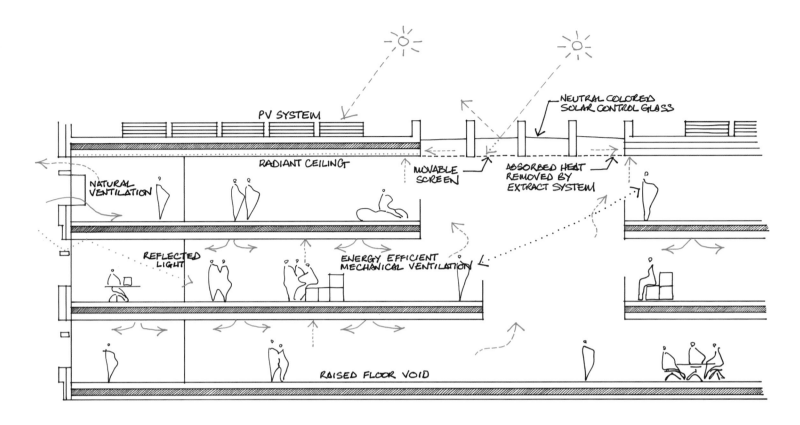

PV SYSTEM

NEUTRAL COLORED
SOLAR CONTROL GLASS

RADIANT CEILING

MOVABLE
SCREEN

ABSORBED HEAT
REMOVED BY
EXTRACT SYSTEM

NATURAL
VENTILATION

REFLECTED
LIGHT

ENERGY EFFICIENT
MECHANICAL VENTILATION

RAISED FLOOR VOID

Fig. 6.88

Fig. 6.89

Fig. 6.88
Adidas office building,
energy concept

Fig. 6.89
Adidas office building,
internal view based on
DMAA rendering

Fig. 6.90
Kuala Lumpur tower,
floor plan

enclosure offering a three-dimensional working environment (Fig. 6.88). Strategically placed voids introduce and distribute natural light and the entire roof is used for solar electricity production. The reduced grey energy, as a result of the compact form and much reduced façade area together with the increased energy production of the large roof surface, more than compensate for the increased artificial lighting in the internal zone of the building, so that we were able to demonstrate that the proposed design not only offers a new type of spatial environment which meets the special needs of the company, but also achieves enhanced energy performance (Fig. 6.89).

Figure 6.90 shows the conceptual floor plan layout for a tower in Kuala Lumpur with Coop Himmelb(l)au architects, for a competition held in 2012. Vertical garden atria are inserted into the tower in the east- and west-facing areas with high solar radiation, while the office areas are positioned on the more favorable orientations. Decentralized air conditioning units are located in the garden atria to serve the individual office floors, thus saving valuable space for shafts and plant rooms.

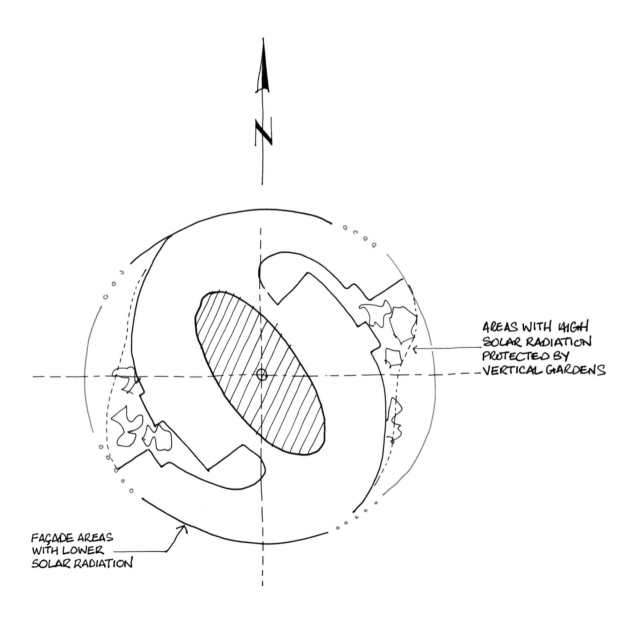

AREAS WITH HIGH
SOLAR RADIATION
PROTECTED BY
VERTICAL GARDENS

FAÇADE AREAS
WITH LOWER
SOLAR RADIATION

Fig. 6.90

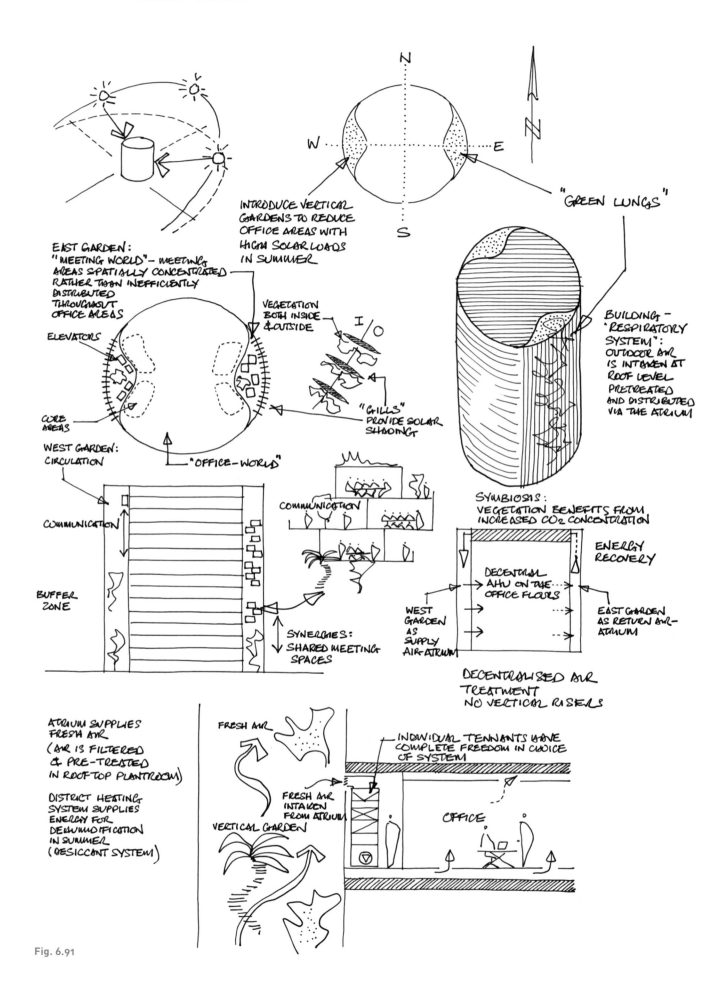

N

W — E

S

"GREEN LUNGS"

INTRODUCE VERTICAL GARDENS TO REDUCE OFFICE AREAS WITH HIGH SOLAR LOADS IN SUMMER

EAST GARDEN: "MEETING WORLD" – MEETING AREAS SPATIALLY CONCENTRATED RATHER THAN INEFFICIENTLY DISTRIBUTED THROUGHOUT OFFICE AREAS

VEGETATION BOTH INSIDE & OUTSIDE

I/O

ELEVATORS

CORE AREAS

"GILLS" PROVIDE SOLAR SHADING

WEST GARDEN: CIRCULATION

"OFFICE-WORLD"

BUILDING – "RESPIRATORY SYSTEM": OUTDOOR AIR IS INTAKEN AT ROOF LEVEL PRETREATED AND DISTRIBUTED VIA THE ATRIUM

COMMUNICATION

BUFFER ZONE

COMMUNICATION

SYNERGIES: SHARED MEETING SPACES

SYMBIOSIS: VEGETATION BENEFITS FROM INCREASED CO_2 CONCENTRATION

ENERGY RECOVERY

DECENTRAL AHU ON THE OFFICE FLOORS

WEST GARDEN AS SUPPLY AIR-ATRIUM

EAST GARDEN AS RETURN AIR-ATRIUM

DECENTRALISED AIR TREATMENT NO VERTICAL RISERS

ATRIUM SUPPLIES FRESH AIR (AIR IS FILTERED & PRE-TREATED IN ROOFTOP PLANTROOM)

DISTRICT HEATING SYSTEM SUPPLIES ENERGY FOR DEHUMIDIFICATION IN SUMMER (DESICCANT SYSTEM)

FRESH AIR

INDIVIDUAL TENNANTS HAVE COMPLETE FREEDOM IN CHOICE OF SYSTEM

FRESH AIR INTAKEN FROM ATRIUM

OFFICE

VERTICAL GARDEN

Fig. 6.91

Fig. 6.91
Gateway gardens tower,
conceptual approach

Fig. 6.92
Gateway gardens tower,
based on CHBL rendering

Using a similar approach in the first-prize-winning entry for the 2014 Gateway Gardens competition with Coop Himmelb(l)au, we started out with a massing which fits onto a difficult site surrounded by a challenging local environment near Frankfurt airport, including nearby connections to the autobahn with attendant issues of noise and air pollution. Two vertical garden atria as buffer zones on the east and west sides were inserted into the volume, so that the office areas could be located on the north-and south-facing sides where the thermal loads are lower and the conflicts between solar shading requirements and daylight and views are easier to deal with. The vertical garden spaces are employed in the climate control concept to allow the building to breathe at this difficult location, one serving as a supply air path, the other for the collection of return air, and to accommodate circulation and shared meeting spaces (Fig. 6.91). In addition to their energetic and functional attributes, they also provide the often-missing element of vertical spatial connectivity in the skyscraper typology (Fig. 6.92).

In recent years, the principal design moves have been increasingly concerned with the way the building is configured; i.e. the way the building program is organized within the building volume. **Configuration** is an increasingly important word in my work and this is possibly the most interesting area in architectural design with regard to energy performance and the whole notion of form follows energy. Basically, configuration is about how the program is put together and arranged. We have already encountered some examples above where this was part of the approach.

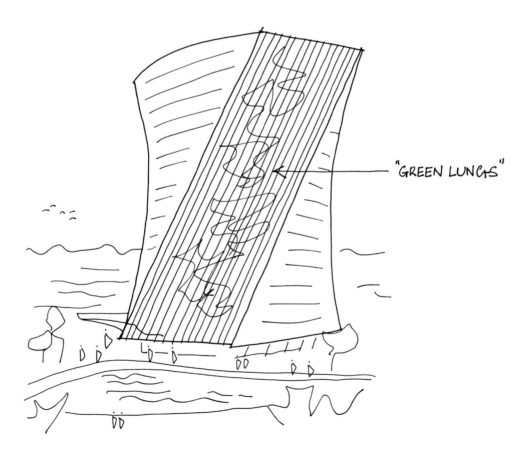

"GREEN LUNGS"

Fig. 6.92

In the competition proposal for the OEVAG bank headquarters building in Vienna city with Carsten Roth Architects, a completely new typological solution for an atrium building was arrived at. The site was a typical perimeter block development structure in the center of Vienna. Some of the façades were listed and to be retained. At our first meeting in Hamburg, I pushed the design in the direction of a central atrium instead of an open courtyard. Besides the energetic advantages of compactness, this would give the bank a representative space and a central communication zone. Years of experience with both of these standard typologies (open courtyard and atrium), however, had taught me that the perceived difference in the quality of the working spaces between the office spaces facing the street and the office spaces facing the courtyard or atrium leads to problems (Fig. 6.93). Experience had also shown that with these types of solutions, the interaction between the atrium and adjoining offices means that either the atrium works well as a communication zone and the adjoining offices less well, or the atrium becomes a sterile space with little life and little communication so that the adjoining offices are allowed to function better. Also in these conventional solutions, the spaces requiring more intensive building services infrastructure such as conference rooms, meeting points, communication areas etc. tend to be dispersed throughout the floor plan and thus necessitate a more complex and less efficient MEP systems distribution network.

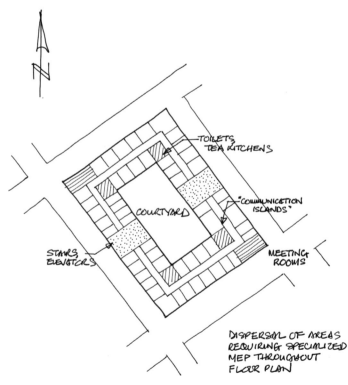

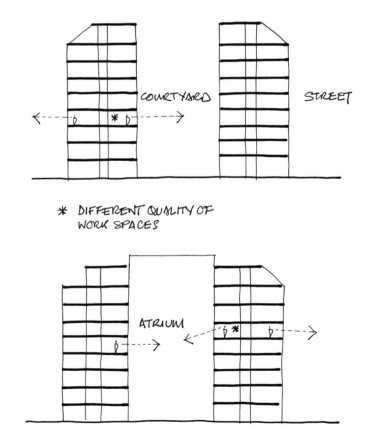

Fig. 6.93

Fig. 6.93
OEVAG Bank HQ, Vienna,
conventional approach

Fig. 6.94
OEVAG Bank HQ, Vienna,
conceptual approach

From this point of departure a means of organizing the space suggested itself, which we developed into a new type of typology in the proposed design which won the architectural competition in 2006. The cellular offices form an external ring facing the streets. Both the special areas described above and the circulation elements form independent structures that are inserted into the large interstitial atrium space within the office ring which serves as a communication center (Fig. 6.94). The design ensures equal quality for all work places. It also creates a dynamic vertical atrium space which encourages and supports informal communication and incorporates circulation elements and shared areas (meeting rooms etc.). The special areas requiring a more intensive building services infrastructure are grouped together and are thus more efficiently served.

In terms of energy demand, the solar load for the special areas is significantly reduced and the compact design reduces the transmission heat losses of the building considerably, as the area of the atrium roof is only approx. 20 % of the area of the skin between offices and atrium. This new typology combines the principle of the combi-office originally developed in Sweden (concentrated working in small cellular offices and shared spaces in a communication zone in the interior), with the concept of an atrium as a vertical city and communication space. The building was completed in 2010. In this case the influence of energy performance strategies on form is not visible in the outer building form or in the façade composition, but it is evident in a subtler way – in the configuration of the building, in its floor plan and section.

In the design of the NRW archive building in Duisburg, Germany with Ortner + Ortner architects, one of the most important design decisions was taken at the start of the design process during the competition phase in 2007. The program was archive space for the storage of important government papers, together with the necessary office working space. Due to

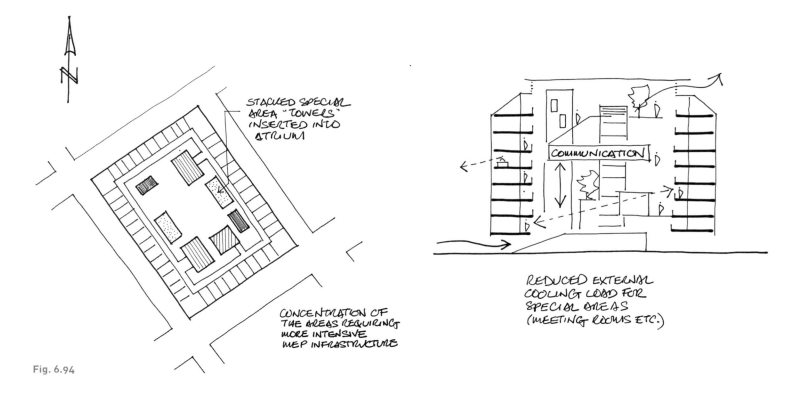

STACKED SPECIAL AREA "TOWERS" INSERTED INTO ATRIUM

COMMUNICATION

CONCENTRATION OF THE AREAS REQUIRING MORE INTENSIVE MEP INFRASTRUCTURE

REDUCED EXTERNAL COOLING LOAD FOR SPECIAL AREAS (MEETING ROOMS ETC.)

Fig. 6.94

Fig. 6.95

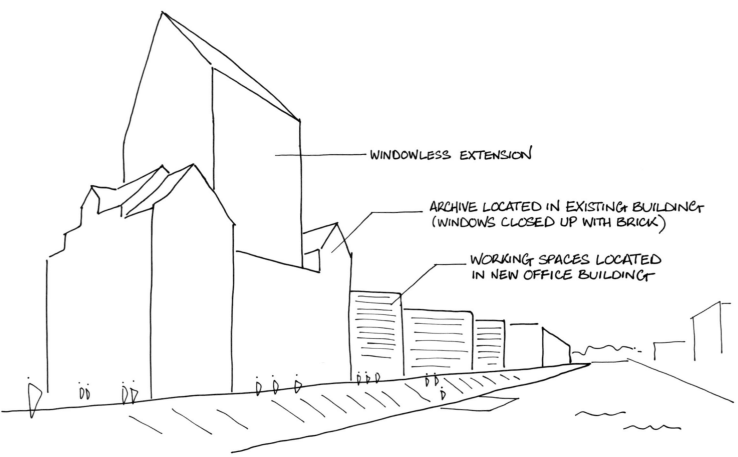

WINDOWLESS EXTENSION

ARCHIVE LOCATED IN EXISTING BUILDING
(WINDOWS CLOSED UP WITH BRICK)

WORKING SPACES LOCATED
IN NEW OFFICE BUILDING

Fig. 6.96

the hygroscopic nature of paper, constant internal environmental conditions must be maintained in order to prevent damage to the documents (especially harmful are rapid fluctuations in relative humidity) and thus this type of building is usually fully air conditioned. An old corn storage building was located on the site and was to be preserved (Fig. 6.95). In initial discussions within the design team we considered daylighting requirements for the work spaces and the possibility of enlarging the relatively small windows. However, very early on, we decided on the following radical approach: close up all the windows in the existing corn storage building on the site, use this building as the archive and provide the working spaces for the employees in a new office building alongside this (Fig. 6.96). In effect, the approach was to separate completely the two functions of document storage and office working, thus altering the conventional organizational structure. By removing the external thermal loads via the windows and the internal thermal loads by providing no working spaces in the archive facility itself, so that people only enter through air locks to collect or return the documents, it was possible to maintain the necessary stable environmental conditions in the archive with help of the exposed thermal mass of the structure and with minimum energy input and technical systems (Fig. 6.97). After winning the competition, design and construction proceeded. The existing windows were closed up and replaced with brick wall to match the existing façade and thermal insulation was added. The necessary thermal conditioning is achieved largely by passive measures. The move which made this possible was the decision made at the outset, to configure the program such that the office spaces and the archive are separated and housed in structures with very different characteristics. The configuration also meant that the existing historical structure could be used to maximum effect. The building was completed in 2013.

The conventional department store typology is essentially a box with all façades on the upper floors closed to block daylight which relies on extensive levels of artificial lighting (Fig. 6.98). In a competition for the renovation of an existing department store with Astoc architects in 2014, we proposed to turn this typological structure around and place the circulation zone, normally in the internal zone of the building, on the outside

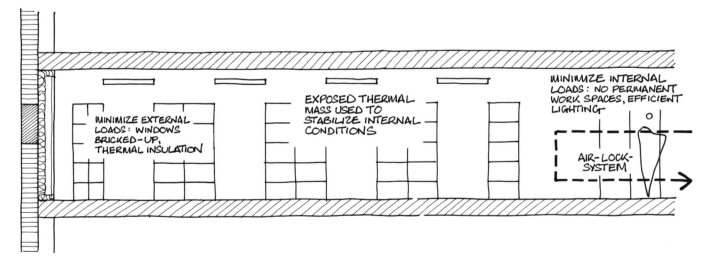

MINIMIZE EXTERNAL LOADS: WINDOWS BRICKED-UP, THERMAL INSULATION

EXPOSED THERMAL MASS USED TO STABILIZE INTERNAL CONDITIONS

MINIMIZE INTERNAL LOADS: NO PERMANENT WORK SPACES, EFFICIENT LIGHTING

AIR-LOCK-SYSTEM

Fig. 6.97

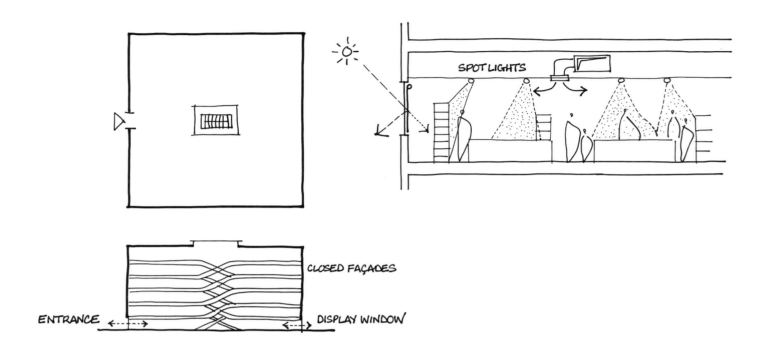

Fig. 6.98

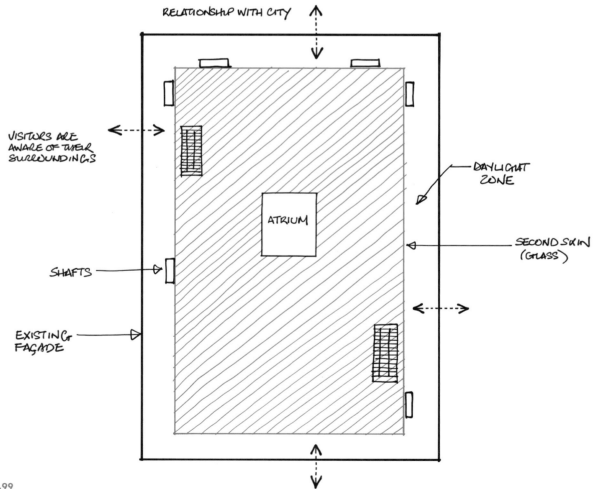

Fig. 6.99

Fig. 6.98
Department store,
conventional approach

Fig. 6.99
Department store renova-
tion, Germany, conceptual
approach

Fig. 6.100
Med Campus Graz, Austria,
energy supply systems

(Fig. 6.99). In this way, the façades can be opened up and natural daylight used to provide lighting of the external zone. This arrangement also allows the visitors to orientate themselves with respect to the surrounding city as they move around the store, and at the same time it breathes life back into the façades, making the building's exterior more interesting to passers-by on the city streets. Besides the energy advantages associated with the use of daylight, the relationship between the store and the city and the spatial experience of the visitors is greatly enhanced. As the activity of shopping increasingly shifts to the virtual world, you could argue that, in order to draw people out of their homes and into department stores, the spatial quality might well be a vital factor. A transparent second skin was proposed between the external circulation zone, which includes cafés, changing rooms and other areas and the internal zone, so that the external zone also acts as a climatic buffer and the existing historical façade does not need any major renovation. The multi-layered approach to the building envelope also alleviates the issues discussed in chapter four regarding the desire to have an inviting entrance without excessive energy loss by infiltration.

The configuration of the MEP systems also offers enormous potential regarding symbiotic relationships and synergies which can be exploited in the development of the energy systems. This is an important aspect of the concepts we developed for the new campus of the Medical University of Graz, in collaboration with the architects Riegler Riewe and completed in 2017. Figure 6.100 shows the concept for the energy supply systems.

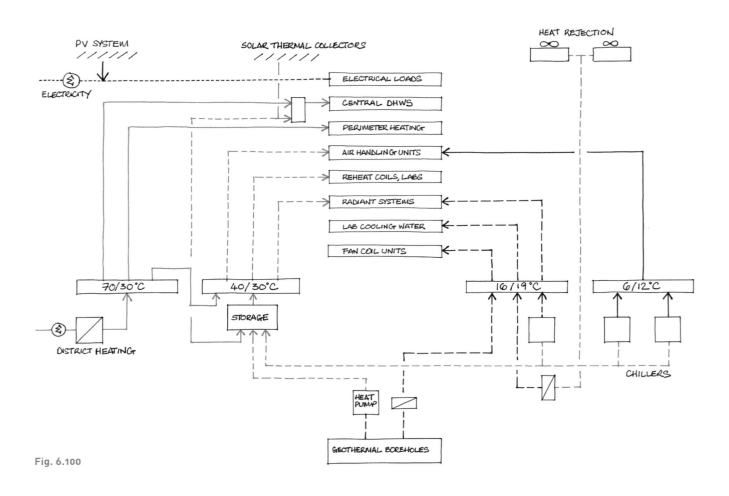

Fig. 6.100

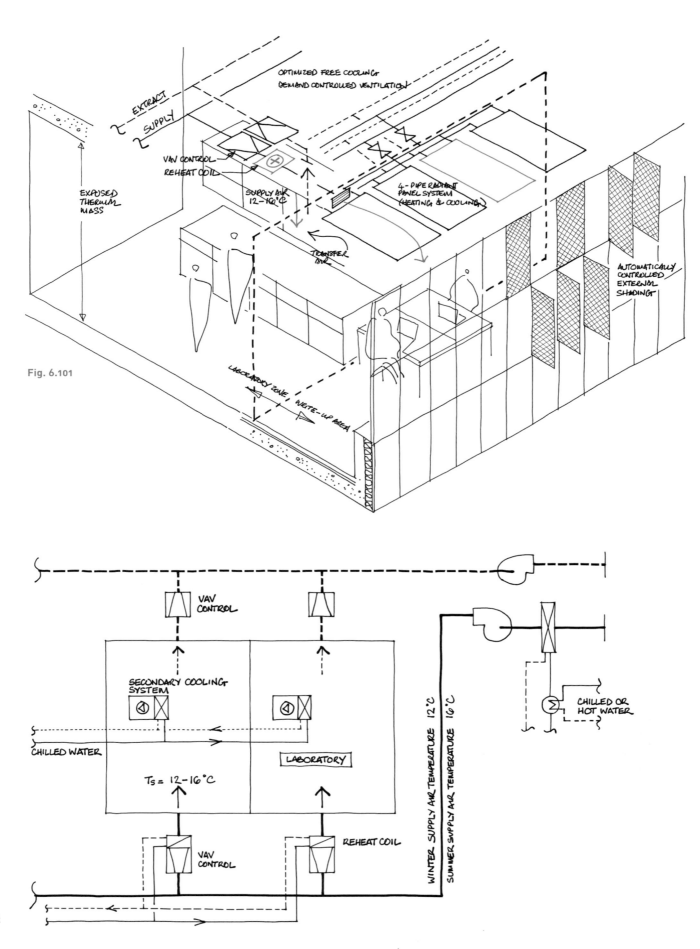

OPTIMIZED FREE COOLING
DEMAND CONTROLLED VENTILATION

EXTRACT

SUPPLY

VAV CONTROL
REHEAT COIL

EXPOSED
THERMAL
MASS

SUPPLY AIR
12-16°C

4-PIPE RADIANT
PANEL SYSTEM
(HEATING & COOLING)

TRANSFER
AIR

AUTOMATICALLY
CONTROLLED
EXTERNAL
SHADING

LABORATORY ZONE

WRITE-UP AREA

Fig. 6.101

VAV
CONTROL

SECONDARY COOLING
SYSTEM

CHILLED WATER

LABORATORY

$T_S = 12-16°C$

VAV
CONTROL

REHEAT COIL

WINTER SUPPLY AIR TEMPERATURE 12°C

SUMMER SUPPLY AIR TEMPERATURE 16°C

CHILLED OR
HOT WATER

Fig. 6.102

Deceptively simple strategies can save considerable amounts of energy and resources. In the laboratory areas, a system was developed which employs the supply of cooled air and the use of reheaters to meet the individual demands of the laboratory spaces instead of the conventional HVAC system type utilized in Central Europe with isothermal supply air and secondary cooling systems, ensuring a greater utilization of free cooling and thus saving thermal energy and increasing energy performance (Fig. 6.101, Fig. 6.102). The floor plan is so configured that the office spaces and write-up areas are positioned in the regions with the best daylight conditions (Fig. 6.103). The daylight openings in the façades in the lab areas are provided at two levels, at mid-level to provide views at the write-up areas and at high level to provide daylight to the laboratories behind. The configuration and size of the openings in the façades depends on the specific location within the dense urban structure and the use of the spaces behind the façade. The offices are naturally ventilated and heated and cooled via suspended radiant ceiling panels (Fig. 6.104). On account of wind considerations related to microclimate the buildings are orientated with the long axis running north-south (see chapter three). The external shading devices were therefore designed as automatically controlled vertically aligned perforated metal elements which allow daylight and views while blocking solar radiation (Fig. 6.105).

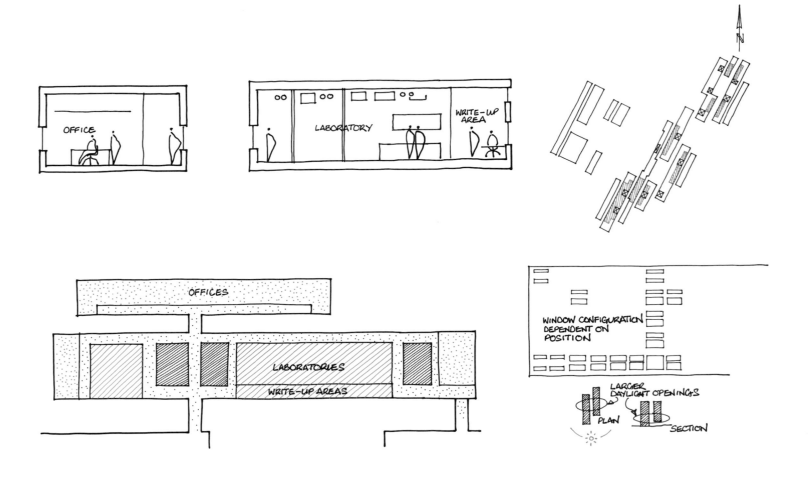

Fig. 6.103

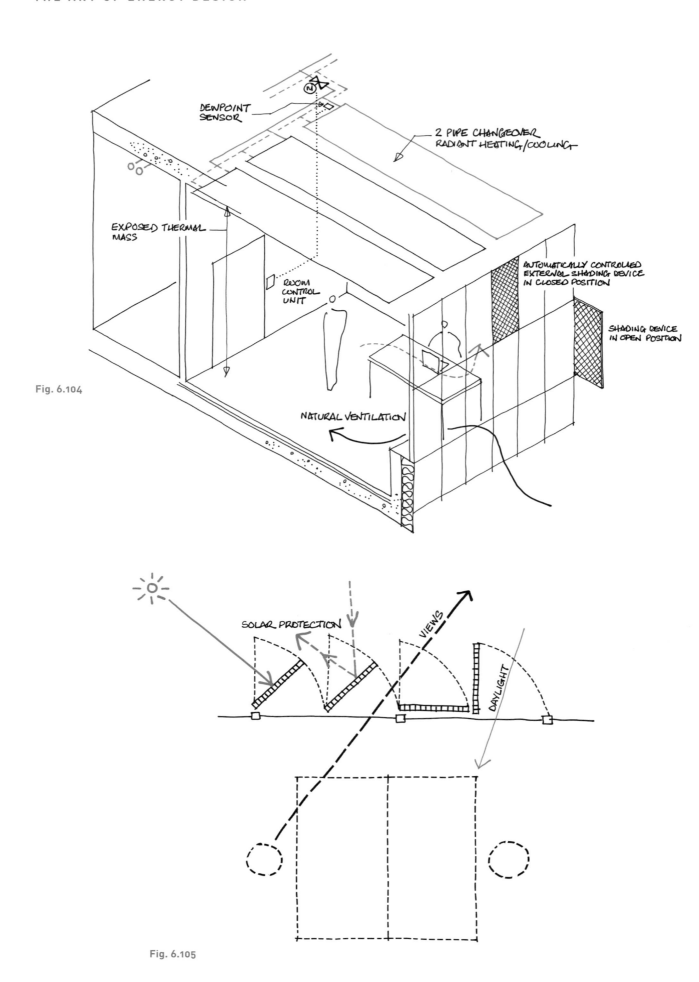

DEWPOINT SENSOR

2 PIPE CHANGEOVER RADIANT HEATING/COOLING

EXPOSED THERMAL MASS

ROOM CONTROL UNIT

AUTOMATICALLY CONTROLLED EXTERNAL SHADING DEVICE IN CLOSED POSITION

SHADING DEVICE IN OPEN POSITION

NATURAL VENTILATION

Fig. 6.104

SOLAR PROTECTION

VIEWS

DAYLIGHT

Fig. 6.105

Figure 6.106 shows the approach used on a competition proposal for a project on a site in Unterföhring, near Munich, Germany, developed in 1999 with MVRDV architects in Rotterdam, in which we proposed an "Interior City" – a complex of office buildings to be situated within a large glass climate envelope, creating a new type of urban environment. Positioning the circulation systems for people and technical systems outside the office volumes allowed the creation of "core-less" open plan office spaces. In the end, the office buildings were all built but without the additional climate envelope, mainly due to concerns regarding cleaning costs.

On the new Ecole Centrale Paris university building in Saclay, Paris, which won first prize in the architectural competition held in 2012 and was completed in 2017, we worked with OMA architects to develop a new university campus building typology which achieves high energy performance by utilizing synergetic interactions between the various uses while creating a new form of campus space under a "climate envelope". The building comprises teaching spaces, laboratories and offices for an engineering school, all enclosed within a climate envelope so that the in-between spaces form an indoor campus. Compared with traditional typologies, the design offers major advantages in terms of communication amongst

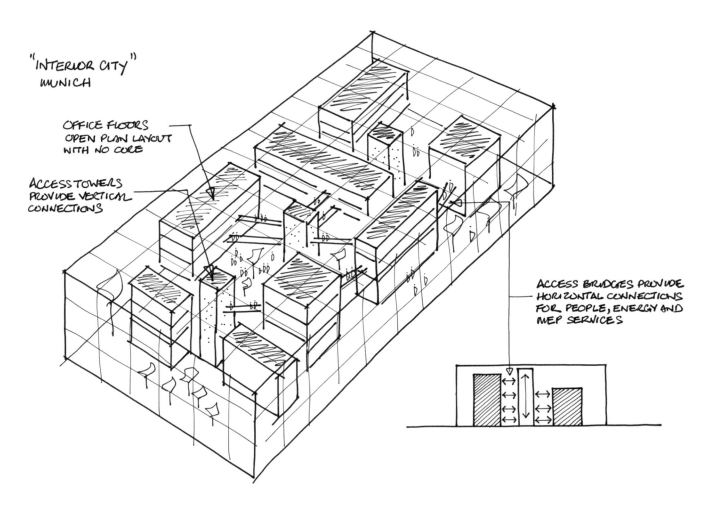

"INTERIOR CITY" MUNICH

OFFICE FLOORS OPEN PLAN LAYOUT WITH NO CORE

ACCESS TOWERS PROVIDE VERTICAL CONNECTIONS

ACCESS BRIDGES PROVIDE HORIZONTAL CONNECTIONS FOR PEOPLE, ENERGY AND MEP SERVICES

Fig. 6.106

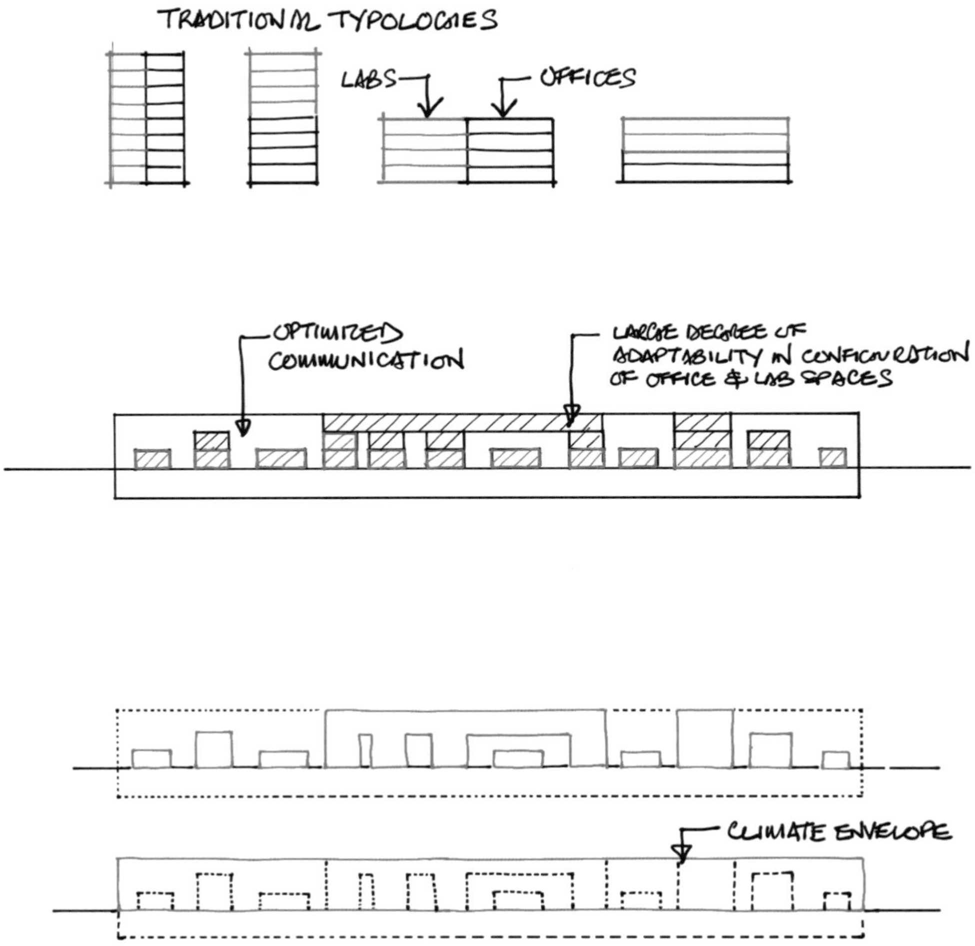

TRADITIONAL TYPOLOGIES

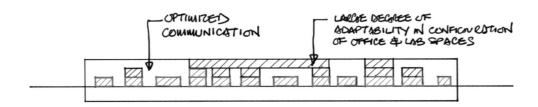

LABS — OFFICES

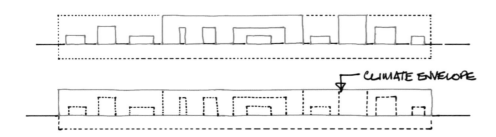

OPTIMIZED COMMUNICATION

LARGE DEGREE OF ADAPTABILITY IN CONFIGURATION OF OFFICE & LAB SPACES

CLIMATE ENVELOPE

Fig. 6.107

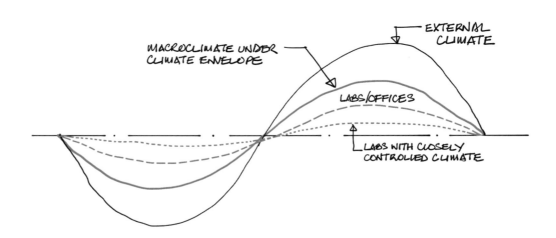

EXTERNAL CLIMATE

MACROCLIMATE UNDER CLIMATE ENVELOPE

LABS/OFFICES

LABS WITH CLOSELY CONTROLLED CLIMATE

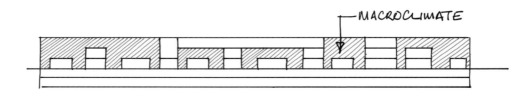

MACROCLIMATE

Fig. 6.108

research staff and students, and flexibility and adaptability regarding future changes in the use and configuration
of offices and laboratories (Fig. 6.107). Placing the climate
envelope around the whole building volume instead of
around the individual office and laboratory cells increases
building compactness, reduces the amount of heat transfer area to outside and creates a unique space between
the office and lab cells (Fig. 6.108). Within the climate envelope, composed of a PTFE foil roof and glass façades, a
macroclimate is created, largely by passive means, which
is not as closely controlled as the internal environments
within the laboratories and the offices. The roof design
reacts to the requirements of the various spaces below by
combining highly insulated opaque areas with transparent
areas and optimizing their placement and distribution to
reflect the distribution of the building program in the hall.

Figure 6.109 shows a conceptual approach for ac-
tively enhancing the macroclimatic conditions in the hall
space underneath the climate envelope. A hydraulic system in the hall captures the absorbed solar energy in
summer and transfers it into a geothermal energy storage system in the ground for use in winter. The relatively
high temperature of the geothermal heat store, combined
with the relatively low temperature of the radiant systems,
allows an efficient thermodynamic operation of the heat
pump system. A water based system providing process
cooling in the laboratory areas can also be integrated into
the system. Fig. 6.110 shows a concept for an adaptable
ETFE roof envelope, combining solar shading and energy
production (a similar concept was used for the DSD pavilion at the EXPO 2000, described above, however using frit-
ting on both layers instead of PV).

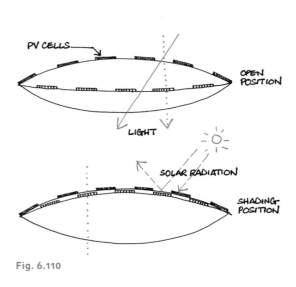

Fig. 6.110

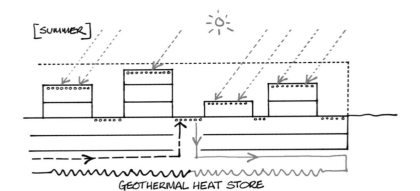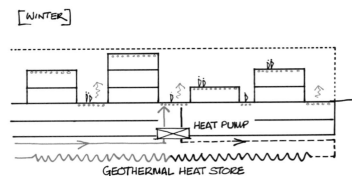

Fig. 6.109

The air handling units are equipped with energy recovery systems and located on a dedicated technical floor in the first basement. Here, outdoor air is treated and supplied to the spaces. Extract systems within the laboratories remove air via extract hoods to maintain the negative pressure required to prevent the possibility of contaminated air entering the shared spaces. The exhaust air is discharged at roof level. The large hall space under the climate enclosure is naturally ventilated via a system of automatically controlled dampers which allow air to enter at low level and leave the space at roof level. The teaching and office areas are mechanically ventilated but can also be naturally ventilated by operable windows. Return air from the offices and teaching areas is utilized to temper the hall.

The hall is a transitional space between the internal and external environments, supporting and enhancing the campus atmosphere and informal communication. It is thought that a large part of the important communication which leads to innovation, new ideas and knowledge at institutions such as universities and large companies occurs in the in-between-spaces between the actual personal work spaces. In the climate of Paris, the potential for enhanced communication possibilities offered by the macroclimate of the campus within a climate envelope such as that proposed at the Ecole Centrale is significantly increased (Fig. 6.111). The typology works to enhance both communication between people and synergetic energy flows between the many diversified uses under its roof, transferring surplus heat from the laboratories to spaces which require

Fig. 6.111

Fig. 6.111
ECP Paris, internal view,
based on OMA rendering

Fig. 6.112
ECP Paris,
energy diagram

heat such as the offices (Fig. 6.112). A major potential in the specific architectural typology of the Ecole Centrale building is to be found in the design of the energy interactions between the internal blocks and the hall volume. For example, excess heat from laboratory spaces can also be removed via a water-based cooling system and used to heat the hall in winter via the radiant floor system.

As we have seen in many examples above, in addition to their spatial function, transitional spaces can be used to increase the energy performance of a building by acting as a thermal buffer, serving as a return air or fresh air path to replace a mechanical system, supporting systems of natural ventilation or enabling synergetic energy relationships between different uses. The next project uses transitional spaces to develop **symbiotic relationships** between man, nature and technology, which is becoming an increasingly important theme in recent work. It is also evident in the research project Hyper-Building-City discussed in the previous chapter.

The proposal for the new headquarters building for Amore Pacific in Seoul, South Korea, developed in 2010 with DMAA was conceived as a "living machine", designed to capture the natural resources and energy flows in its surroundings and employ them to provide optimal environmental conditions for its occupants (Fig. 6.113). The form of the building departs from the standard orthogonal floor plans of the conventional skyscraper to improve the use of daylight and create vertical sky gardens on all sides of

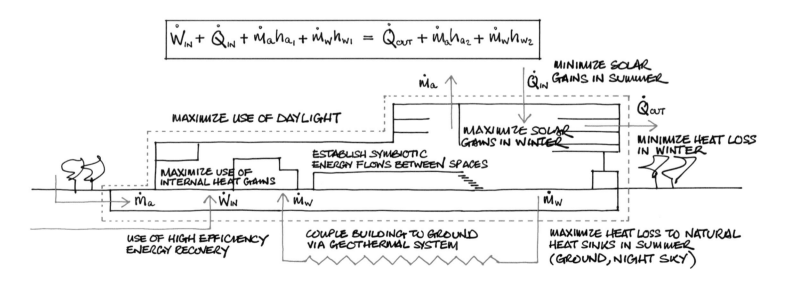

$$\dot{W}_{IN} + \dot{Q}_{IN} + \dot{m}_a h_{a_1} + \dot{m}_w h_{w_1} = \dot{Q}_{out} + \dot{m}_a h_{a_2} + \dot{m}_w h_{w_2}$$

MINIMIZE SOLAR
$\dot{Q}_{IN}$ GAINS IN SUMMER

$\dot{m}_a$

$\dot{Q}_{out}$

MAXIMIZE USE OF DAYLIGHT

MAXIMIZE SOLAR
GAINS IN WINTER

MINIMIZE HEAT LOSS
IN WINTER

ESTABLISH SYMBIOTIC
ENERGY FLOWS BETWEEN SPACES

MAXIMIZE USE OF
INTERNAL HEAT GAINS

$\dot{m}_a$ $\dot{W}_{IN}$ $\dot{m}_w$

$\dot{m}_w$

USE OF HIGH EFFICIENCY
ENERGY RECOVERY

COUPLE BUILDING TO GROUND
VIA GEOTHERMAL SYSTEM

MAXIMIZE HEAT LOSS TO NATURAL
HEAT SINKS IN SUMMER
(GROUND, NIGHT SKY)

Fig. 6.112

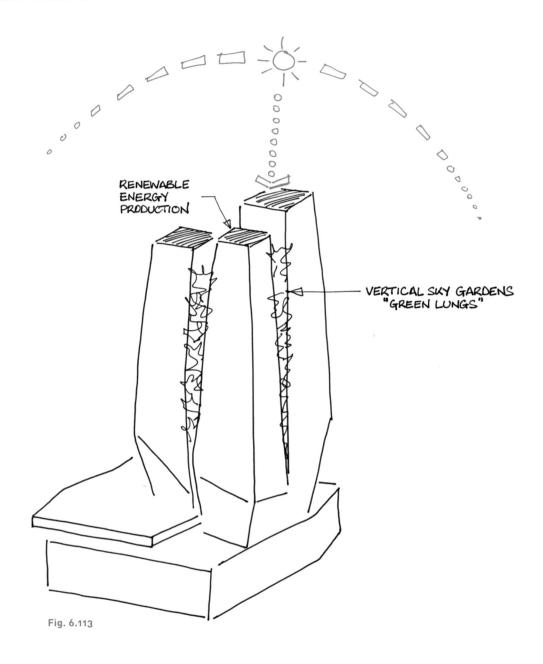

RENEWABLE
ENERGY
PRODUCTION

VERTICAL SKY GARDENS
"GREEN LUNGS"

Fig. 6.113

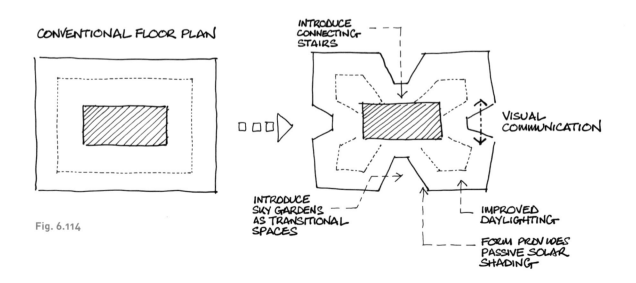

CONVENTIONAL FLOOR PLAN

INTRODUCE
CONNECTING
STAIRS

VISUAL
COMMUNICATION

Fig. 6.114

INTRODUCE
SKY GARDENS
AS TRANSITIONAL
SPACES

IMPROVED
DAYLIGHTING

FORM PROVIDES
PASSIVE SOLAR
SHADING

the building which can be thought of as the building's "green lungs" (Fig. 6.114). They mediate as transitional spaces between inside and outside and provide the office spaces with filtered and tempered fresh air. Vertical landscaping extends planting, vegetation and biodiversity from the Yongsan park in the east vertically skywards and constitutes at the same time an important element of the buildings climate control system (Fig. 6.115).

Ground water is used to temper the incoming air and dehumidify it in summer. The water is piped through coils aligned vertically in the sky gardens so that outdoor air flowing through the coils is cooled and dehumidified in summer and preheated in winter. The resulting condensate in summer is used directly for irrigation of the planting and vegetation. This process represents a symbiotic relationship between humans and nature in which the humans receive the dried, cooled air, and the vegetation the condensed water (Fig. 6.116). The leaves and foliage block incident solar radiation in summer. After further conditioning via on-floor decentral units, the air is distributed to the building spaces without the use of any conventional ductwork systems. This modular configuration with an interconnected cell structure ensures high energy performance and adaptable, flexible and ro-

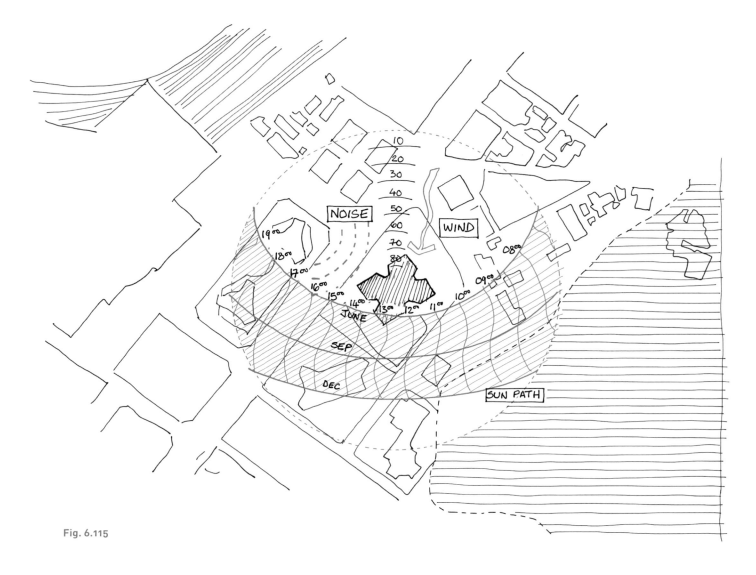

Fig. 6.115

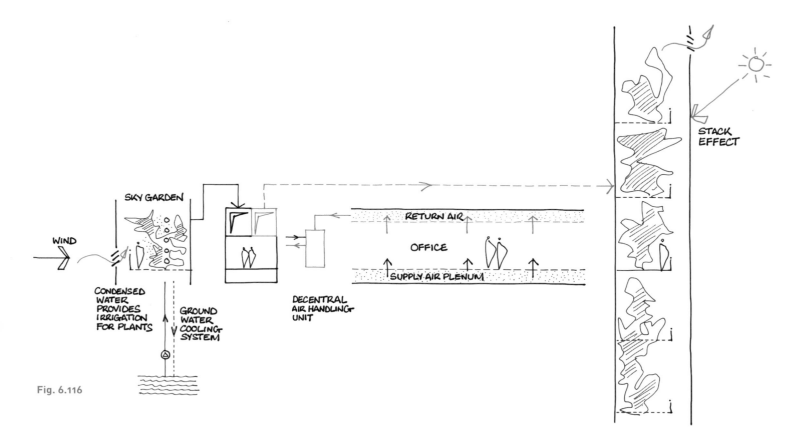

Fig. 6.116

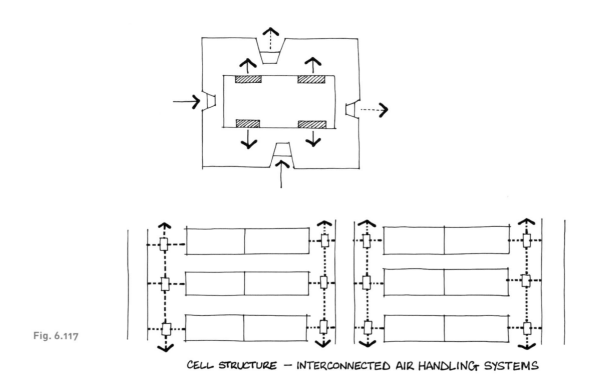

Fig. 6.117

CELL STRUCTURE — INTERCONNECTED AIR HANDLING SYSTEMS

Fig. 6.116
Amore Pacific HQ,
climate control concepts

Fig. 6.117
Amore Pacific HQ,
interconnected air
handling systems

bust system operation (Fig. 6.117). In winter, collected rainwater is used for irrigation. The vertical landscaping improves the microclimate, absorbing carbon dioxide and producing oxygen through photosynthesis, providing some filtration of the air as well as humidification in winter and evaporative cooling and shading in summer. In addition to the climatic and energetic aspects, the sky gardens and the connecting stairs located adjacent to them enhance communication, create visual interest for the occupants and provide a sense of vertical connectivity in the office tower.

Instead of the conventional central air-conditioning systems commonly employed in high-rise office towers, the concept employs decentralized air handling units on the office floors. The major advantages associated with this system are flexibility of use and substantial energy savings due to reduced operating hours and reduced system pressure drop. Air is delivered into pressurized floor plenums and from there into the spaces through low pressure displacement ventilation supply diffusers. The sky gardens, in combination with raised floor and suspended ceiling voids, are used to distribute the necessary air quantities required for ventilation without using conventional ductwork, providing substantial savings in material and installation costs for ductwork and reducing fan energy use. The supply and extract systems of the individual decentralized air handling plants are interconnected via controllable dampers to allow the benefits of applying diversity factors in sizing as well as advantages associated with standby capacity and adaptability. Dampers in the floor and ceiling voids can be used to interconnect the various floor zones. The fresh air and discharge duct systems are interconnected in the core area. The systems are zoned so that the perimeter zone is treated independently from the internal zone, in order to achieve maximum performance regarding energy savings and flexibility in use.

The proposed building envelope is composed of highly selective solar control glass panels and highly insulating opaque panels in a relationship which varies according to orientation, position (e.g. at the corners) and elevation (building height), in order to optimize building energy performance. The placement of these in the pattern which determines the building skin's appearance was influenced by considerations pertaining to optimum daylight use, views, solar control, glare protection, thermal insulation, natural ventilation and noise protection. By solving these issues in a single layer skin, embodied energy is reduced and wind problems associated with external shading devices are avoided. By varying the position and proportion of the glass and opaque façade elements and the characteristics of glass used, an optimal performance with regard to daylighting, solar control and thermal insulation can be achieved.

Another recurring theme in recent work which the design for the Amore Pacific building illustrates well is that of **dynamic adaptability.** As explained above, all buildings exist in a very dynamic environmental context. The variation range depends on the location and climate zone. The Amore Pacific building itself is, as are most buildings, a static object in a sea of ever-changing conditions. However, the building skin and systems react to these conditions in a dynamic manner (Fig. 6.118). Fresh air for the building is drawn in via the sky gardens, in which the conditions at the given time are most suitable. The fresh air intakes of the decentralized air

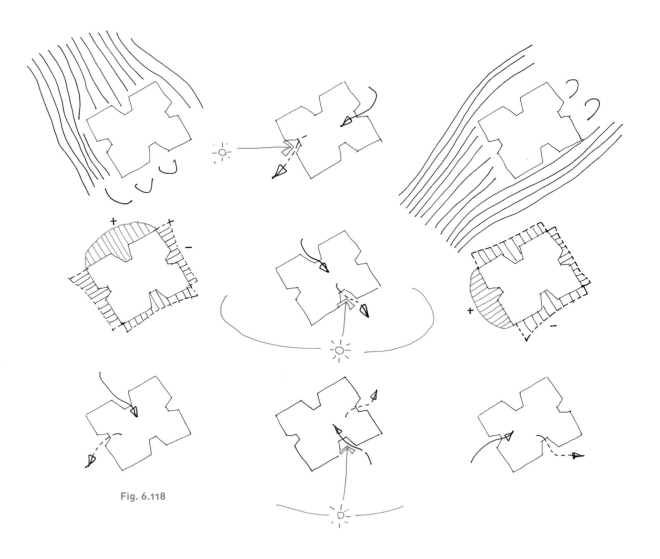

Fig. 6.118

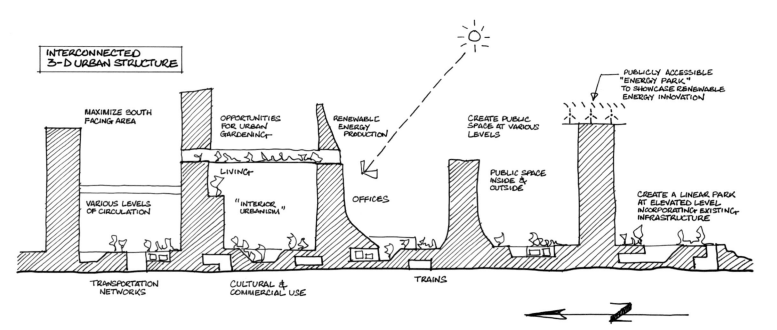

INTERCONNECTED
3-D URBAN STRUCTURE

MAXIMIZE SOUTH
FACING AREA

OPPORTUNITIES
FOR URBAN
GARDENING

RENEWABLE
ENERGY
PRODUCTION

CREATE PUBLIC
SPACE AT VARIOUS
LEVELS

PUBLICLY ACCESSIBLE
"ENERGY PARK"
TO SHOWCASE RENEWABLE
ENERGY INNOVATION

LIVING

VARIOUS LEVELS
OF CIRCULATION

"INTERIOR
URBANISM"

OFFICES

PUBLIC SPACE
INSIDE &
OUTSIDE

CREATE A LINEAR PARK
AT ELEVATED LEVEL
INCORPORATING EXISTING
INFRASTRUCTURE

TRANSPORTATION
NETWORKS

CULTURAL &
COMMERCIAL USE

TRAINS

Fig. 6.119

Fig. 6.118
Amore Pacific HQ,
dynamic adaptability

Fig. 6.119
Urban design proposal,
Berlin, conceptual
approach

handling units installed on the office floors draw air from the sky gardens. These are interconnected on each floor so that the orientation of the fresh air intake is dynamically adapted to suit the prevailing conditions. In winter, outdoor air is taken from the sky garden with the highest temperature, in summer from the area with the lowest temperature. The sky gardens are also utilized to support the driving pressure required to distribute air to the occupied spaces by employing the stack effect on the hotter side of the building (sky gardens connected vertically) in combination with the static pressure of the prevailing wind.

All of the designs described above are the result of a specific response to particular challenges with many influencing factors; climate, location, local context, architect etc. On all the projects, the four elements introduced in chapter four – building form, building skin, climate control systems and energy supply systems are optimized to maximize performance. On some of the projects, one or more of the elements may be dominant, yet strategies for all four elements are always part of the final solution. As explained in chapter four, climate is an important factor, but the challenges of the specific site and the intended use of the building as well as the cultural context are equally important for the development of the solution. No two concepts are really alike, except in spirit and approach. The bad news is, there is no patent recipe. Actually, that is the good news. It means that we can maximize energy performance and minimize the use of resources and at the same time continue to create a diversified range of architectural projects which enrich the urban environment.

In the last chapter, I discussed the possibilities for generation of form on an urban scale. This can be seen in the research work on optimal urban density, teleworking and in particular on the Hyper-Building-City project. I will close this chapter with a concept for a project with Coop Himmelb(l)au, which we proposed in a two-stage competition process for a large urban site in Berlin Gleisdreieck in 2015 (Fig. 6.119). Building on the research work described in chapter five, we proposed an interlinked three-dimensional urban structure with various levels of public access and circulation, incorporating an elevated linear park at low level as a connecting element. This park level ties the development into the existing infrastructure located at the site, including railway lines, new transport connections, diverse cultural and leisure facilities as well as commercial units. Atria, courtyards and other elements connect the various levels to the linear park. The vertical structures above comprise mixed-use buildings with office and residential use, with the residential units primarily situated on the upper floors. The buildings are orientated for optimal energy performance with the main façades facing north-south. The structures include commercially operated greenhouses for food production, but also space for use by residents for informal urban gardening. A diverse range of public places is located at various elevations throughout the interlinked structure, both as outdoor space and in glass-enclosed volumes. Solar energy generation is integrated into the building envelopes. At the rooftop level, an "Energy Park", similar to that proposed for the projects in Vienna and Prague (see chapter five) is proposed with space for leisure activities combined with the opportunity for residents and visitors to experience the new renewable energy technologies (solar, wind) used to power the development.

Fig. 7.1
Relationship between
productivity and comfort

How we as a society measure and evaluate energy performance in the built environment and reward or punish the various strategies and concepts employed to achieve this will influence the future development of architecture. The development of intelligent methods for the evaluation of energy efficiency in the area of the built environment is therefore very important.

The term "energy efficiency" in the building sector is unfortunately often misunderstood, misused and confused with energy demand/consumption. Low energy consumption is often falsely equated with high energy efficiency. Frequently, efforts in research and practice are directed towards minimizing energy demand and not towards maximizing energy efficiency. This misconception is fundamental and needs to be corrected in order to avoid future misguided developments. Maximizing energy efficiency involves more than simply minimizing energy consumption. In order to properly evaluate performance, we must consider the benefits obtained from the energy "consumed". Efficiency is the relationship between output (benefit) and input (resources).

In the context of the thermal performance of buildings, **energy efficiency** can be understood to be the relationship between the quality of the internal thermal environment and the quantity of energy used to maintain this. The economic importance of the relationship between thermal comfort and productivity has become increasingly recognized. Figure 7.1 shows in a qualitative manner the relationship between thermal comfort and pro-

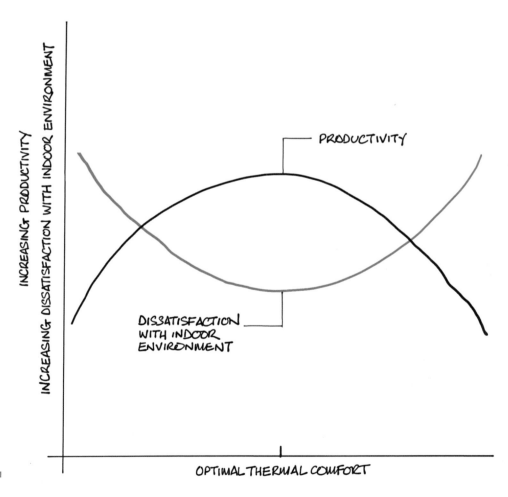

Fig. 7.1

ductivity in an indoor environment such as an office or a classroom. There is a body of research produced by a large international research community which supports the existence of this fundamental relationship in many different ways. Therefore, the real challenge in energy efficiency is achieving a good indoor environment with low energy demand.

Unfortunately, the legal instruments and regulatory devices currently employed to regulate the achievement of energy efficiency in buildings deal solely with energy demand or consumption, and not with energy efficiency. A certificate with an energy demand rating, however, means little if information about the quality of the associated internal environment is not available. The current one-sided approach which concentrates on energy consumption can lead to situations whereby seemingly high energy efficiency is only being achieved on paper. If the indoor environment is not acceptable, systems will be adjusted or new systems added to achieve better internal conditions at the cost of higher energy consumption.

When I developed the BEEP (Building Energy and Environmental Performance) methodology in 2007, the aim was an evaluation method which would allow the true energy efficiency of a building or a building design to be determined and thus compared with alternative design options or other buildings. The BEEP method quantifies the relationship between the quality of the internal thermal environmental conditions and the quan-

Fig. 7.2

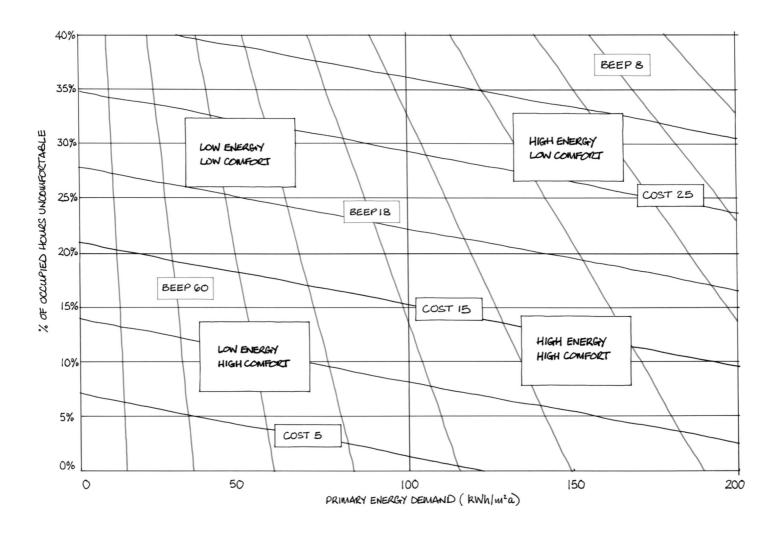

Fig. 7.2
BEEP chart

tity of primary energy required to achieve and maintain these. It takes into account the physical limitations of the façade of the building considered as well as those relating to the building's construction materials and its HVAC systems. It was the first evaluation method worldwide, and is to my knowledge still the only one which can measure the real energy efficiency in a building as defined above.

In order to measure energy efficiency, it is necessary to relate the quality of the internal environment to energy demand. In the BEEP methodology, the number of hours wherein comfortable conditions are not achieved is used to indicate the quality of the internal environment. This in turn is measured by determining how many hours the comfort index "Predicted Percentage Dissatisfied" (PPD) is greater than 10%. The PPD expresses the percentage of people likely to be dissatisfied with the thermal environment. A PPD of 10% means that statistically 10% of the people in the space can be expected to be dissatisfied with the internal environment. The horizontal coordinate of a given point on the BEEP chart represents the primary energy demand of the building design for heating, cooling, lighting and fans and the vertical coordinate the percentage of occupied hours in a year wherein conditions are uncomfortable (Fig. 7.2).

The evaluated energy performance (BEEP value) is calculated as the ratio of the number of hours with comfortable conditions to the primary energy demand and is expressed in the physically meaningful units of comfortable hours per kWh/m²a primary energy demand. The BEEP curves connect points (building spaces) with the same energy efficiency. The higher the BEEP value, the higher the energy efficiency of the solution. The resulting BEEP chart can be thought of as comprising four quadrants. The goal of building designers should be a **high BEEP value positioned in the bottom left quadrant**. Often decisions seem to be between the bottom right and the top left quadrants. Obviously, the top right area is to be avoided.

The COST lines connect buildings which have similar economic implications in operation. These are calculated as the sum of the energy costs and the effect of the loss of productivity due to non-optimal internal conditions. A lower COST value means lower costs in operation. The underlying simplified assumption is that there is a 1% loss in productivity whenever the PPD is greater than 10%. These economic curves are primarily displayed to indicate tendencies and to show the vast difference between the energy and economic efficiencies (demonstrated by the different slope of the curves).

Energy prices would need to increase radically before decisions which are made based on energy performance and decisions made based on operating cost lead to the same result.

Figure 7.3 shows the comparison of four alternative design options for an office building in Vienna city on the BEEP chart. The first design option has façades with a 70 % window-wall-ratio (WWR) and external blinds and is air-conditioned with non-operable windows. The second is fully glazed with selective solar control glazing and internal shading devices. It is also air-conditioned with non-operable windows. The third design option has a 40 % WWR, external blinds, operable windows and is heated only. Exposed concrete slabs and night-time ventilation are used to limit summertime temperatures. The fourth design option has the same façade design as the first option, but combined with exposed concrete slabs, night time ventilation, a cooling system and operable windows.

Energy demand was calculated using dynamic thermal simulation software. When the alternative solutions are ranked in terms of the BEEP value, the results are surprising when compared with a ranking based on intuition; for example option 1 has a higher BEEP value and therefore a higher energy performance than option 3. From an economic point of view, option 1 has the lowest operating costs (although the costs of system maintenance would also have to be considered) while the operating costs for options 2 and 3 are similar. Option 4 has the highest BEEP value and is the only "low energy high comfort" solution. Note that while the energy demand of 3 and 4 are similar, the total performance of option 4 as measured by the BEEP value is significantly higher. Option 2 is the worst type of solution; high energy and low comfort.

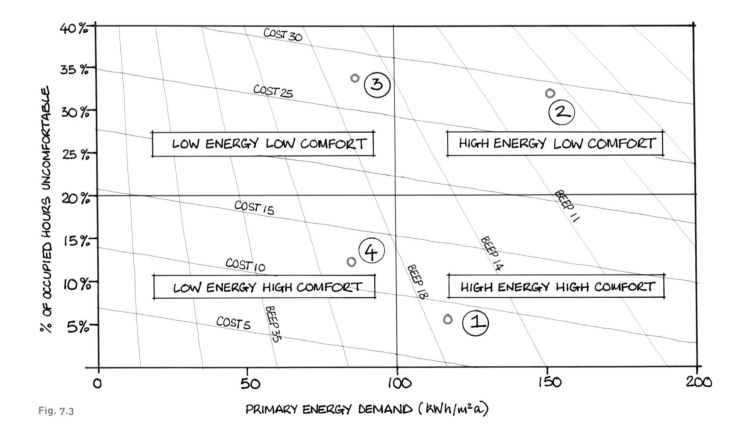

Fig. 7.3

The results show that we need to compare options comprehensively and understand energy efficiency not as energy use alone, but as the relationship between energy use and value in terms of the quality of the internal climate achieved. This should be part of a total approach in which the capital and running costs, the functionality and the architectural quality of the various options are also compared with each another. In terms of conserving energy, or possibly even from an ecological point of view, concentrating on reducing energy demand is possibly a legitimate approach; but is it really sustainable? Achieving sustainability is a complex task, and consideration of the economic and social aspects may mean that conserving energy at the expense of a lower quality of internal environment is not the most sustainable approach.

Figure 7.4 shows the results of another study, this time of three alternative solutions for the renovation of an existing office building. In all three solutions, the windows are replaced. In two solutions, thermal insulation is added to the external walls and in one of these solutions, mechanical ventilation is also installed. The BEEP value for both solutions is higher than for the existing building. Adding mechanical ventilation increases comfort, but also increases primary energy demand, leading to a lower BEEP value than the solution with natural ventilation. The highest energy performance (high BEEP value in the "low energy high comfort" quadrant) is attained by a third solution in which thermal insulation is not added, but motor controlled windows to achieve nighttime ventilation and a cooling system are provided.

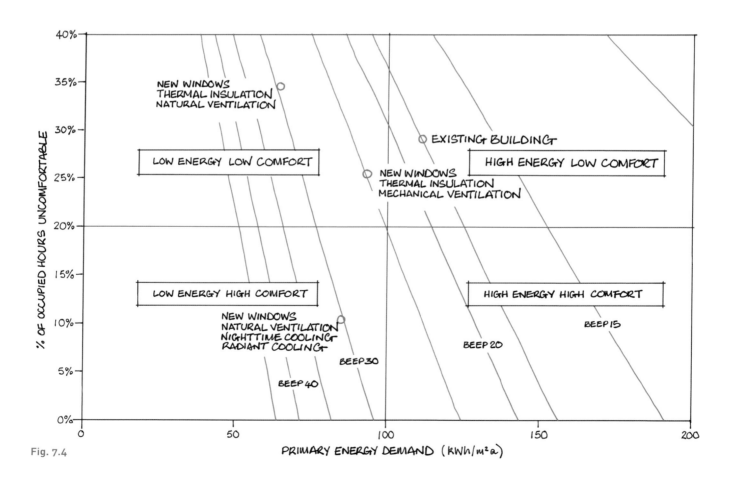

Fig. 7.4

The results of case studies examined using the BEEP method show that low energy consumption cannot be equated with high energy efficiency and that the use of a more sophisticated evaluation method such as BEEP in place of the methods currently in use would influence the future development of architecture. This method is fundamentally different to the methods thus far proposed to judge the energy efficiency of buildings. Methods which define energy efficiency as the relationship between the total primary energy input and the heating and cooling energy demand of the space, for example, merely measure the efficiency of the HVAC and energy supply systems in meeting the energy demand required to produce the same internal environmental conditions in a space. Such methods must assume that it is possible to achieve these conditions in all building design options which are to be compared, and this is the fundamental flaw in the thinking. Different architectural designs, but also the design and configuration of the proposed HVAC systems, often mean that the same internal environmental conditions cannot physically be achieved for all options.

Further research in the area of performance evaluation is needed. Future development of the BEEP method could lead to a much more complex instrument in which the quality of the internal environment achieved – including factors such as air quality, lighting levels and acoustics but also psychological issues such as the effects of daylight, operable windows etc. – is related to total primary energy demand over the total life cycle of the building (including embodied energy etc.). Capital costs could be factored into the economic curves. Space – like energy and materials – is also a resource and this should also be evaluated (see chapter five). For example, is the use of very thick walls to reduce heating energy demand really efficient?

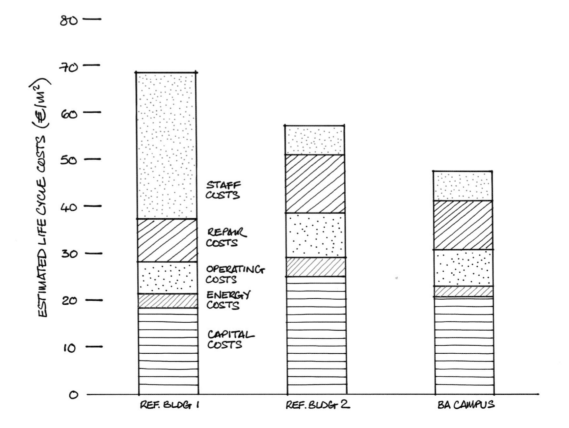

Fig. 7.5

Fig. 7.5
Life Cycle Costs

The BEEP methodology is more than a tool for the evaluation of the performance of buildings. It is a way of thinking and an approach to building design. Figure 7.5 shows a simple Life Cycle Analysis carried out at the competition stage for the new Bank Austria HQ in Vienna, briefly described in chapter six. By factoring in the operating costs into the calculations, including the costs of reduced productivity as a result of lower thermal comfort, it could be shown that while the proposed design was more expensive in capital cost terms, it was the better option in the long-term. In a similar way, the optimization of the energy performance of a city entails balancing the relationship between the social qualities and economic productivity of the city entity and the magnitude of inputs (energy, resources, water, food etc.) and undesirable outputs (pollution, waste etc.) required to maintain these.

Primary energy demand is often used as a metric when evaluating energy efficiency. Each country has its own values for converting final energy use to primary energy demand. These are called primary energy factors and vary not only spatially from country to country but also with time as the energy supply systems in a location are developed and expanded. For example, in Austria the primary energy factor used for electricity is very low compared to other countries, owing in large part to the sizeable share of hydroelectricity in the national mix. The data should however always be used critically. For example, renewable energy production in Austria is significantly higher in summer on account of the increased contributions from hydroelectricity and photovoltaic systems. If heat pumps use electricity in winter to heat buildings, the electricity consumption – and the peak demand – in winter will rise. This increased demand is then likely to be met – at least at the present time – by fossil fuel thermal power plants. The actual primary energy demand and associated CO_2 emissions will thus be less favorable than the calculated value using a primary energy factor averaged over a complete year. In our research work, we use a relationship of 1:3 for the primary energy comparison of thermal energy versus electrical energy, as this relationship is a good representation of the present global situation. More importantly, it reflects the fundamental thermodynamic relationship with regard to the quality of available energy or the exergy of these two forms of energy better. Figure 7.6 shows the 1:3 ratio between thermal energy and electricity for a fossil fuel thermal power plant. Also shown is the relationship for renewable solar energy. With the same physical area, roughly 1 kW of electricity or 3 kW of heat can be generated by solar panels, again giving the 1:3 relationship. The cost ratio between these two forms of energy also hovers around this factor of 3 in many locations.

Together with low energy demand and high quality internal environmental conditions, **architectural quality** is a vital component in energy-efficient architecture. Unfortunately, the architectural quality of many of the so-called low-energy buildings constructed in recent years has left a lot to be desired. On the other hand, a sustainable development cannot by definition proceed with a simultaneous loss in the architectural quality of our built environment. Energy efficient architecture must be understood as a triad comprising minimized energy consumption, optimal internal conditions and excellent architectural quality (Fig. 7.7). As described above, it is possible with the BEEP method to combine the first two parameters and objectively determine the best combination. The third parameter can and should also be evaluated.

A related issue to the evaluation of performance is the importance of **feedback loops**. The building process today operates essentially without any feedback loops. How effectively can we achieve progress in an environment without feedback? I will close this chapter with an example of a project on which two important feedback loops were integrated, contributing to the success of the project.

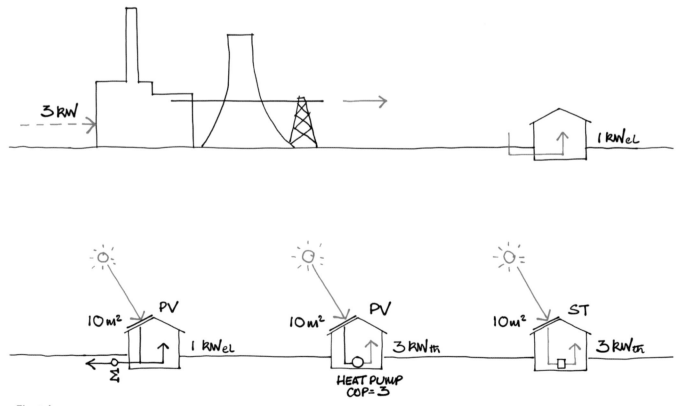

Fig. 7.6

Fig. 7.6
Primary energy factors

Fig. 7.7
Triade of energy-
efficient architecture

While completing the design of the low-energy building in Berlin that was briefly described in the last chapter, the aspect of user behavior was considered. Empirical studies and experience show that buildings often do not achieve the performance for which they were designed. This is often ascribed to improper or non-optimal behavior of the users. In the specific context of post-wall East Berlin in the early 1990s, this aspect seemed particularly important. Driving around the area in the depths of winter revealed a lot of open windows, reportedly as a result of heating system designs which did not include thermostatic valves and instead relied on windows to regulate the temperature while the heat output of radiators remained more or less constant. The proposed design already included control strategies to optimize performance, such as window contacts which ensured that the heating system was shut off when windows were opened etc.; but was this enough? We began to think about how the future occupants could be integrated into the design. This led to the idea of incorporating a small visual display screen into each apartment which would provide information on the status of the various systems; e.g. temperature data, whether windows were opened or whether the heating system was on or off (Fig. 7.8). Most importantly however, detailed information regarding heating energy consumption could be displayed, and to increase the effectiveness of the strategy we had this converted directly into financial currency. The aim was to achieve a heightened level of awareness for the users with regard to the effects of their behavior on the thermal behavior of the building, and to strengthen their relationship with the building.

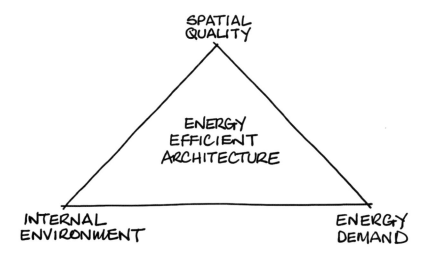

Fig. 7.7

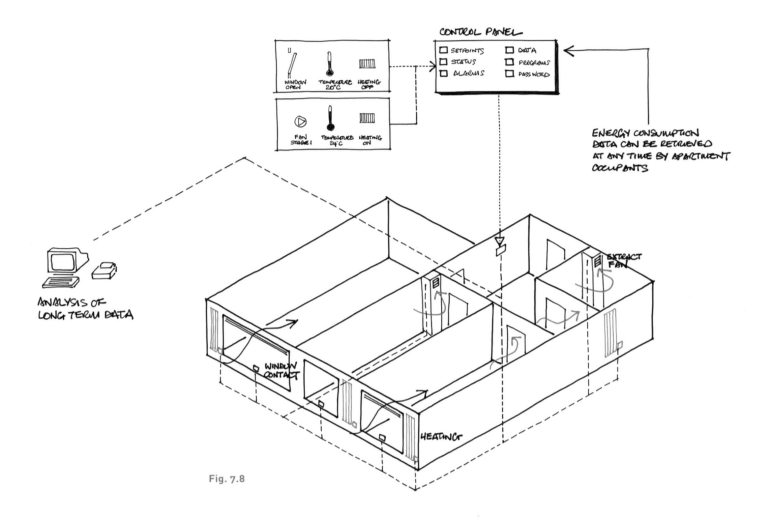

Fig. 7.8

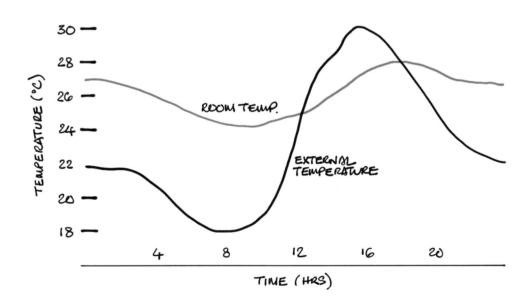

Fig. 7.9

Fig. 7.8
Feedback loops,
Low Energy Building,
Marzahn, Berlin

Fig. 7.9
Simulated summertime
temperatures, Low Energy
Building, Marzahn, Berlin

This was the first feedback loop. The second was that the data was also transferred back to our office via modem, allowing not only direct feedback to the user but also to the designer, thus on the one hand enabling lessons to be learnt with regard to the effectiveness of the various strategies, e.g. comparing summertime temperatures in operation with simulated values (Fig. 7.9), but also on the other hand allowing us to collect information on non-optimal use of the building which could then be passed on to the occupants. The goal was an optimization of the total system of building and occupants. A financial grant from the city of Berlin enabled this to take place. It should be noted that this all took place back in the 1990s, before the widespread use of smart phones etc. The information and communication technology available at the time was generally a lot more limited than today. For example, the visual display units installed in the apartments were a lot less user-friendly than we had intended. Today, there exists a vast – largely untapped – potential to use widely available technology for optimizing communication between buildings and users and thus maximizing energy performance.

The pleasure of turning on a tap on a cold day to wash your hands, and feeling the warm water flow over your skin; a warm relaxing shower or a long, hot bath; a warm fire on a cold night; the refreshing coolness of an air-conditioned space after coming in from the hot humid city on a summer's day; reading a book at night in good light; the taste of a cool drink on a hot day; the feel of a powerful car engine underneath you; the myriad pleasures made possible by electrically powered equipment in the name of entertainment, which also make work easier. Do you want to give that all up?

I didn't think so. We are addicted to energy use – on a large scale: a scale that is impossible to produce using your own muscle power. And as we have seen, you would need a lot of servants to do it for you. We are addicted to energy, and thus we are also addicted to fossil fuels – since the vast majority of our present energy demand is met by these. As we have seen in chapter one, the rate of energy use in a typical European country is approx. 4400 W per person or roughly 10 liters of oil per day. We could achieve the same standard of living with lower energy consumption by increasing the energy efficiency of the various processes involved: However, today, in many parts of our world, there are many people using less than 1 liter of oil a day. Over a billion people on the planet have no access to electricity at all. Over 20 000 people starve due to a lack of food every day. If we include preventable diseases, twice that number dies daily. Remembering the fundamental relationship between economic productivity and energy demand described in chapter one, it becomes evident that in absolute terms, we will need to increase and not reduce the amount of energy being used on our planet in order to ensure that the fundamental needs of all humanity are met.

According to leading scientists in the field of climate change, we need to eliminate CO_2 emissions by the end of this century in order to prevent potentially disastrous consequences regarding climate change. Figure 8.1 shows a basic calculation of global carbon emissions; the mathematical product of world population, Gross Domestic Product and the factors for energy and carbon intensity as discussed in chapter one. You might say that GDP is not the best way to measure the state of development or happiness of a society. After all, included in this means of measuring economic output are factors such as cleaning up oil spills, etc. There are other – and probably better – proposed ways of measuring the useful output of a society. However, regardless of how we measure output, if we want to reduce CO_2 emissions we need to do one or more of the following:

- reduce world population (P)
- reduce economic output or productivity ($/P)
- reduce energy intensity (W/$)
- reduce carbon intensity of energy production (kg CO_2/W)

As we have seen in chapter 1, the first parameter in the equation in Figure 8.1 is going to increase substantially until at least mid-century, and is much more likely to be larger rather than smaller at the end of this century than it is now. For the reasons given above, the second parameter needs to be increased on a global scale and not reduced. Therefore, we will have to operate with the last two parameters, knowing that the first two will probably increase substantially. Reduction of energy intensity can be achieved either by increasing productivity for the same energy demand, or reducing energy demand for the same productivity (or both simultaneously). In building design, this basically comes down to increasing energy performance. Many possible solutions for increasing energy performance in building design and on an urban design scale have been discussed in this book.

However, there are also fundamental thermodynamic reasons preventing the reduction of energy intensity beyond certain physical limits which exist for the various ways we use energy. Also, we have to be wary of the so-called rebound effect, whereby increasing the energy efficiency of a certain service leads to its increased use, and therefore to a stagnation of absolute energy demand. Therefore, it is the last parameter which will have to be reduced to zero or a near-zero value. This does not mean, however, that we can neglect the optimization of the third parameter. Assuming that nuclear energy is not the answer, we are left with renewable energy sources, primarily wind and solar. As we have seen in chapter five, there are many technical challenges here, particularly relating to storage and the large land area required due to the low energy yield density of these sources. Then, there is also the issue of the energy required to build the renewable energy infrastructure, which is often forgotten but is not negligible. As an example, consider a PV module with a primary embodied energy demand of 4000 MJ/m² and an expected lifetime of 25 years. Assuming a primary energy conversation factor of 3 (see chapter seven) and an annual electrical energy yield of 100 kWh/m²a for a PV module in Central Europe, the actual electrical energy yield available for external use is approximately 85 kWh/m²a, if the energy required to manufacture the re-

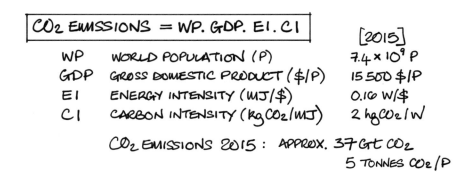

Fig. 8.1

Fig. 8.1
Global carbon emissions

placement module is deducted from the yield. The land areas calculated in chapter five would then need to be around 20 % larger. It is evident that we need to undertake everything possible to increase energy efficiency at the same time as we convert to carbon-free energy sources.

Is there enough renewable energy available to meet our energy needs? You will have often read or heard statements to the effect, that the Sun delivers more energy to the Earth in an hour than we consume in a year or 10 000 times more energy in a year than we need in the same time period. As we saw in chapter three, the average solar radiation reaching the Earth's surface is approximately 1000 W/m². The portion of the Earth's surface receiving this radiation at a particular time can be approximated as a disc with the Earth's radius of 6371 km. If we multiply this surface area by the energy received from the Sun and sum this for 8760 hours in a year, we arrive at a figure of approximately 4 000 000 EJ, which is roughly 7000 times higher than the present global energy consumption of 570 EJ. By this estimation, the sun delivers 459 EJ in one hour, so it would take roughly 1.2 hours to supply the energy used by us in one year on the Earth at present.

This energy is, however, not distributed evenly over the Earth's surface, and roughly 70 % of that surface is water. Perhaps the answer to the following question would provide more insight: What magnitude of land area would be required to meet Europe's energy consumption today? If we assume 1500 kWh/m² annual global radiation for a sunny location in Europe, a conversion efficiency of 10 % solar to electrical energy and a factor of 3 to convert to equivalent primary energy demand, the land required to meet present primary energy consumption (approx. 70 EJ in 2015) is only about 1 % of the total land area in the EU. While this fraction seems very small, in absolute terms this is an area roughly half the size of Portugal. Plans to outsource Europe's solar energy production to climatically more favorable desert areas in Africa have also been discussed. Recalling our discussion of energy security in chapter one, the geopolitical implications of such policies are obviously an issue to be considered.

As discussed in chapter five, combined heat and power plants (CHPs), running on biomass fuels and feeding district heating networks in cities, will probably be an important element in our future **energy supply infrastructure** – at least for the foreseeable future – on account of the energy storage challenges associated with wind and solar energy, and also because many countries have sizable biomass resources. Figure 8.2 shows a possible future energy supply system which could be implemented in a typical European country. In this scheme, hydro, solar, wind and biomass energy sources supply energy into an electrical grid. A district heating system is fed by solar-thermal and geothermal sources as well as waste heat from CHP, industry, waste water treatment, data centers, etc. Surplus electrical energy which cannot be stored can, until such time as a more effective means of storing electricity is found, be converted into heat and stored in this form which is technically easier. The district heating network is therefore used to store energy and to transport heat from places where waste heat is produced to places where heat is needed.

The next question is the time frame. Fossil fuel resources are finite and therefore the need to devise a new energy system is unavoidable. Yet there are almost certainly enough fossil fuels left to release sufficient carbon dioxide to cause irreversible damage to the planet. How can we reduce the use of fossil fuels in the current political and economic situation, in which fossil fuels are so much cheaper than the alternatives? There are two fundamentally different approaches: The first is to subsidize renewable energy sources; the second is to allocate the external costs of fossil fuel energy to the real sources and/or place appropriate taxes on carbon emissions. The first approach is being followed in several developed countries of the world – with mixed results. The second is theoretically a better approach, but practically speaking it does not appear plausible in the near future that all countries could agree to implement such a system (and implementing it on a partial basis would inevitably lead to major problems in international business). A technical possibility which would theoretically allow us to continue burning fossil fuels without – or with greatly reduced – CO_2 emissions is Carbon Capture and Storage (CCS). Practically, this technology has yet to be proved on a sufficiently large scale.

I do not believe, as some people would seem to want us to believe, that future energy solutions are all about sacrifice or about having to accept a reduction in the quality of life. I believe we can improve the quality of life, while at the same time solving the challenges the energy problem poses. It is important to recognize that part of the human condition, and therefore part of humanity, is a continual drive for growth and betterment. While individuals may express that they are content with what they have – or even express the possibility of less – and sometimes, however rarely, actually back these sentiments up with actions, we must accept that this does not apply to humanity at large. Human history is a story of a continued drive for more, which is not fully explained by Darwinian selection, Maslow's hierarchy of needs or the second law of thermodynamics.

Sustainability is a much-used term these days; perhaps too much used and with too little meaning. The approach taken to this topic is also

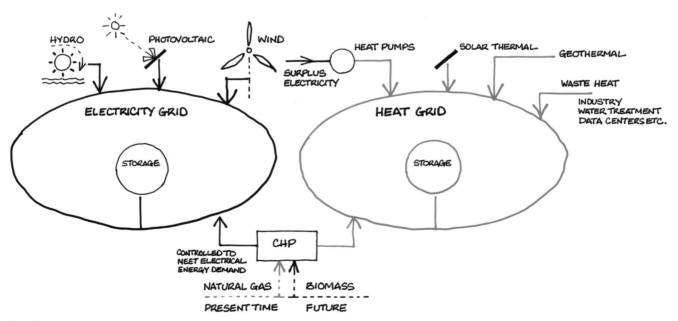

Fig. 8.2

Fig. 8.2
Possible future energy
supply system

often very conservative and seems to have the primary aim of maintaining things more or less as they are. Given the human condition as mentioned above, I believe that such an ambition is fundamentally not suitable for motivating a society at a deep level, and is therefore destined to failure. While a form of development in which the natural environment is not further damaged is certainly laudable, why not strive to develop and improve the quality of both our manmade and natural environments at the same time?

As explained in this book, we can use natural forces instead of devising ever more effective means of protecting ourselves against them. Instead of concentrating on minimizing the negative impact on the environment of the buildings we design, we need to maximize their positive impact. Whether form follows energy or energy follows form, the relationship between the built environment and energy is obvious, omnipresent and important. Buildings are one of the main contributors to world energy demand, and therefore architecture makes up a large part of probably the most central problem facing humanity today and for the foreseeable future – the fair distribution of the world's resources. Therefore, architecture must be a large part of the solution. Never before has the architectural discipline been provided with such an opportunity to take up a central role in the history of mankind. Besides being a tangible expression of a society's cultural values, priorities and aspirations, which good architecture must be, it can also provide the physical solution to this major – and possibly existential – challenge. One could say that this is a merely fixing a self-caused problem. However, this is a quick leap to the wrong conclusion. Architecture is not fine art, but a necessity; we need places to live and work, and this is what architecture at a fundamental level provides.

All of the project examples described in this book are to be seen within the context of a real-life construction industry, and have to deal with many issues besides energy performance. None of them lay claim to the perfect form in terms of energy, yet the parameter of energy performance is clearly visible in the form-finding process and the final architectural proposals. In our work in pure research, for example on naturally ventilated tall buildings or the Hyperbuilding-City-Model, the influence is even more visible.

- We need to think in systems.
- We should not be afraid of complexity.
- We should strive for simple solutions, but not oversimplified representations of the problem.
- We should be beware of following conventional wisdom blindly.

The fact that my contributions have influenced the form and appearance of many buildings and building designs is a source of some pride. Yet it is the question of how well the building really performs and functions on an energetic, spatial and aesthetic level which is much more important to me. A design in which the influence on the building's appearance is less discernible, but which performs very well both in energy efficiency and architectural terms is more satisfying than a design which works less well. Happily, experience has shown that in most cases the two go hand in hand, and that is the central hypothesis of this book – the creating of energy-efficient buildings does necessitate the creation of new forms.

APPENDIX

Acknowledgements

I would like to extend my sincere thanks to my staff at the Institute of Buildings and Energy at Graz University of Technology, at the Energy Design unit at the University of Applied Arts in Vienna, at the engineering design firm Energy Design Cody and to my former colleagues at Arup.

I would also like to thank all my students, from undergraduate to PhD level, for their interest, their questions and their ideas.

The architects with whom I have collaborated over the years deserve a special mention, as a large portion of the work described in this book would not have been possible without their creativity, openness and dedication. Many of these architects and their projects are mentioned in the book.

I would especially like to thank my whole family for their continued support, encouragement and love.

Project List

The following projects were mentioned in this book (in order of appearance).
The architects are named in the text. Climate zones given are indicative only.

Project	Country	Climate zone	Engineer	Status	Start	Completed	Chapter
WU Campus, Vienna	Austria	Temperate	Arup	Completed	2008	2013	2
GSW tower, Berlin	Germany	Temperate	Arup	Completed	1991	1999	2
MCUR museum, La Reunion	La Reunion	Tropical	Arup	Competition proposal	2006	-	2
Hyundai Motorstudio Goyang, Seoul	South Korea	Subtropical	Energy Design Cody	Completed	2012	2017	2
Ecole Centrale Paris	France	Temperate	Energy Design Cody	Completed	2012	2017	3, 6
Med Campus Graz	Austria	Temperate	Energy Design Cody	Completed	2010	2017	3, 4, 6
Braun HQ, Kronberg	Germany	Temperate	Arup	Completed	1996	2000	3, 4, 6
Taiyuan Botanical Gardens	China	Subtropical	Energy Design Cody	Under construction	2015	-	4, 6
ESPCI Paris	France	Temperate	Energy Design Cody	Competition proposal	2013	-	4, 6
The V Tower, Prague	Czech Republic	Temperate	Energy Design Cody	Under construction	2014	-	4
Shenzen Bay Tower	China	Subtropical	Energy Design Cody	Competition proposal	2012	-	4
School building, Berlin	Germany	Temperate	Energy Design Cody	Competition proposal	2014	-	4
House of Music, Aalborg	Denmark	Temperate	Arup	Completed	2003	2014	4
Neues Museum, Berlin	Germany	Temperate	Arup	Completed	1997	2009	4
Dutch Embassy, Berlin	Germany	Temperate	Arup	Completed	1997	2003	4
Office tower, Vienna	Austria	Temperate	Arup	Competition proposal	2005	-	4
Museum Schloss Oberhausen	Germany	Temperate	Arup	Completed	1995	1998	4
Fronius building, Wels	Austria	Temperate	Arup	Completed	2006	2011	4, 6
Bigova Bay, Masterplan	Montenegro	Subtropical	Arup	Under construction	2008	-	5
Office building, Schwedlerstr.	Germany	Temperate	Arup	Completed	1993	1995	6
Central Bank of Azerbaijan, Baku	Azerbaijan	Subtropical	Energy Design Cody	Under construction	2010	-	6
European Central Bank HQ, Frankfurt	Germany	Temperate	Arup	Completed	2003	2014	6
Fudan University, Shanghai	China	Subtropical	Energy Design Cody	Under construction	2011	-	6
IKA Library, Adlershof, Berlin	Germany	Temperate	Arup	Completed	1998	2002	6
MOCAPE Shenzen	China	Subtropical	Arup	Completed	2007	2016	6
Dalian International Conference Center	China	Temperate	Arup	Completed	2008	2012	6
Residential tower, Manhattan, NYC	USA	Subtropical	Energy Design Cody	Stopped	2013	-	6
Grand Egyptian Museum, Gisa	Eygpt	Subtropical	Arup	Competition proposal	2003	-	6
Patna Museum	India	Subtropical	Energy Design Cody	Competition proposal	2011	-	6

Project	Country	Climate zone	Engineer	Status	Start	Completed	Chapter
Health care facility in Doha	Qatar	Subtropical	Energy Design Cody	Competition proposal	2013	–	6
Dubai Design District	UAE	Subtropical	Energy Design Cody	Competition proposal	2014	–	6
House in Doha	Qatar	Subtropical	Energy Design Cody	Design	2013	–	6
New Parliamentary Building, Tirana	Albania	Subtropical	Energy Design Cody	1st prize in competition	2011	–	6
Convention Center Baku	Azerbaijan	Subtropical	Energy Design Cody	Completed	2013	2015	6
Duales System Pavilion, EXPO 2000	Germany	Temperate	Arup	Completed	1998	2000	6
Guangzhou opera house	China	Subtropical	Arup	Competition proposal	2003	–	6
Beethoven hall, Bonn	Germany	Temperate	Arup	Competition proposal	2008	–	6
Mediahub Tower, Singapore	Singapore	Tropical	Arup	Competition proposal	2008	–	6
Bank Austria Campus, Vienna	Austria	Temperate	Energy Design Cody	Under construction	2011	–	6, 7
Intercontinental hotel site, Vienna	Austria	Temperate	Energy Design Cody	Competition proposal	2013	–	6
Central Park Taopu, Shanghai	China	Subtropical	Energy Design Cody	Competition proposal	2014	–	6
Walkerhill Spa & Resort, Seoul	South Korea	Subtropical	Energy Design Cody	1st prize in competition	2016	–	6
Busan Cinema Center	South Korea	Subtropical	Arup	Completed	2005	2012	6
Central Park Baku	Azerbaijan	Subtropical	Energy Design Cody	Competition proposal	2014	–	6
University Campus Baku	Azerbaijan	Subtropical	Energy Design Cody	Competition proposal	2014	–	6
Active energy building, Vaduz	Liechtenstein	Temperate	Energy Design Cody	Under construction	2010	–	6
Glass pavillion, Montreal Botanical Gardens	Canada	Temperate	Energy Design Cody	Competition proposal	2014	–	6
Low Energy Building, Marzahn, Berlin	Germany	Temperate	Arup	Completed	1994	1997	6, 7
Sunbelt Management building, San Diego	USA	Subtropical	Arup	Stopped	2001	–	6
Infineon Asia Pacific HQ, Singapore	Singapore	Tropical	Arup	Completed	2002	2005	6
Adidas office building, Herzogenaurach	Germany	Temperate	Energy Design Cody	1st prize in competition	2014	–	6
Rainbow tower, Kuala Lumpur	Malaysia	Tropical	Energy Design Cody	Competition proposal	2012	–	6
Gateway Gardens Tower, Frankfurt	Germany	Temperate	Energy Design Cody	1st prize in competition	2014	–	6
OEVAG Bank HQ, Vienna	Austria	Temperate	Arup	Completed	2006	2010	6
NRW state archive, Duisburg	Germany	Temperate	Arup	Completed	2007	2013	6
Department store renovation, Germany	Germany	Temperate	Energy Design Cody	Competition proposal	2014	–	6
Interior City Munich	Germany	Temperate	Arup	Completed	1999	2003	6
Amore Pacific HQ, Seoul	South Korea	Subtropical	Arup	Competition proposal	2010	–	6
Gleisdreieck Berlin, masterplan	Germany	Temperate	Energy Design Cody	Competition proposal	2015	–	6

Index

Notes

1.

Data from the following sources was used in this chapter:

Energy: www.eia.gov
CO_2 emissions and GDP per capita: databank.worldbank.org
Population: en.wikipedia.org/wiki/List_of_countries_and_dependencies_by_population

2.

David MacKay used a similar diagram to represent global CO_2 emissions in his seminal work "Sustainable energy – without the hot air" – see bibliography.

3.

The data for reserves is taken from "BP Statistical Review of World Energy June 2016" (https://www.bp.com). These are the total proven reserves which can be extracted economically from the ground. There are probably significantly more fossil fuels in the ground which could be extracted. The calculation assumes that world population and energy demand grow at annual rates of 0.6 % and 1 % respectively. The point made by the diagram is that, regardless of the assumptions made, fossil fuels are a very finite resource and will not be sufficient to meet energy demand in the foreseeable future.

4.

More information on the research work carried out at the Institute for Buildings and Energy at Graz University of Technology described in this book can be found at www.ige.tugraz.at.

5.

The modified sine curve diagram is based on a diagram made by Victor Olgyay in the 1960s – see bibliography.

6.

The data for this model is taken from the official statistics for Austria for the year 2013 (https://www.bmwfw.gv.at)

Bibliography/ Further Reading

Energy
Coley, David. Energy and Climate Change, Creating a Sustainable Future. Chichester. England. 2008.
Andrews, John. Jelley, Nick. Energy Science, principles, technologies, and impacts. Oxford University Press. Oxford. 2007.
MacKay, David J. C. Sustainable Energy – without the hot air. UIT. Cambridge, England. 2009.

The Science of Energy Design
Cengel, Yunus A. Boles, Michael A. Thermodynamics, An Engineering Approach. McGraw-Hill. Boston. 2007.
Cengel, Yunus A. Cimbala, John M. Fluid Mechanics, Fundamentals and Applications. McGraw-Hill. Boston. 2010.
Cengel, Yunus A. Heat Transfer, A Practical Approach. McGraw-Hill. Boston. 2006.

External and Internal Environment
ASHRAE Handbook, Fundamentals. Atlanta, GA: American Society of Heating Refrigerating, and Air Conditioning Engineers, Inc. 2013.
CIBSE Guide A: Environmental Design. London, CIBSE, 2007.
Smithson, Peter. Addison, Ken. Atkinson, Ken. Fundamentals of the physical environment. Routledge, New York. 2002.
Speckmann, Erwin-Josef. Hescheler, Jürgen. Köhling, Rüdiger. Physiologie. Urban & Fischer, Munich, 2013.

Buildings and Energy
ASHRAE Handbook, HVAC Applications. Atlanta, GA: American Society of Heating Refrigerating, and Air Conditioning Engineers, Inc. 2015.
ASHRAE Handbook, HVAC Systems and Equipment. Atlanta, GA: American Society of Heating Refrigerating, and Air Conditioning Engineers, Inc. 2016.
Olgyay, Victor. Design with Climate, bioclimatic approach to architectural regionalism. Princeton University Press. Princeton. 1963.
Recknagel. Sprenger. Schramek. Taschenbuch für Heizung + Klimatechnik. Oldenbourg 2016.

Author

Brian Cody is professor and head of the Institute of Buildings and Energy at Graz University of Technology in Austria, and founder and CEO of the consulting firm Energy Design Cody – also based in Graz – which is responsible for the development of innovative energy and climate control concepts in construction projects all over the world. He is also visiting professor and head of the Energy Design unit at the University of Applied Arts in Vienna. Before his appointment at Graz University of Technology in 2003, he was Associate Director of the international engineering consultancy Arup with over 13 000 staff in over 35 countries and Design Leader of their offices in Germany. He remained as consultant to Arup until 2010, when he set up his own engineering design company. His focus in research, teaching and practice is on maximizing the energy performance of buildings and cities.

Univ. Prof. Brian Cody

Concept, text, sketches and diagrams: Brian Cody
Acquisitions Editor: David Marold, Birkhäuser Verlag, A-Vienna
Project and Production Management: Angelika Heller, Birkhäuser Verlag, A-Vienna
Proofreading: Alun Brown, A-Vienna
Lithography: pixelstorm, A-Vienna
Layout, cover design and typography: Martin Gaal, A-Vienna
Printing and binding: Holzhausen Druck GmbH, A-Wolkersdorf

Library of Congress Cataloging-in-Publication data
A CIP catalog record for this book has been applied for at the Library of Congress.

Bibliographic information published by the German National Library
The German National Library lists this publication in the Deutsche Nationalbibliografie;
detailed bibliographic data are available on the Internet at http://dnb.dnb.de.

This work is subject to copyright. All rights are reserved, whether the whole or part of the
material is concerned, specifically the rights of translation, reprinting, re-use of illustra-
tions, recitation, broadcasting, reproduction on microfilms or in other ways, and storage in
databases. For any kind of use, permission of the copyright owner must be obtained.

Although the author and publisher have made every effort to ensure that the information
in this book was correct at press time, the author and publisher do not assume and here-
by disclaim any liability to any party for any loss, damage, or disruption caused by errors
or omissions, whether such errors or omissions result from negligence, accident, or any
other cause.

This publication is also available as an e-book (ISBN 978-3-0356-1411-4).

© 2017 Birkhäuser Verlag GmbH, Basel
P.O. Box 44, 4009 Basel, Switzerland
Part of Walter de Gruyter GmbH, Berlin/Boston

Printed on acid-free paper produced from chlorine-free pulp. TCF ∞

Printed in Austria

ISBN 978-3-0356-1405-3 (Softcover)
ISBN 978-3-99043-202-0 (Hardcover)

9 8 7 6 5 4 3 2 1
www.birkhauser.com